CRIMSON SKIES

THE HISTORY OF A TWENTIETH CENTURY ENGLISH WORKING MAN

by

Charlie Framp

with a Foreword
by
Lord (Len) Murray

19 88

RICHARD KAY PUBLICATIONS
80 Sleaford Road • BOSTON • Lincolnshire • PE21 8EU

LIFE IN LINCOLNSHIRE TITLES:

   This book is the fifth of these titles which are biographical or auto-
biographical accounts of the lives of men or women who have an interesting tale to tell and who have spent a major part of their lives in Lincolnshire (the 'Old' Lincolnshire). Details of other titles will be found on the
back flap of the dust-jacket or inside the back cover. The publishers are
always pleased to hear from authors who have material appropriate for
these titles.

© Charles Framp 1988
Foreword: © Lord Murray 1988
ISBN 0 902662 82 1 (cased edition)
ISBN 0 902662 83 X (paperback edition)

British Library Cataloguing in Publication Data

Framp, Charlie
    Crimson skies : the history of a twentieth century English
    working man.
    1.   England.   Framp,   Charlie.
    I.   Title
    942.082ʹ.092ʹ4

This book has been set throughout on an AppleMac DTP system, using a Laser-
Writer Plus laser printer, in a package supplied by Gestetner Ltd. The main body
of the text is set in 10 point Bookman type.
Printed by **The Echo Press** • 25 Swan Street • Loughborough • Leics. LE11 0BT

CONTENTS

Foreword

by
Lord (Len) Murray, O. B. E.

I have never met Charles Framp, but I feel that I know him well through this impressive book. I recognise in his pages so many of the children I grew up with in just such a village, so many of the infantrymen I knew during the war, so many trade unionists I worked with – and sometimes argued with. The war was a major influence on our generation. I have never read a more gripping account of the war as experienced by a private soldier – and that was the real perspective. Private Framp sets out in an understated – and therefore all the more telling – way, the experiences which shaped him, and left him shattered in body and resolute to prevent a recurrence of the agony of war, critical in mind, but remarkably unembittered. The qualities that war discovered in him – comradeship, a concern for fairness, loyalty, determination, even stubbornness – are those that later led him to become a shop steward.

To some people war service came to represent a peak of experience and achievement which left them content to go on reliving those years for the rest of their lives. Not so for Charles Framp. To him they were a spur, a warning, and a reminder. Certainly that shared experience set apart him and his generation, as was reflected in the support which, as a steward, he found among the wartime ex-servicemen in the works (as Harold Macmillan always felt closer to those, on either side of the party division, who had served in the first war; surely some of the polarisation of politics in recent years is due to the passing of a generation who, whatever their other differences, had served together).

But for Charles Framp war memories were never a substitute for action. Notably, it was less a deep prior ideological commitment than his revulsion from the waste of war that led him to spend a few years in the Communist Party. With him – as with me – it was no more than a flirtation: neither of us would have made a thorough-going Stalinist. But he readily pays tribute to the way the CP, at an important stage, contributed to his understanding of the world and to his intellectual development, and expresses his 'debt of gratitude for that first awakening of my interest in reading and learning and for the heightening of my awareness of the larger world.' "Then felt I like some watcher of the skies . . ."

Nor did his newfound joy in books inhibit his instinct for action: rather it seems to have sharpened his desire and his capacity to serve. In seeking election as a bricklayers' shop steward he had come a long way from his earlier war-time conviction that 'I was a born private, tailor-made for the rank.' It was his innate belief in fairness, and his resentment at the bad conditions in the steelworks, that led him into active trade unionism. Not that he had any illusions about working men of the sort harboured by ultra-lefts of middle or upper class origin; he was ready enough to attack phony overtime against the short-sighted opposition of many of his own members.

At the heart of Charles Framp's trade union beliefs, as of trade unionism itself, was 'the right of the ordinary steelworker . . . to have his say also in the affairs of his industry . . . the dream of generations of working-men for a greater say in and control over the economic forces which govern their lives'. Industrial democracy is as valid and as necessary as political democracy itself. He is, I believe, unduly critical of the experiment with Worker Directors in the steel industry. He came under the influence, for a time, of the Institute of Workers' Control, but his practical trade union commonsense obviously cut through the divisive nonsense of the ultras' doctrine that unions are to be attacked because they merely come between members and their aspirations. Unions must be the servants of their members, accountable to their members, democratic in their structure and actions, but without leadership, loyalty and discipline they are nothing.

This book mirrors the man and his age. Charles Framp does not seek to embellish his private's-eye view of the war or his working-man's view of industry and trades unionism. He recounts, as it happened, a tale which is valuable in itself and will provide invaluable material for those who tell the broader story of our life and times. We are all in debt to this English infantryman and shop steward both for what he did and for his account of it.

Loughton 14 February 1988

PART ONE

THE BOY

Once I knew a youth, but long ago,
Long gone is he beyond my aid.
More's the pity life had it so,
For I am the man he made.

C. Framp

1.

MAM'S HAIRBRUSH

IF IN THE GREAT MASTER PLAN of human genealogy you had been scheduled to make your debut into the world in the years between 1918 and, say the mid 1920s and it had also been decreed therein that you were to be born in Europe of native European stock, then you were lucky, damned lucky, if you made it. Many millions didn't – their luck ran out prematurely with the advent of The Great War of 1914-18, which did so much to change the face of Europe and much too, to change its faces.

Following history's massive convulsion of 1914-18, the European section of the great master plan had to be hugely revised and hastily rewritten. Many, if not most, Europeans alive today owe their existence to that re-casting of the genealogical programme.

I myself was among the lucky. My father, though twice wounded and disabled in the war, survived it, so to ensure the continuance of his line and my own eventual safe arrival into the world - which great event, predetermined or otherwise, occurred on the last day of July 1922.

I was born the third of five children. There should have been six but mother, desperate in the desperate circumstances of the time - the late 1920s - decreed otherwise and procured an abortion for herself - so to live out the rest of her life ever companioned by guilt and remorse.

My birth was the signal for no great outburst of national rejoicing – indeed, there was little enough of that even within the confines of my immediate family. I was but another mouth to feed at a time when the times were hard – for my parents, bloody hard! And by all accounts mine was no small mouth, weighing in for the battle of life as I did at a staggering eleven and a quarter pounds – a feat for which mother was never able to wholly forgive me.

In later years when perhaps a friend or neighbour had dropped in for a cup of tea and a chat and the conversation had got round to such matters, as it almost invariably did, mother would let her gaze rest reproachfully upon me for a moment or two and then, to my acute embarrassment, proceed to inform her audience that I'd been the only one of her 'five' to lay her up for longer than the statutory eight days. In the event it had been three weeks – and her 'with two more kiddies under three and a husband also to see to!' I felt extremely guilty about the whole business.

At the same time as mother informed dad of my impending arrival into the world they also had a stroke of good luck – they acquired the keys to a home of their own – rented, of course!

The house was no 'semi with mod. cons.' nor yet a 'quaint old cottage in an English country lane'. It was a small terraced house, the middle one of a row of thirteen, fronted by an identical row on the other side of the street and backed by an almost identical row belonging to the street behind it, with a dirt ten-foot between.

The property was the usual three up, three down type, that is, if you classed the tiny scullery and the equally tiny bedroom above it as rooms. It had no water laid on – that was obtained from a shared pump behind the house. Consequently there was no bathroom either. There was no gas or electricity, the cooking was done on an old black-leaded Yorkshire range in the kitchen, which also served to heat the house. In the scullery was the ten-gallon capacity copper which provided the water for mother's washdays and our weekly baths. The bucket closet was down the yard behind the pig sty.

Primitive as it was, to mam and dad, after three years of living in the suffocating atmosphere of one room, it was nothing less than heavenly. There was, however, as there always seems to be with all good fortune, a sting attached to it – the house required furnishing, which, in turn, required money, and that was the sting, they had none.

True, dad was working, but the meagre wages he was earning

as an unskilled labourer were gobbled up, almost as quickly as he'd got them home, by his hungry family, his hungry landlady and the equally hungry creditors he'd incurred in the getting together of the few sticks of furniture they already possessed. But he was a resourceful man and never more so than when the odds were stacked against him. He got himself over that particular hump in life by the simple expediency of cashing in his war pension in exchange for a lump settlement. And that, coupled with an extension of his credit, enabled mother to purchase enough of her household needs for us to be able to move into the house without her having to advertise our poverty too blatantly to her new neighbours.

And that's how it was a few weeks later that I came to be born in the upstairs front bedroom of the house in which mother lived the rest of her life. She died in it fifty-seven years later at the age of eighty-three.

Dad was a Londoner born. He'd arrived, newly-married, in the booming steel town of Scunthorpe in 1919, almost straight from the booming steel guns of France. He'd learned of the town's prosperity and its job potential from a fellow soldier while the two of them had, for a brief hour or two, shared the same shell-hole in France. He'd made up his mind then that when that particular war to end wars was finally over and done with – always supposing he survived it which, at the time, appeared to be highly unlikely – that would be the place for him to make for. He'd reasoned that a land fit for heroes, which they were going to build right after the war was finished, would also require, amongst a lot of other things, an awful lot of steel. Scunthorpe sounded like it was just the place to be and, who knew, he might even live there happily ever after, like they did in fairy stories.

What in 1936 was to become known as the Borough of Scunthorpe was, at the time of my birth in 1922, comprised of five quite separate communities, strung like a row of beads in a straight line running from north to south, about four miles in length overall. Ashby, the village in which I first saw the light of day, was the most southerly of the five.

To the north and east of the five parishes were the steelworks – known simply as 'The Works'. These consisted of a huge complex of giant sheds, blast furnaces, tall chimneys, cooling towers and the like which, together with their ancillary workings, mines etc, and associated industries, formed a huge arc about the villages and covered an area of ground no less great. The workforce for this huge concentration of industry was drawn from practically the whole of north Lincolnshire and the nearer parts of South Yorkshire.

Over the steelworks by day hung a thick grey-brown pall of dust and smoke, belched into the sky from the tops of the monstrously tall brick chimneys, which cast its shadow and its fallout over the surrounding country for miles around and also provided, for the early morning workers, some weird and wonderful sunrises.

By night, every night and all through the night, the skies above the five parishes were constantly stained a bright crimson as the never-ending trains of huge slag ladles were hauled to the tops of the mountainous slag banks by fiercely determined works locos and there, like so many monster buckets, unceremoniously up-ended, to send their fiery contents cascading down the steep slopes in exact likeness of the lava-flow of erupting volcanoes and, similarly, to light up the sky for many miles around – and incidentally to provide the inspiration for the Borough of Scunthorpe's motto, 'The Heavens Reflect our Labours'.

Our house was about a mile and a half from the nearest of the steelworks – as the crow flies, that is. We three boys of the family, all born within eighteen months of each other, shared the middle bedroom. We also shared the same bed. It was a large, iron-framed double with brass knobs at the corners and it might have been designed with us three especially in mind – it took all the punishment we, with our constant fighting and wrestling and other trampoline-like activities, handed out to it, without ever showing the slightest sign of collapse. The brass knobs, too, were ideal for securing the corners of the sheets, when we played tents.

On the cold winter nights mother always warmed the bed before putting us into it by means of one of the oven plates wrapped in an old blanket and placed under the covers. And there, with dad's old army great-coat, still complete with brass buttons, also placed on the bed for extra warmth, we slept 'as snug as bugs in a rug'.

Some of my earliest memories in life are associated with that old, brass-knobbed bed. I can close my eyes and see now the three of us lying in it, scarcely daring to whisper and trying to smother our giggles after mother, short of temper no doubt after a hard day's wash or whatever, had finally succeeded in restoring quiet to the bedroom with the flat of her hairbrush, after her re-peated warnings from the bottom of the stairs had been just as repeatedly ignored by us - such occasions were by no means rare.

I can remember too the wild winter nights when the west wind gusted fiercely across the wide Trent valley to rattle alarm-ingly the loose-fitting frames of our bedroom window and drove the rain clouds, thick and low, through the skies above the five villages, intercepting the surging crimson light ere it had left the bank sides and throwing it back to earth still at its brightest. Then the black nights were suddenly transformed into bright red days and the falling rain into a glittering cascade of crimson jew-els, through and beyond which the brightly gleaming rooftops and the sharply silhouetted chimney stacks and pots of the row of normally drab houses behind ours took on the magical quality of a fairyland.

To us small boys of Ashby, the vast acres of farmland about the village and those of the rough, uncultivated common land which lay between it and the steelworks, were adventure play-grounds of the greatest delight. Almost every field had its water-ing pond for the cattle – many of them quite large. These ponds teemed with life of all kinds – frogs, toads, newts and, in the larger ones, sticklebacks. Dragon- and damselflies seemed to be as abundant in those places as house and horse flies. About the ponds cowslips were then almost as common as buttercups and daisies. The high hedgerows and trees rang with birdsong – such rarities today as snipe, shrike, yellow wagtail and curlew were then not at all uncommon in the neighbourhood. Their eggs were considered to be no great find by the egg collectors among us.

We gathered everything in season – elderberries, blackberries, crab apples, hazelnuts, even walnuts and, of course, conkers. Watercress grew by the becks and mushrooms you could find in almost every field. We spent many happy days gathering this rich harvest of the fields and the hedgerows, with scarcely a soul to say us nay, other than the occasional bull.

Happy the times we spent fishing for sticklebacks in the larger ponds and with no more tackle than a length of cotton thread dangled into the water from the end of any old stick broken, as often as not, from one of the innumerable pussy-willows which grew about the place. On the other end of the thread a worm wriggled frantically for its life as the sticklebacks manouvred about it for the attack – poor old worm!

On the long hot days of the summer, when we'd tired of the fishing, then off came our clothes and we joined the sticklebacks in the water. The fact that we'd brought along neither bathing costumes nor towels to dry ourselves with afterwards bothered us not one little bit. Such genteel refinements weren't for us – besides, the carrying of such bulky articles would have inhibited the free use of our 'weapons' – catapults, mostly, but also bows and arrows and spears, all made by ourselves and mostly unreliable. Even so, we potted at anything and everything which moved as we went from place to place, even the old bull.

The animals were in no danger, our noisy approach had driven to cover those which might have been within the limited range of our weapons and those that were beyond it knew perfectly well they were! But, to gratify our boyish instincts, we potted at them just the same and then, instincts gratified, honour upheld, we continued on our noisy way to seek other quarry or interests.

Today all that land of my boyhood delight is no more. It lies buried beneath a profusion of housing estates, industrial estates, steelworks expansions and all the rest of it. Television sets, computers and hi-fi equipment generally seems to be poor compensation for the kids of today's Ashby for the loss of such a wonderful world of adventure and discovery. Even if such a thing were possible, I wouldn't swop my boyhood for theirs. In that respect at least, we were luckier than they.

But even in those early days, life wasn't all sweet dreams and play – albeit the hardships and the struggles of our parents trying to bring up a large family on small wages – in many cases no wages – largely escaped us. Just occasionally some extra precipitously delivered bolt of misfortune would pierce the screen of our childhood games and preoccupation with each other to make us suddenly aware of the fact that there were other forces in the world, forces as powerful as mums and dads, dark, evil forces which even they quailed before – and then you were afraid yourselves.

One such incident happened to me when I was about seven years old. I'd been 'bod eggin', bird's nesting that is. I'd raced excitedly up the yard of our house, through the back door and into the kitchen to show my brothers the results of my latest foray, only to be brought to a shocked standstill just inside the kitchen door, by the sight of my mother lying prostrate on the hearthrug before the old Yorkshire range. She was sobbing bitterly, head cradled in her arms. There was, I remember quite distinctly, no fire in the grate but of course I'd been too young to make the connection between the two events. There was no fire because there was no coal. There was no coal because there was no money with which to buy it. This would also be about the time my mother procured her abortion.

If the circumstances of our family could be described as desperate at the time, then there were many other families about us whose circumstances were not a whit less desperate. And, scarcely a hundred yards from our house, in the field at the bottom of the street which is now a children's play park, other families lived in broken down caravans and put-together shacks. Gypsies, we called them, but kiddies were born there and grew up there and with never the sight nor sound of gypsy merrymaking around a gypsy fire beneath a romantic gypsy moon to the wild rhythm of gypsy music – they were paupers, pure and simple. Their water was obtained from a spring at the bottom of the field, their toilets were holes in the ground, poorly screened by sacking nailed to wooden poles, but they reckoned it was still better than the workhouse.

Mother was forever chastising us for bringing home our friends who lived in these abodes and she fiercely forbade us to visit them in their homes. She said they were infested with lice and fleas, which was only too true, almost all of them were, as we often discovered to our own discomfort when we'd flouted our mother's strict instructions to stay away. But it was hard for us other children of the neighbourhood to do that – their homes always seemed to be much more interesting than our own. One boy there had a pet jackdaw which flew freely about the field. Another kept rabbits. But a favourite attraction was a mass of live eels kept in an ordinary dolly-tub which had a wooden lid, by a man we called Wingy. He'd only one arm, having lost the other, so it was said, in the war. He would himself lift off the lid to let us view the eels. The lure of such wonderful attractions was such that even the flat of mum's hairbrush was often unable to counter it.

Not surprisingly, in view of the primitive living conditions of the time and the prevalence of pig sties, pigs and stacks of pigshit in the neighbourhood, disease was as rife as the poverty it thrived on. Scarlet fever, diptheria, consumption, polio, Erysipelas and rickets, too, were common. Scarcely a household escaped for long a visit from one or another of these agents of death.

I've known whole, or almost whole families to be wiped out almost overnight following their visitations. And the loss of the breadwinner by any means was a disaster of truly catastrophic proportions to a family, sometimes leaving the surviving members of the family with no other option than the workhouse. A late friend of mine remembered, as a small boy, walking all the seven miles from Ashby to the workhouse at Brigg, in company with his mother and two sisters, to ask that they be taken in there, following the death of his father.

8.

Mother herself made much of us kiddies' clothing from materials she'd sometimes had given to her, sometimes she'd bought at a jumble sale but also, quite often, from her own meagre wardrobe – which fact, if dad noticed and questioned, would cause her to reply tartly and with a true mother's logic – 'Nobody sees me but the kids they do.'

Many, many nights as a small boy I've drifted off to sleep to the reassuring sound of mother's old sewing-machine whirring eighteen to the dozen in the kitchen immediately below our bedroom, in which she spent many long hours making and mending and with no more light than that provided by the oil lamp on the table before her and the flickering fire in the grate behind.

I remember once, when I was eight, maybe nine, years old, my ungrateful self throwing a fit of temper because *again* she hadn't put flies in the pair of trousers she'd just made for me. I wanted to be the same as the other boys at school and not have to hitch up my trouser leg whenever I wanted to wee!

Always, because the trousers had no pockets either, she'd tuck a piece of clean, white, freshly ironed cloth through one of the criss-cross braces of the trousers, upon which to wipe our noses, before packing us off to school. She was having no ragged-trousered, snotty-nosed little brats to shame her – and neither did she, ever!

Behind the curtains of the bay window of our front room, on a tall wooden stand, stood a large aspidistra. Behind that again, apart from an old Victorian mirror on the wall above the fireplace, a couple of framed prints on the walls and a carpet by the door, there was nothing else in the way of furniture. But there was one other thing in the room – an old belt-driven motor cycle which dad had hopes of restoring to working order. I don't recollect that he ever did.

In the evenings, after we kids had been put to bed, this room occasionally became the venue for mysterious meetings of gruff-voiced men. The first we'd know that one of these meetings was about to commence was when we heard the repeated knockings on the front door, followed by the sounds of it being opened and closed again and the voices of the men as they greeted each other. We didn't know what the meetings were about but from the little we could hear and judging from the fact that his voice appeared to be the most prominent of all the voices, our Dad seemed to be very important and we felt quite proud of this. We were, in fact, listening in to our first trade union meetings.

Following the defeat of the General Strike in 1926 – or, as our Dad would have it, the betrayal of it by its leaders, trades union organisation on the Works had all but collapsed. Men deserted their unions by the thousand but a few, like Dad, retained their faith and their loyalties and attempted still to pursue their age-old dreams of improving wages and working conditions by collective action – in the circumstances following the collapse of the General Strike, this by the men on the spot, trades union members or otherwise. And because these trades union stalwarts, once their activities became known to the bosses, themselves became marked men, they preferred to conduct their business away from the prying eyes of those bosses and the ever cocked ears of gaffers' narks. Hence their meetings in such places as our front room.

A favourite tactic of the men, in dealing with a grievance they were unable to solve in any other way, was the 'lightning midnight' strike. The idea being that a boss fetched from a nice warm bed and maybe a nice warm wife in the middle of the night would probably be readier to make concessions than one fortified by a good night's sleep and a hearty breakfast served by a contented wife. Many a time I've had a chuckle over his reminiscences of the encounters between men and bosses in the early hours of the mornings.

Inevitably, there came the day when Dad became identified by the bosses as one of their 'trouble-makers' and, as such, he was included in the next lay-off.

These lay-offs were a regular feature of the 1920s and 1930s steelworks employment and were the source of much distress in the town. They could last for days, for weeks or for months — in the case of the 'trouble makers', for ever. In their cases it was victimisation pure and simple but the way in which it was carried out made it impossible to prove, not that that would have helped much anyway in the circumstances of the time.

There were three major steelworks at Scunthorpe and once a man became blacklisted by one of these he also found it impossible to obtain work with either of the other two. Although the works employment officers always denied the keeping and circulating, amongst themselves, of a blacklist of names, everybody knew they did. In the same way, they operated a 'gentleman's' agreement, amongst themselves, not to poach each other's labour. They also combined to put pressure on the local authority, through their agents on the councils, not to let other industries into the area which might provide alternative work. These practices they also denied. Scunthorpe was a 'one horse' town and they wanted to keep it that way. It danced to the tune called by the steel barons. You refused to dance to your own and your family's cost, that was the stark message of the blacklist.

To augment his meagre dole allowance, Dad obtained an evening paper round, travelling around the ill lit streets of Ashby on his bike, calling out his arrival several times in each one and finding change by the light of the carbide light on his machine. Occasionally he also found a day's, or perhaps even a week's work with one of the local builders or farmers – hod carrying, ditch digging or whatever. But little enough did the income from all these activities combined contribute to the household budget. I very much doubt if he declared any of it to the Labour Exchange clerks – his circumstances were much too reduced for him to be able to entertain such genteel notions of honour or of 'playing the game'.

As reduced and precarious as our family circumstances were at this time they were, as far as I can remember, never so desperate that we had to have recourse to the soup kitchens, which made their re-appearance on the streets in the early 1930s after being absent from them since the General Strike of 1926. One of them operated no more than a hundred yards from our own house at the Working Men's Club just around the corner of the street. I think maybe Mother would have died of shame had they been.

We, however – that is, we children – did go along to the Salvation Army's Joy Hour sessions which were held once or twice each week in the wooden Hall behind the Club, where, for the price of a few hymns and a halfpenny, you could get a hot roast potato or a mug of pea soup with a hunk of bread — and no matter if you hadn't the halfpenny, you were fed just the same. After a time lapse of over half a century, I can still hear those shrill child voices of ours raised in the singing of such old hymn favourites as 'Tell me the old, old story', 'Onward Christian Soldiers' and 'Jesus wants me for a sunbeam' – sung under the direction and watchful gaze of the stern old heavily-moustached Captain. They were indeed Joy Hours!

When I was about twelve years old, Dad's connection with the newspaper trade suddenly brought him a real stroke of luck. He secured the agency for a small business of his own, selling Sunday newspapers.

The business was only small but it was still large enough for us three boys of the family to be able to have small paper rounds of our own, in addition to the rounds of the three or four older boys who came with the business. As well as being able to make a small but very much needed contribution ourselves to the household finances, for the first time in our lives we also had pennies of our own to jingle in our pockets. Such affluence we'd never known!

Our front room, as bare as ever it had been – even barer, for it was no longer graced by the presence of the broken down old motorcycle – became now the venue for the business.

Each and every Sunday morning that came we'd be up with the larks – as early even as the early morning shift workers themselves were preparing to set off for the first shift of the day – ready and eager – to begin with anyway – to accompany Dad to the railway station at Scunthorpe in the small service bus he'd hired for the occasion to fetch the papers. We felt most important as we manfully half dragged, half carried the heavy bundles of tightly bound papers from the station platform to the waiting bus

12.

for Dad to complete the final loading.

Back at the house, papers unloaded, bus dismissed, Mother would have breakfast waiting for us and no half egg breakfast either but the full treatment with bacon and tomatoes and her own homemade bread to boot. It would be mid-afternoon before we would be able to sit down to the next hot meal.

Added all together, the money Dad made from the Sunday newspaper business, the occasional day's hod carrying and his dole allowance at least equalled what he would have earned had he been in full-time work. Which state of affairs was considered by somebody, somewhere in the dole office to be a very shocking state of affairs indeed which, if allowed to progress, might easily lead to the dissolution of the whole of the working class and, ultimately, even to the complete bankruptcy of the entire country.

Accordingly, that somebody, somewhere in the dole office acted swiftly to avert this catastrophe looming over the country – he stopped Dad's dole. Which dastardly act in turn shocked Dad – but not so deeply as to rob him of his senses. He lodged an immediate appeal against the stoppage, which led to the matter being referred to a tribunal. Not as quickly as all that, but eventually. Now that his dole was well and truly stopped, the immediacy had gone out of the situation as far as the dole office mandarins were concerned.

But the day did come when Dad's case was to be heard by the tribunal sitting, not in Scunthorpe but in, if I remember correctly, Gainsborough, fourteen miles away. Nothing daunted, he mounted his bike and rode off to do battle with 'them' on behalf of 'us', taking with him nothing more than Mother's fervent prayers for his success and his own resourcefulness – and perhaps also a couple of bob in his pocket with which to buy a pint or two afterwards to wash down the packed lunch Mother had provided for him.

The case against him was that, as he was now running a business in his own right, he was no longer entitled to unemployment benefit. No mention was made of his occasional moonlighting forays or of his evening paper round which, for Dad,

13.

enormously simplified the whole business of his defence. He was able to argue that he served his dole masters faithfully for the six days of the week for which they paid him but that on the seventh, the Sunday, he was compulsorily rested by them and for that day they neither paid him any money nor had he sought to be paid for it. Therefore the Sunday was his own, to do with as he wished. By selling papers on Sundays, he argued, he was no more in contravention of the laws governing the payment of unemployment benefit than were the unemployed men who cultivated their allotments on that day and sold the produce, or the man who sold his piglets on the same day for profit. Which brilliant defence won him the day. His dole, with full back pay, was restored.

Dad's lucky stars were staging a comeback from the cold on the other side of the galaxy where they'd been hiding for many years. It was scarcely any time at all after his brush with the dole office before he obtained a job, a regular job, with a pressed concrete firm. The work was very heavy and very dirty but he was no stranger to those kinds of conditions.

Ernie, my eldest brother, left school at Christmas 1934. He wasn't fourteen years of age really until the January but as his birthday fell in the school holidays, it counted. He began work as an apprentice bricklayer, which work can also be heavy and dirty, especially at that time of the year. But if he wasn't accustomed to the conditions, he soon became so – though Mother wept for him when she saw his hands at the end of his first week's work. They were all cracked and bleeding, due to the combined action of lime and water. She hadn't wanted that for him, she said. But Ernie was a sticker and, apart from his stint in the army during the war, he's worked at the trade ever since.

With our new found affluence, Mother was able to make a start on furnishing the front room in the way she'd always dreamt of doing one day. But first she wanted the papers out, so out they went. We cleaned out the pigsty, which wasn't a pig sty really, we'd never kept pigs in it, though others along the ten foot did in theirs. It was built of bricks with a high, slated roof and enclosed an area about nine feet by nine feet. After we'd white-washed the inside and furnished it with one or two old tables upon which to place the papers, it served our purpose quite well.

In July 1936, having attained the ripe old age of fourteen, I too left school. I could read, I could write and I'd also learned how to do some simple arithmetic. I was therefore pronounced fit and ready to enter the real world beyond the school walls, the world of doing rather than of swotting – wild horses wouldn't have dragged me back to it.

I'd never been anything of a scholar, even amongst the eleven-plus scholarship failures I'd schooled with – my heart had ever been in the great outside where the sun shone and people were free. Mother had tried to instill a little learning into us her-self. She'd bought us books when she'd had the money. Books like Peter Parly's Tales of Greece and Rome, The Broad Highway and the Books of Knowledge – but her efforts were largely wasted. we looked at the pictures and then discarded them.

There was no chance of obtaining a job on the steelworks – they employed nobody under the age of sixteen. My first job then was with the Co-operative Society – I became a baker's boy. I as-sisted the 'baker' to deliver bread and cakes around the houses from a horse-drawn van. He wouldn't have known a bowl of dough from a bowl of soapsuds – he obtained his title from his practice of throwing open the doors of houses and bawling 'Baker!' into the interiors to announce his arrival. I did the same on the other side of the streets.

They were proud moments for me when he allowed me to take the reins and drive the van. I felt very important as we smartly clip-clopped through the streets on our way back to the bakery, just dying to be seen by my former school friends or my brothers. Of course, the baker was taking no chances by placing the reins in my inexperienced hands and neither was the horse. It knew every step, stop and start of the round and especially did it know its way back to its warm, comfortable stall and its feed of oats after the day's deliveries were over. It did the driving, not me. If I made mistakes with the reins it ignored them and went its own way and always at its own pace. It was very much in charge. It, and the baker, knew it was – it was only I who didn't.

He was a clever old horse in other ways too, was Jim – for that was his name. If we lingered a little too long for his liking at any of our calls he'd snort his displeasure and paw the ground with his offside foreleg and then if we still didn't take the hint, he'd take the van on himself to the next stop, so causing the baker and me extra leg work. How I laughed at him on such occasions – but when I patted him on the nose to pacify him, he wouldn't have any of it, he'd lower his head and nudge me with such force as to almost throw me off my feet. He'd neither be patronised nor laughed at.

Jim, Dick, Killer, Floss, Sam and others of their stablemates eventually became the downfall of me and several of the other baker's boys. It happened like this.

After we'd finished each day's deliveries we returned to the bakery where the horses were unhitched from the vans and ridden by us boys back to the stables, which were about half a mile away. There were always several vans arrived back at the bakery at the same time, consequently there were also several boys to take back to the stables several horses. Boys and horses, all anxious to be done with the day's work and back in their own homes and stables, tucking in to a good feed.

We began to make a race of it, the journey back to the stable. The horses needed no urging and once clear of the bakery we let them have their heads. We thundered along one of Scunthorpe's busiest roads several horses abreast in a manner reminiscent of the Light Brigade. There wasn't nearly as much traffic on the roads as there is today – even so, cyclists, hearing the rapidly approaching thunder of iron-shod hooves on the metalled surface of the road behind them, first threw startled glances over their shoulders and then hurled themselves and their machines frantically onto the footpaths, there to shake furious fists at us as we thundered by them.

Of course, such a dangerous sport had to be stopped immediately. All of us boys were gathered together and fiercely warned

16.

of the consequences to ourselves if we continued with it – it was to be instant dismissal for the next lot caught. Nobody thought of getting the horses together and giving them the same lecture. They'd been as bad as we had.

And, sure enough, perhaps no more than a couple of days later, it happened again and it was the horses which started it – they couldn't understand the slow plod back to the stables. One decided to take his head and that was enough for the others, they all did and the next moment we were all thundering along the road like the United States Cavalry after Geronimo and this time the consequences really were disastrous. One of the horses, squeezed in by the others, collided with the side of a bus, throwing its rider who suffered a fractured skull. It could have been much worse.

We'd been warned and we were sacked – and the real culprits, the horses, who wisely kept their mouths shut, were kept on.

As I mentioned earlier, a clever old horse was Jim. When I returned him to his stable for the last time and after I'd watered him and led him to his stall where his feed of oats awaited him, whereas at this point he'd always, previously, lost interest in me as he buried his muzzle into the oats, this time he didn't. He turned his head away from the oats towards me and nuzzled me affectionately several times before turning back to the oats. He knew we were parting for the last time.

2.

THE MONKEY WALK

MY NEXT JOB was with the same firm of builders my brother worked for – I too became an apprentice bricklayer.

The blueprint for this firm might have been lifted straight from the pages of Tressal's '*Ragged Trousered Philanthropists*' – its organisation and work practices were a carbon copy of those employed by Rushton and Co. – and so were its characters. They were all there – the Crasses, the Slymes, the Newmans and the Philpots, right down to the Besotted Wretches and the apprentice boys. The only one missing was Hunter, the head foreman – our boss and owner of the firm was his own Hunter. Indeed, a Nimrod and 'a mighty hunter before the Lord' – and as greatly feared by his men and boys.

His speciality was cheap labour. He never employed a skilled man to do what a semi-skilled man could do, or a semi-skilled man to do what an unskilled man could do and none of them to do what a boy could do. Consequently, the firm swarmed with boys.

Backender, our boss – he obtained the name from his extraordinary habit of constantly reaching one hand behind him to scratch his anus, often lifting one or other of his legs to gain better access. It was said he suffered severely from piles but because he was unpopular most of the time and unmarried all of the time, there were those who hinted darkly at other causes of his discomfort – but there was no evidence to support the charge. Most of his men settled for the piles – he was a queer bugger, they agreed, but not that 'queer'.

He'd set up business in Scunthorpe as an undertaker at the end of the First World War, in which he'd served as a conscientious objector, for he was a deeply religious man and a 'shining light' in the church, in whose affairs he played a leading role. He was too a staunch member of the Conservative Party and a Borough Councillor. In short, he was a 'pillar of society'.

Under his vigorous direction the firm had grown from its humble beginnings of undertaking into, by the time I joined it in late 1936, one of the largest building firms in the area, though it still retained the undertaking side of the business. No job was too small for it and no job too large. Its activities, which covered the whole spectrum of the building trade, ranged far and wide even beyond the borough boundaries. Its men, handcarts and one lorry were to be seen everywhere about the town and all of them were visited frequently during the day by Backender in his car. You never knew when he was likely to arrive on any job so you took no liberties!

It was his proud boast that he could take a boy and make a skilled tradesman of him – good enough for himself anyway – in half the time it took his rivals and it was a boast he largely made good by the simple expedient of either sacking outright or relegating to other work those boys who didn't measure up to his requirements.

I remember once myself, at the age of sixteen, in company with another boy of fifteen, being sent from the 'yard' to build a garden wall for a lady who lived not too far away. When we arrived there she asked me where the bricklayer was and when I told her I was the bricklayer, she wouldn't even let us start on the job. 'I'm paying for men,' she said, 'not boys.' I could have done it but I couldn't persuade her of that.

Away from his church and from his business and political cronies, Backender was a foul-mouthed bully and possessed of a fearsome temper. His yelling and cursing could be heard a hundred yards away and once, at least, *was*, by his vicar, who had come in search of him. He threw up his hands in horror, 'Mr Backender, Mr Backender!' he cried in shocked tones, 'really, must you use such language?'

There was, of course, no trades union organisation on the job. The mere suggestion of such a thing would have been enough to have caused Backender to have apoplexy. Consequently we apprentice boys were never properly indentured. The mere suggestion of that too would have had the same effect – it would have been too much like incurring certain obligations himself and he was too smart for that.

There were no regular rises, annual or otherwise, for us as we progressed in age or skill. When you thought you were worth more money than he was paying you or you had been assured such was the case by the older boys or men, you just had to screw up your courage and tackle him about the matter yourself. It was very like Oliver Twist's asking for more – you knew just how he must have felt. You had to pick your moment to approach him carefully. Sometimes we waited for days for the right one, to catch him when he was in a 'good' mood and then he would peer down at you through his rimless glasses as if you were something that had crawled out of the woodwork as you put your request to him. Maybe he'd lift a leg and give his arse a couple of scratches and then, without uttering a word by way of an answer, he'd climb into his car and drive away. You didn't know until the Friday pay day whether or not you'd been granted the rise or if it was as much as you'd asked for. You opened the envelope and it was either in or it was not, there was no arguing either way.

If you approached him at the 'wrong' time, the reception you were given could be very different. I remember one youth who miscalculated in this way – he'd be about eighteen years old. He'd approached Backender in the usual deferential manner and asked him, 'Please, Mr Backender, do you think I could have a rise?' 'No, I bloody well don't!' Backender snapped back at him, badtemperedly. The lad was taken aback by the abruptness and tone of the answer but he was a spirited youth who, incidentally, won himself a Military Medal in the war a few years later, and he flushed and then replied, 'Then, Mr. Backender, do you think I could have my cards?' Backender paused a long moment this time before answering, and then he replied, 'Yes, you can have your cards,' and then suddenly and fiercely added, 'and your bloody father's as well!' The boy's father worked for him too, as a builder's labourer.

Occasionally, Backender received his come-uppance. Such an occasion arose when the church, his church, decided to build itself a new church hall, a very large and spacious church hall and therefore a very costly one. Backender had absolutely no doubts about just who would get the contract to build that, it could only be himself. Was he not one of the church's leading lights? Did he not sing in the choir? And did he not let the vicar occasionally borrow one of his men or boys to carry out some repair to the church? The good Lord was now about to reward him for his past munificence towards the church and, as he was so certain to be awarded the contract, he could afford to up the ante a bit, a sort of bonus like. He did, he submitted the highest price he dared for the work and lost the job to one of his arch rivals. The old vicar had done for him.

Backender called fire and brimstone down upon his head and upon his church too and never went there again. He found himself a new vicar and a new church in the next parish and, for all I knew, a new God too. That was Backender – nobody ever crossed him and got away with it, not even vicars or churches or Gods.

For us fifteen and sixteen year olds of the later 1930s, Scunthorpe High Street was the place to be on Sunday evenings, that's where the action was. Hair plastered back with vaseline above our pimply faces, wearing sports jackets and flannel trousers so baggy they resembled divided skirts more than they did trousers, and our feet crammed into patent leather winkle-picker shoes, we paraded endlessly up and down the High Street – it was our 'Monkey Walk'.

There we met girls, who also paraded endlessly up and down the street, attracted there by the same primordial urge as ourselves, the instinct to mate. As yet but an instinct, our encounters with the girls were usually characterised by an exchange of mild insults and juvenile, very juvenile witticisms lifted, as often as not, straight from the latest Hollywood film to hit town.

Those boys amongst us who thought they could pass for eighteen year olds, put it to the test in the pubs where, with the beer, came free cheese or potted meat sandwiches. Occasionally, just occasionally, because maybe you'd entered the place too early, before it was sufficiently filled, and thus made yourselves more noticeable, and because you were obviously under age, you had to suffer the humiliating experience of being refused service and being escorted to the door by one of the waiters.

No matter, there were other attractions in the High Street besides pubs and girls – like public meetings. If my memory serves me correctly, most of these meetings were staged by Mosely's Blackshirts, with the Labour Party and the Communist Party less often staging counter meetings.

As far as we young teenagers were concerned it was all good knock-about stuff. We joined in the cheering or jeering at the meetings as the fancy took us, without really understanding just what it was we were cheering or jeering at. Occasionally there were scuffles in the crowd but the speakers were always well protected by 'bouncers' and attempts to haul them off their soap boxes usually failed. We boys soon learned to have a healthy respect for these bouncers who weren't above landing you one across the earhole if your jeering became too frequent and too loud. We learned to do it from a safe distance and to be ready to bolt for it should the bouncers make towards us. In short, we added nothing at all to the great democratic debates of the day.

One of the prime subjects of these meetings was the Spanish Civil War. The Mosleyites were pro-Franco and the Labourites and the Communists anti-Franco. I think I'm right in saying it was the two latter parties which combined to set up the Republican Aid Committee in Scunthorpe.

This committee was formed by Republican sympathisers not only to raise cash for the Republican cause but to raise volunteers to fight for it as well in the ranks of the British Battalion of the International Brigade. It met with a fair success on both counts.

It recruited a number of men in Scunthorpe, most of whom took the first available opportunity, after the effects of the drink had worn off, to unvolunteer themselves again. Even so, there were still those made of sterner stuff who did make it all the way to Spain, which was in itself no small achievement, as the British Government of the day and their enemies everywhere put every possible obstacle in their way. This small band of stalwarts from Scunthorpe eventually did see service with the British Battalion of the International Brigade until it was disbanded at the end of the war, or almost at the end. Amongst them was one Charles James Framp, my father.

It was a thousand pities a man of Dad's undoubted high intelligence had never enjoyed the supportive background of a stable upbringing and a good education. His own father had died in 1905 when Dad had been only eight years old and because of his family circumstances – he was one of seven children, four of whom were younger than himself – he'd never attended school after he was twelve years old.

In August 1914, at the age of seventeen, he'd joined the Norfolk Regiment, in which he served out the war. He'd been wounded twice, each time by bullets, once shot through the face and once through the leg. He was discharged from the army in April 1919 on a small pension, having attained the rank of Corporal.

Dad's early life had been a hard, harsh one, made bitter by extreme poverty, but he'd never allowed himself to become embittered by it. Indeed, the picture many had of him was one of carefree independence, even irresponsibility.

About the same time as I changed jobs, from baker's boy to brickie's boy, Dad, too had changed jobs. His high intelligence and 'gift of the gab' generally had so impressed the Managing Director of a brewery company, who had visited the Working Man's Club which Dad frequented, that he'd promptly offered him a job as a brewery representative with the company. It wasn't a job in any sense of the word which Dad had ever understood. For a start, it was a white collar and he'd be able to work the hours of his own choosing. Also, it was salaried, which in itself was considerably more than his present earnings with the pressed concrete firm, on top of which would be his commission on sales and, to crown it all, he would have an expense account and a brand spanking new car to travel about in. How could he refuse such an offer?

Mother hadn't been as keen on the job as he was, it worried her. Dad had been drinking more and more since he'd been in full time work. With three wage earners now in the family and the Sunday newspaper business going well, life had never been better for us – she was quite happy with things as they were. Dad's new job would be tantamount to granting him a licence to spend the whole of his time in the pubs and clubs and that's what worried her. When he accepted the job she was filled with forboding.

The first casualty of Dad's sudden rise in the world was his Sunday newspaper business, he just lost interest in it. Within six months of his becoming a brewery 'rep', under pressure from the main agent, he handed the business over to an old friend of his but with the proviso that we three boys would be able to keep our delivery rounds for as long as we wanted them – for which we were grateful as we could earn by them on Sundays, almost as much as we could during the week on our full time jobs.

The second and last casualty was himself. Returning home, the worse for drink, in his car one day from an out of town jaunt, he failed to negotiate the sharp bend at the foot of a steep hill. His car, or rather the brewery's car, finished up lying on its back in a field – it was a complete write off. Surprisingly, amazingly, Dad himself was, apart from a few scratches and bruises, unhurt. But this latest accident in a succession of accidents with his car, all due to Dad's over-indulgence in his own wares, was the last straw – the same director who had hired him, fired him.

He'd held the job for little more than twelve months, during which time all Mother's fears had been realised. How she slated him, but even then not as much as he did himself. He knew what he'd done, he'd blown everything, his job, his Sunday newspaper business and almost his marriage. Had it not been the International Brigade, it might well have been the French Foreign Legion for him – or whoever would have taken him at the age of forty.

We at home knew nothing of Dad's Spanish connection until

24.

Mam received a letter from him announcing his arrival in that country, which came as a bit of a shock to her. She first railed at him and then she wept for him. It appeared to us boys that she didn't know her own mind regarding him.

To Ernie, my elder brother, and myself now fell the responsibility of supporting the family. Dad's sudden 'demise' and his departure had left a great hole in the family fortunes which was going to take an awful lot of filling. True, through the auspices of the Republican Aid Committee, Mother received an allowance but I seem to remember it wasn't very much at all, certainly nowhere near as much as Dad's wages would have been.

We were now right back to square one. Ernie was earning about sixpence an hour and I about fourpence, mere boy's wages, though we both needed the outfitting and feeding of men. Dad's forsight in protecting our Sunday newspsper rounds, when he'd handed on the business, now proved to be a godsend to the family, though the pocket money we'd formerly enjoyed was severely cut – it was all needed in the house.

Donald, my younger brother, left school at Easter 1938, which improved our family income a little bit. He became a butcher's boy and through him Mother was also able to obtain meat at a cut rate, which also helped. One way and another we got through.

The Spanish Civil War came to an end in the spring of 1939, with the defeat of the Republican cause. To escape Franco's retribution, Dad, like thousands of other International Brigadeers, popped quickly across the Pyrenees into France where he was, as quickly, popped into an internment camp by the French and where he stayed for several long weeks, while the French and British Governments wrangled over what to do with him and his fellow internees of the ex-British Battalion of the International Brigade. In the end, weary of each other's stupidity, they let him come home, which he did in April 1939, having suffered no harm from his adventure in Spain other than a dislocated shoulder, incurred when he'd been shot out of a tree by one of Franco's sharpshooters.

If he'd expected a hero's welcome from Mother when he returned home, he was very much mistaken. He blew it again. He'd brought a friend home with him, a buddy from the International Brigade. He returned from one war to another. Mam wasn't having that. This swearing of eternal friendship and my home shall be your home stuff might have sounded fine in a last stand split trench overlooking the Ebro river but it had no practical application back here in Scunthorpe. She gave her unwelcome guest a night's lodging and then booted him out and that was the last we saw of him. Franco might have feared the International Brigade – but our Mam didn't.

In 1938 unemployment and short-time working in Scunthorpe still cast their blight over the town but the scent of change was in the air, blowing on the chill wind of re-armament. Re-armament meant steel and steel meant Scunthorpe. But before you can have steel you need steelworkers and before you get steelworkers you need houses for them to live in. In 1938 a mini building boom hit the town and Backenders became swamped with work – building council houses.

Backender himself granted rises to his lads, who well knew when they were on to a good thing, like he'd never done before. He knew too that this was no time to risk the loss of any of his valuable crop of apprentices to rivals who, themselves bunged out with work, wouldn't hesitate to poach them – they were, after all, Backender trained.

There was much talk of war and of peace, with most people, Chamberlain's assurances of peace in our time notwithstanding, believing more and more that we were heading for a major clash with Germany. I remember the older men gravely shaking their heads over the news items then coming from the Continent, as they ate their sandwiches in the site cabins. A few of them had served in the First World War, they knew what it would be like should there be a repeat of that – Chamberlain spoke for them.

I was at work on a small building site in the town centre when I first heard the eerie, blood-curdling wail of the air raid sirens and wondered what on earth it was. It was only a test but nobody had warned us of it. This would be late July or early August of 1939, by which time I think nearly everybody had come to believe that war with Germany was now but a matter of time.

Conscription for the armed forces had been introduced that year and my brother Ernie, still two years below the call-up age of twenty, had joined the Territorial Army and Scunthorpe rehearsed its black-outs. Nobody doubted that if war did come, then, as a major steel-making town, it would become a prime target for Hitler's bombers. But how did you black-out such a large complex of steelworks? You couldn't switch furnaces off and once the tapping process had begun it must continue. You could confine the tipping of slag to the daylight hours but there were also a million other lights, glares and glows which all needed to be masked. What a headache! But, because it had to be done, it was.

Came the first day of September 1939 and Britain was still far from ready for war – but Hitler would wait no longer, his patience was exhausted. He fired the gun for the war to begin, right into the face of Poland and immediately followed it up with a ferocious punch to that luckless country's solar plexus. Which dastardly and cowardly acts so outraged the gentlemanly Chamberlain that he gave Hitler twenty-four hours to get out of Poland or face the consequences. Hitler chose the consequences and the war was properly on.

The first effects upon our household of Chamberlain's declaration of war upon Germany were two in number. Firstly, Ernie, as a Territorial soldier, was yanked clean out of it by the army and packed off to a place of safety called 'somewhere in England'. Secondly, Dad completed making the blackout shield for the kitchen window downstairs, which wasn't a moment too soon, for that very night the air-raid sirens sounded their warning and scarcely had they sounded when something, which in itself sounded like a whole stick of bombs, exploded on our backdoor. It was the street's air raid warden, who incidentally looked not a little like Hitler himself. He also had pretty much the same manners. 'Put that bloody light out!' he yelled, above the deathly hush which had fallen upon the street. Dad did.

That same week I went along to the Army Recruiting Office in Scunthorpe to join up but the sergeant wouldn't accept me without the written permission of my parents. Mother almost had a fit when I took the papers home for her and Dad to sign. She tore them into shreds right in front of me. She'd had her fill of war and one soldier in the family, she said, was enough.

3.

GOING FOR A SOLDIER

WITH THE OUTBREAK of war came the Essential Works Order and all building work not essential to the war effort was immediately stopped. Houses and other types of dwellings were abandoned, often more than half built, for the duration of war, the sites becoming overgrown with weeds and the unfinished buildings becoming looted and vandalised until they became indistinguishable themselves from the bomb-blasted ruins, which came eventually to mar the inner areas of our great cities.

Backenders switched from building houses to building shelters, the schools having priority – their shelters we built below ground level but those for the general public we built above ground. These latter were scattered about the town, strategically placed at street corners and road junctions. This work kept us busy well into 1940.

The air raids, which everybody had predicted would come, didn't. Though the sirens sounded their chill warnings almost every night to begin with, eventually people took to ignoring them. The greatest inconvenience of the war, at this early stage, was the blackout.

In the spring of 1940 we began work upon a combined First Aid Post and Casualty Clearing Station at Ashby. Somebody, it seemed, still retained faith in Hitler's bombers. We knew it would be nearly our last job in the town – practically all the shelters which were scheduled to be built were built, there was little prospect of more work. Which gloomy outlook caused Backender, as he surveyed his business prospects for the remainder of 1940 and perhaps even beyond, to divert much of his scratching from his anus to his head without, so far as I was able to observe, discovering anything which might have brought a little cheer into his life. There was, I supposed, always the possibility that the undertaking side of his business could be set to enjoy a boom but even that prospect, at the time, appeared to be doubtful.

He still visited us on the sites – or rather, those of us who still remained in his employment. Many had dived for safety into the steelworks, even before the war had commenced, to obtain reserved occupation status for themselves, and a couple of his older boys, at least, had answered the call-up. Even so, he still retained, in his employment, as late as April 1940, some fifty per cent of his old workmen. But he was no longer the yelling, cursing Backender he had formerly been. He'd arrive on the job and stand a while, moodily surveying the work and then clamber back into his car, quite often without saying a word to anybody. Even I felt a touch of sympathy for the old sod – not much of a touch maybe, but a touch.

Came April, came Norway and the war, which everybody thought, and still more hoped, was fizzling out, suddenly took off with a tremendous whoosh. And Hitler, who was no slouch when it came to war, immediately followed that up by taking a tremendous swipe at Holland and Belgium, so bringing to an abrupt end the snoring emanating from the depths of the Maginot Line, the rumbling of which, it has been said, given the right wind direction, could be heard on the Channel coast of England. And suddenly the war was very real once more. A young militia lad out of the next street to ours was killed in Norway and another, who lived next door to us, was killed in Holland.

In June 1940, we had the 'miracle' of Dunkirk, which wasn't a miracle at all but a débâcle. And Winston Churchill himself had to tell the British people who even at that late date, still hadn't properly grasped what war was about, that that's what it was. 'Victories,' he said, 'aren't won by evacuations.' Which any man who had ever shit himself in battle could have told him.

The trouble with miracles in war – unless maybe they're harmless ones like the Angel at Mons – is that people get to believing in them, consequently, when they get into trouble they tend to sit about waiting for one to happen. Churchill, who was no slouch either when it came to war, had no time for that. He wanted victory and he wanted it as quickly as possible. As far as he was concerned, miracles were out, that war and 'blood, toil, tears and sweat' were in and, of course, he was right – you can't meet bombs with Bibles, unless you really do believe in Heaven.

After Dunkirk the British people, under Churchill, buckled down properly to the job of winning the war, though their military leaders, not being so quick on the uptake, took a little longer, as witness the later débâcles of Singapore and Dieppe.

For Hitler, it was next stop, Britain. It had to be if he wanted to end the war. His war planes, which, up until July 1940, we'd scarcely seen, now made their appearance in the British skies by the thousands, chiefly in the south.

I was eighteen years old on 31 July 1940. At that age I could enlist in the army without my parents' consent and I was resolved to do just that and Mother knew I was – she did everything possible to counter my intention.

Backender was still finding odd jobs to do for the few of us he still employed, but it wouldn't be, it couldn't be, very long before the firm was compelled to close down. I decided to defer my enlistment until that moment, as I thought it would be easier for Mother to accept. My last job for the firm was at Backender's own home. The two or three of us still working for him had the job of extra strengthening his own Anderson shelter. By the time we'd completed the work, an atom bomb would have been hard put to crack it. When we'd finished the job he gave us the customary two hours notice, which he was legally compelled to do, and then, without so much as a thank you, a goodbye or kiss my arse, he paid us off for the last time.

Now unemployed, I went to the Labour Exchange to sign on. Not surprisingly, thay had no vacancies for bricklayers, except on the steelworks, furnace building. Accordingly I was directed there. But I had a prior engagement, at the Army Recruiting Office.

The recruiting Sergeant accepted my enlistment but he also advised me to take the job at the steelworks, as it might be several weeks before I actually entered the army – which surprised me. But I took his advice, which turned out to be good advice – it was to be more than two months before I finally got off.

At the steelworks they wouldn't offer me a job with the brick-layers as I was under twenty-one. Instead they offered me a job in the 'pool'. This was a gang comprised of unskilled workers upon which all other departments could draw whenever they needed extra help. I didn't argue, I took the job – it would only be for a matter of a few weeks, I thought.

Although the red skies had been banished from over Scun-thorpe, they'd reappeared over Hull, sixteen miles away, as the bomber flies, as that city burned under a rain of Nazi bombs and incendiaries.

That late summer of 1940, while I waited to go into the army, I'd sometimes be awakened during the nights by the steady rat-tling of our loose-fitting bedroom window frames and I'd know at once that 'they' were bombing Hull again and then, in the far dis-tance, you'd hear the rumble of the ack-ack and the thud of the bombs, and, if you dressed and went outside and looked north-east, you'd see the glow in the sky as that city burned.

I've heard it said that Goering, the head of the Luftwaffe, trained his bomber crews over the Humber before sending them to London and other big city targets.

Almost no bombs fell on Scunthorpe and those that did were not really meant for it – rather, they were jettisoned by German crews, too afraid to drop them on the better defended targets of Hull or Sheffield or wherever. But, of course, the citizens of Scun-thorpe weren't to know that – their town could be on Goering's hit list on any night of the week. So each night the sirens let out their blood curdling wail they wondered, could this be it? Their nights too were dark and long and filled with dread.

PART TWO

THE SOLDIER

Hark the Master of the Revenue
demands of every man his due,
of some less, of others more,
but of none they pay another's bill,
but the Master of Life has a different law
imposes He a harsher will,
if a generation does not pay his tax,
then it He takes from the next!
C. Framp

4.

THE STRAWBERRY FIELD

I ENTERED THE RANKS of the British Army in December 1940 at the age of eighteen years, when I was directed to join the 70th Battalion of the Leicestershire Regiment, which was then stationed at Kettering in Northamptonshire.

The 70th Leicesters was a young soldier's, or boy's Battalion. Its intake of recruits, all volunteers busting a gut to get into the war, was confined to the sixteen to nineteen year age group. They were held and trained in the Battalion until they reached the age of twenty, which was at that time the official call-up age. They were then transferred to the regiments of their own choosing.

Its officers and senior NCOs were mostly ageing regulars or reservists, a number of whom wore the medal ribbons of the First World War. They complemented our equipment exactly – it was all vintage 1914-18 stuff. Our webbing was the broad-belted, multi-pouched type of pre-Bren gun times, our weapons were the five-round capacity Canadian Ross rifle and the Lewis gun. Out on the march we resembled nothing so much as a ghost battalion of World War 1!

We did our basic training – foot drill, arms drill and the rest of it in the back streets of Kettering, accompanied as often as not by excited gangs of kids and dogs.

Towards the end of January 1941 we moved to Peterborough, where we were accomodated in the town's Drill Halls. There we learned how to fire our rifles and Lewis guns and how to make 'Molotov Cocktails' – petrol bombs, that is. We went on route marches and we did a few field exercises. We also provided the occasional 'crash guard' for the RAF. These were placed on an aircraft which had come down in the area, British and German, until such time as they or their remains could be salvaged by the RAF recovery crews.

About the end of March our training was considered to be sufficiently well advanced for us, that is C Company of the Battalion, to be entrusted with a real job of work. We were charged with the responsibility of the preparing and manning of the defences of Sutton Bridge airfield in South Lincolnshire, ready to meet the coming invasion by the Germans – and nobody doubted it was coming!

The area was of crucial importance to the defence of the country as a whole – it was fen country, as flat as a pancake and therefore ideally suited to the landing requirements of Hitler's airborne divisions – in which event our airfield would undoubtedly become a prime objective of the enemy.

The three platoons of the company were billetted separately at widely scattered points about the airfield, my own in what had formerly been the officer's married quarters. The nearest of the other two platoons was billeted a mile or so away over on the other side of the airfield.

We 'mucked in' with the RAF for grub – their food in their dining-hall – and what an eye opener it was for us! No soggy helpings of indifferently cooked food dumped into mess tins to be taken away and eaten in cold, draughty marquee dining halls for them. The food was out of this world – beautifully cooked and served on clean, white, pre-heated plates and always a choice of desert. The dining-hall itself was warm and spacious and beautifully decorated. The tables contained all the condiments, including a variety of sauces – not just your jam jar half filled with damp salt on the occasional table, such as we'd been accusomed to. And to cap it all, at one end of the dining room was a raised stage upon which a group of Air Force musicians played on stringed instruments the whole of the meal break. None of your trash music either, real Viennese stuff it was they played. It was to us uncultured lot as if we'd entered another world!

We'd been there no more than a week when the RAF cook sergeant, apparently concerned about his too rapidly dwindling food stocks, stood by the serving counter in the dining-hall in order to count for himself the number of soldiers he was feeding. It should properly have been about a hundred and twenty but when he'd counted almost half as many again as that and made himself hoarse with arguing, he suddenly lost his temper altogether and flatly refused to serve anyone else in khaki that mealtime. This incident led to us Leicestershires being each issued with a numbered disc which we had to hand over to the cook sergeant each meal break in order to get served even once, which provoked a fierce resentment amongst us as we were certain the RAF men with no similar check were also going round twice.

Every day, rain or fine, we were up at the crack of dawn and out on the job improving the defences of the airfield. These consisted of strong points – which we called 'localities' and which were numbered 1 to 12. At the core of each strong point was a concrete pill box which was designed to hold a Vickers machine gun crew. About the pill boxes we dug slit trenches for the ordinary riflemen and erected barbed wire barricades to protect them in turn. Each pill box, as the command point of each locality, was also connected by telephone to Company headquarters on the airfield itself.

The invasion was expected daily – or so we were told. Ceaselessly we toiled, digging trenches and erecting barbed wire barricades and rehearsing our defence drills – there was no time for 'bullshit'. All formal drills and parades were abolished. Every day that came we took along our haversack rations and stayed on the jobs until our officers were satisfied our work was on schedule. Sometimes a Church Army or Salvation Army mobile canteen would visit us and we would be allowed a short break to take advantage of its presence. For a copper or two you could buy a 'wad and a char' – that is, a rock bun and a cup of tea.

At night fifty per cent of our strength was on guard duty patrolling the defence localities and the airfield itself, while the other fifty per cent slept. On the nights you were 'off' you'd tumble into your bed – made up on the floors of houses which accomodated us – dog tired after a hard day's work and scarcely any sleep the previous night, hoping against hope that there would be no invasion alarm that night, either for real or for practice.

If we were unlucky, we'd be awakened again perhaps in the small hours of the morning by the guard commander's shrill whistling, the sound of doors being violently opened and his voice hollering, 'Everybody out!   On the double!' And then in the dim light, all we were allowed, we'd frantically throw on our clothes and equipment, grab rifles and tumble down the stairs.   There every man would be given his particular 'extra' to carry – spare magazines for the Lewis guns, maybe a box of 303 ammunition carried between two men – mine was the tripod of the Vickers machine gun which weighed about fifty pounds.   Someone would lift it onto my back, pointing two of its legs forwards over my shoulders.   I would reach up and grasp the legs firmly, one in each hand, and then set off into the often pitch black night for my particular pill box, about three hundred yards distant.

Always, as I made the fastest possible time, the sling of my rifle would somehow slip down into the crook of my elbow, causing the rifle to swing wildly and the butt of it to fetch me extemely painful raps on my shins, and sometimes, as I negotiated the barbed wire barricades and fences, it would get itself caught on the wire or on a post, so causing my hand to be torn away from the leg of the tripod and myself to fall heavily to the ground.

There were ditches to cross too.   During the day and unburdened it was child's play to stride over them but in the darkness of the night and heavily burdened as we were, it was a different story.   The ditches became filled with cursing, struggling men attempting to retrieve their loads and assist one another out of them.

Then nearing journey's end, you came to the main Sutton Bridge-King's Lynn road which, as this was fen country, was raised considerably above the land each side of it.   If, in the dark and the rush, you missed the steps to the top cut into the bank sides and attempted to climb the bank anyway, you would sometimes get almost to the top and then suddenly lose your footing on the wet, slippery grass and go crashing all the way to the bottom again.

Short as it was, that journey on the dark, rainy nights and the time we were expected to do it in became a fearsome obstacle course in its own right – it tried our normal good humour and high spirits to the limit. Fortunately, most of our alarms occurred on the brightly moonlit nights which made the mad rush for the defences so much easier.

On those nights – of the bright moons – the Germans always stepped up their air activity over the country. Consequently we suffered many false alarms and alerts on such nights – of parachutists descending somewhere, of lights flashing in lonely places, of strange happenings on the coast. It was all invasion nerves, there was seldom any substance to the reports.

As we patrolled the defences in pairs on those bright moonlit nights, we'd hear the constant drone of German aircraft crossing the coastline on their way to bomb targets further inland and then we'd pause to look up into the bright night sky and attempt to pick them out as they passed across the face of the moon. Later, in the early hours of the morning, we'd hear those same planes, missions completed, returning home and follow their flight paths with our gaze far out to sea until gradually the rhythmic throb and beat of their engines died away to a complete silence.

Occasionally, one or another target in our area became the objective for the bombers and once or twice the airfield itself.

One bright moonlit night I was on guard duty, my companion walking perhaps twenty yards in front of me. I heard an aircraft approaching from the direction of the sea – it sounded very low – British or German, I wondered? My uncertainty was almost immediately resolved when the flare path was suddenly switched on. I paused to watch the plane land and then suddenly to my left there was a blinding flash of light. I heard an explosion, then a second flash illuminated the gable end of a farm cottage which stood on the edge of the airfield. The end wall of the cottage collapsed in a swirling cloud of dust and smoke and I could see right into the bedrooms. A succession of other flashes leapt across the airfield – we were under air attack.

The flare path was immediately switched off - somebody had bungled badly. Out of the cloud of still swirling, moonlit dust and smoke my guard mate suddenly appeared. I wondered what on earth he was playing at – he was dancing like a dervish. I still hadn't properly grasped what was happening, so suddenly had it happened, and then I saw that he was dancing with pain and shock – one of his arms had been blown clean off, all that remained of it was a short length of splintered bone which gleamed whitely in the moonlight   He had also, although I didn't realise it at the time, been hit in the stomach. I quickly grabbed hold of him and placed his remaining arm about my neck and I'd no sooner begun to lead him away when a woman in her nightdress ran by me screaming hysterically, followed by a man trying to keep up with her. It was the couple from the cottage. As I made my way to the airfield's medical station supporting my badly wounded mate, other German planes, guided by the fires started by the first, came in low and released their bombs. Again I saw the rapid succession of flashes leap across the airfield as the bombs exploded. The one or two Oerlikon guns – the 'drome's only defence against air attack – had by now got into action, their tracer bullets shot up into the sky and the German air gunners overhead replied in kind. I heard and saw their bullets strike and set to dance the high barricade of concertina barbed wire which I was following. I handed my companion over to the medical orderlies at the station. He was scarcely conscious. I'd half carried, half led him more than a quarter of a mile and I too was drenched with blood – his. I returned to my post to watch the rest of the raid from the safety of a ditch.

A farmer called Soles cultivated much of the land about the airfield. He was known to us as Old Soles, or sometimes more affectionately as Old Regie, but more respectfully to our Captain who, as well as being an officer was also a gentleman, in his not infrequent correspondence with him, as Mr R Soles.

We regularly enjoyed the sound and fury of Old Regie's confrontations with the red faced officers in charge of our digging and wiring parties – our sympathies were unfailingly with him on these occasions. He would no sooner get one of his fields turned over and planted with seed than we lot would descend upon it and dig a line of trenches and erect barbed wire barricades right through the middle of it and the first he would know of it was when he spotted us at work in the field. Then he would descend upon us like an avenging angel, waving his stick over his head as if it was a knobkerry. 'Dig for Victory? Dig for Victory yer buggers!' he would howl at our officers, 'as fast as ah'm getting the stuff int'd ground, yer buggers is tearing it out again!'

Old Regie was also a frequent visitor to our Company office, which was a wooden hut in a corner of the airfield. We always knew what the trouble was when we saw him disappearing into it – he was just plain sick to death of providing free eggs for breakfast for the night guards!

It just so happened that the siting of his hen houses coincided with the meeting point between a couple of the 'prowler' or wandering guards. The two men of each guard coming off 'stag' just before dawn were always reminded by their other mates in the guardroom 'not to forget the eggs' as casually as if they were going to the shop to buy them.

Occasionally Old Regie or one of his men would wait in the hen houses to catch the thieves red-handed and, of course, we were constantly lectured on the subject by our officers. Maybe for a day or two after one of these lectures, or maybe after Regie had been seen lurking in the vicinity of the hen houses, the hens would step up productivity but as a rule they'd slipped back again within the week.

But Old Regie was no quitter, he was a farmer of the old bulldog breed. He never gave up, he fought us in the hen houses, in the fields or wherever he found us on his land. He never surrendered, no matter how heavily the odds were stacked against him. He did, too have his victories. Perhaps *his* finest hour came when he captured a whole platoon single-handed. He sprang out of a ditch and caught the whole bunch of them coolly helping themselves to his newly ripening strawberries!

That same evening, upon their return to the airfield, the platoon found the Captain with Old Regie standing beside him waiting for them. He, the Captain, pitched into them as he'd never done before. He'd told them and he'd told them he told them, until he was sick of telling them he told them, and now he was going to tell them no more. He was going to *act*. He'd decided in consultation with Mr. R. Soles to place a guard over the strawberries until such time as they were lifted by their rightful owner. From that night on, the platoon would, in addition to all its other guards and duties, have to provide still another guard each night to be placed over the strawberries. Well, that was certainly one up to Old Regie – or that's what it appeared to be at the time – but scarcely a week later he was back in the Company office pleading with the Captain to remove the guard. Since they'd taken up their guard duties in the field the strawberry disappearance rate had gone through the roof! I– and everybody else in the Company except the Captain – knew what had happened. The guards had gone into business, 'their' strawberries for the hen house eggs of the other guards. Now all the guards were having strawberries with their eggs for breakfast!

So raged the Battle of Britain in that corner of the country, and then the Germans struck. At a stroke they reduced all our hard work of the defences to naught, they invaded Russia.

Shortly after that particularly cowardly German blow we were posted elsewhere. There was no joyous peal of bells in the area to mark the occasion, I remember. But I also distinctly don't remember there being many tears shed by the local populace when we broke the news to them and especially by the RAF cook sergeant and Old Soles.

For the remainder of that year we messed about on other aerodromes and in other camps, all of which were situated in the East Midlands and all of which bore the same address – 'somewhere in England' – which was convenient because nobody had remembered to put back the signposts and name places anyway after the invasion scare had receded.

In January 1942 I caught the train at Peterborough, along with the rest of the Battalion, for St. Albans to embark upon a crash course of winter training on the heaths outside the town. The snow had been delivered ahead of us and lay everywhere about the town, deep and crisp and even and bloody cold. We mucked about in it for two or three weeks and then we returned to 'somewhere else in England'.

Out on the march one night during our stay at St. Albans we'd passed by Napsbury Hospital. I'd gazed at it with more than a passing interest. It was that same hospital in which Mum had served as a nurse during the First World War and it had been there she'd first met Dad, after he'd been wounded in France in 1918. I tried to picture the two of them in there as young people, never in their wildest imaginings would they have thought that one day, scarcely a generation later, the roads outside the hospital would again ring with the marching feet of the soldiers of a Second World War and that among those ranks there would be marching a son of theirs.

Mother believed in 'second sight', she was always telling the rest of the family how this or that happening had 'broken' this or that dream of hers. It was no doubt a good thing for me that she'd been unable to stretch her second sight that far ahead.

In the wet spring of 1942 rumours began to circulate the camp to the effect that the battalion was to be broken up and we lot, twenty years old or not, were to be sent to the regiments of our choice. True or false? I wasn't particularly bothered, that July I'd be twenty years old anyway and so be eligible for transfer.

I'd put down the Black Watch as my first choice of regiment. It was a popular choice amongst us lads of the 70th Leicesters, all the Scots regiments were. They seemed to be that bit more glamorous than their English counterparts.

I and about half a dozen others of the 70th Battalion of the Leicestershire Regiment were eventually transferred to the 6th Battalion of the Black Watch, or to give it its proper title, the 6th Battalion, The Royal Highland Regiment, that was in August

1942. In peacetime it had been a unit of the Territorial Army. Mustered on the outbreak of war it had seen service in France and Belgium with the 4th Division, to which it still belonged.

At the time we joined it, August 1942, the battalion was stationed at Thurso, right up in the far north of Scotland, as draughty a part of Britain as you could find, certainly no place for kilts! Even our Nissan huts on the cliff tops were tied down with steel ropes to prevent them being blown away. We were pleasantly surprised to discover a large part of the battalion's strength, perhaps a quarter, was comprised of fellow Sassenachs or Englishmen, mostly reinforcements drafted into the battalion after its evacuation from France to make up its losses. There were also a number of ex-70th Leicesters on its strength which all helped to ease our early sense of alienation.

The salt porrige was a bit of a shocker. It was strange too to be soldiering with 'old sweats', many of whom were over thirty and had seen action in France. I felt very junior.

The training was also much tougher than anything we'd experienced in the Leicesters. Looking back on it, it seems to me we spent half our time doubling around the camp in P.T. kit or over obstacle courses in battle kit and the other half squelching over boggy peat moors on route marches, which by Divisional order were never less than twenty-five miles in length and during which we had to march for one hour wearing our gas masks, so frightening half to death the rabbits and the few crofter kids we encountered.

I wasn't sorry when we moved to the kinder climate of the border country in early October. I was sorry when I discovered the reason for the move.

We were there to be trained and toughened up as we'd never been trained and toughened up before at a 'Battle School' situated just outside Hawick. We were accomodated in a brigade sized camp and from the moment we entered it to the moment we left it six weeks later we did everything on the double – all leave was cancelled for the duration of the course. What followed was the toughest six weeks of my life, both before and since. The assault courses and the obstacle courses were truly fearsome, involving the crossing of a river and a large pond and even clambering under the wheel of a water mill in the deep, cold, muddy waters of a racing stream. Ropes had been strung across the river and the pond for the benefit of non-swimmers, albeit that in that respect we were all the same – the weight of our rifles and equipment and the ammunition we carried made swimming impossible for anybody. We covered the courses in sections and in platoons and we had a set time to cover them. If you took longer than that set time, even if it was only by seconds and that by only one man of the section, you all had to do it again and again and again if necessary. Live ammunition and practice grenades were used by the instructors both to simulate the real conditions of battle and to speed us on our way.

Occasionally a man would jib at the obstacles, especially the water obstacles where inevitably you spent some of the crossing time under water. Nobody had any sympathy for them, you were too busy being sorry for yourself. When this happened the instructors would grab hold of the man and hurl him into the water – then hurl a few extra practice grenades into the water after him to make sure he didn't clamber back on to the same bank. As far as they, the instructors, were concerned, we'd a war to win and no lily-livered milk sops were going to jeopardize that on the flimsy pretext that they couldn't swim or breathe or what.

I remember that though I'd carried no spare flesh at the commencement of the course, I'd still lost several pounds in weight by the end of it. So realistic of battle had been the course that we did actually lose a few men on it, killed and wounded.

We followed up that high speed training by embarking next upon a course of invasion training. For this we travelled to Inverary on the western coast of Scotland, where we carried out our exercises on, and in, the icy waters of Loch Fyne and the Irish Sea.

To begin with, we practiced boarding the landing craft from the quayside at Inverary and assaulting the opposite shore of the loch. During these exercises it snowed pretty heavily but nobody thought of calling off the exercises on that count. Always, in our opinion, the sailors of the Royal Navy who had the charge of the landing craft, dropped the landing ramp much too soon, so causing us to wade unnecessary extra yards through the chest high, freezing waters of the loch to the shore, where we completed the exercises by lying about in the snow listening to what sounded like the unending chatter of machine guns but was, in reality, the chatter of our own teeth!

Later, we practiced the boarding of the landing craft from the ocean-going liners out at sea and this too was a dicy business as we discovered. Carrying all our battle gear, we'd climb over the rails of the great ships and on to the huge rope nets draped over their sides for us to clamber down and drop into the landing craft waiting below to receive us – but it was never as easy as that. You had to time your drop from the net into the landing craft just right, heavily burdened and encumbered as you were and restricted for time and for room. It was all too easy, especially in the dark, to miscalculate and so sprain an ankle or even break a leg, either your own or somebody else's. Due to the action of the waves often one boat was rising as the other was falling and while you were trying to figure out just which boat was doing what, the two would drift apart and open up a gap between them into which you could easily drop and be crushed as the two scrunched together again, and finally, while you clung to the net trying to make up your mind, one of the men clambering down above you would like as not crush your fingers beneath his great boot or put the heel of it into your face, so making up your mind for you. It was indeed a dicy business.

Sometime in January 1943 we returned thankfully to the border country, far away from boats and sailors and the icy seas. We were stationed, or rather my Company was, at Abbotsford in the ancestral home of Sir Walter Scott, a very beautiful place surrounded by pine forests. Scarcely had we settled in than it was announced that we were all, the whole battalion, to be granted home leave – embarkation leave.

We were certain this was going to be it – the second front,

the invasion of the Continent. There could have been no other purpose to our recent training.

Upon our return to Abbotsford after the ten days' leave, our platoon commander, Lt Hutchinson, decided that it would be nice if each member of his platoon could have a group photograph of the entire platoon to send home to his family before departing overseas to fight the savage foe.

Accordingly, immediately prior to the photograph being taken and knowing just how scruffy and unphotogenic some of his men could be, Lieutenant Hutchinson had us paraded for his inspection all slicked up in our best battledresses. We stood in three ranks before him while he ran his eye over each man carefully. Only one man failed to pass muster – myself. I was ordered to go to the stores immediately and draw another battledress suit.

At that stage of the war all newly issued battledresses were impregnated with some sort of anti-gas chemical which not only rendered the suit as stiff as cardboard until you'd 'broken them in' but also left them looking almost cream in colour until that too wore off. Result - when the photograph was finally taken and developed, from my position bang in the centre of the platoon, I stood out like a snowman in a platoon of Zulus and mother, when she received it – as full of second sightings and miracle happenings as ever, and Winston Churchill no matter, believed it to be an omen, that God had directed a ray of sunshine or something especially at me in order that I would be saved from the war and brought safely back to her. Oh mother!

5.

THE CONVOY

WE SAILED from Liverpool early in February 1943 on a huge
Dutch liner weighing some 21 000 tons. In the Irish Sea we
rendezvoused with other ships to make up a large convoy which
then rounded the top of Ireland and headed out into the Atlantic,
indeed so far out that rumours began to circulate around the ship
that we were headed for the Panama Canal and then to the far
east to fight the Japs.

Our quarters were right down at the bottom of the ship,
well below the water line, which made us all very nervous. The U-
boat menace was very real; it wasn't then beaten and the Atlantic
swarmed with them.

As we practiced our boat drills, proceeding along the maze of
narrow corridors and up the never ending succession of ladders
in orderly manner until we finally emerged onto the boat deck itself, I couldn't help but wonder how it would all go in a real emergency – how would the men behave then, after the ship had perhaps been torpedoed and water was pouring into the corridors?
Would they then wait patiently at the junctions of the corridors or
at the foot of the ladders for their rightful turns – or would it then
be a mad, undisciplined stampede of every man for himself?

As we sat on our hammocks during the submarine warning
times, each man clutching or already wearing his mae-west, ob-
serving a complete silence in the semi-darkness, you could feel
the tension building up as we sat out the long, long minutes waiting for that apalling crash which would signal that a torpedo had
struck home. I'm sure that at such times it would have taken
very little to start a wild, unholy stampede for the ladders leading
to the boat deck – such was the claustrophobic effect our sunken
quarters had upon us.

On about the tenth day at sea we were graciously informed
of our destination – it was Algiers. We were given another very

useful item of information at the same time – we'd arrived!

My first view of that great, romantic, Mediterranean sea port was obtained from the deck of our great ship as it slowly nosed its way into the harbour. From what I could see of the city, all its buildings appeared to be roofless, box-like structures, ranging in colour from white to dirty grey and scattered higgledy-piggledy one above the other on the shoreline. My first impression of it then was the very unromantic one of a pile of giant teeth in various stages of discolouration scattered by some giant hand of the past over a hillside overlooking the sea.

We disembarked wearing greatcoats and full marching order. We were thankful for the greatcoats – despite the fact that we'd arrived on the southern shores of the Med it was as cold as the Scotland we'd left behind. We marched the four miles to our billets, which were in a disused brickyard, accompanied all the way by hoardes of Arab kids chanting, 'Cigarette Johnnie', 'Chocolate Johnnie'. They did pretty well out of us too.

We didn't stay long in Algiers, less than a week perhaps, but it was long enough for us to be able to take a quick squint at the Kasbah which, as well as being out of bounds, was dirty, squalid and fascinating, and also to witness a couple of air raids on the harbour by German and Italian planes.

The fighting in Tunisia was still going on, though not exactly as planned. The First Army seemed to have got itself pretty well bogged down in the hills. Apparently they were waiting for us to un-bog them. Both sides, the Allies and the Axis powers, were re-inforcing their armies in Africa heavily – it would be the side which won the battle of the reinforcements which would win the Battle of Africa – of Tunisia anyway.

We travelled the first leg of our journey into Tunisia by destroyer, from Algiers to Bone, and it's a journey I'll remember the rest of my life. We'd no sooner left Algiers harbour than a howling gale sprang up. There had been no room to accomodate us below decks, we just had to cling frantically to whatever hand holds we could find for ourselves; there were no safety rails around the ship, only a single rope hung slackly between a few iron posts lay between us and the boiling sea. The destroyer making full speed didn't go over the waves, it sliced straight through them, sending great sheets of ice-cold salt water sweeping over the decks and us. One moment you would be looking up at the sky, and the next, without changing position, you would be looking down at the sea scarcely a yard below your nose. We were soaked to the skin, frozen stiff and as sick as dogs when we arrived at Bone maybe twelve hours later. We could hardly stand up, let alone march.

The remainder of our journey into Tunisia was made by road, which was itself pretty rough travelling. I don't remember how long the journey took us but we eventually arrived at a bleak and desolate part of the country, which became known to us as Cow Valley, where we bivouacked for the night. I'd no idea we were so close to the front itself until it became dark – then we saw the quick flashes of light in the distance. Sometimes there were several flashes in quick succession and if you listened carefully you could hear a thudding in the distance – it was the guns. I couldn't remove my eyes from the horizon upon which their lights twinkled from time to time. I must have watched it for hours before I finally gave up and retired to my blankets. I eventually fell asleep wondering how I would behave under fire – what would it really be like?

We had arrived at the Beja sector of the front. Our Battalion was to take over a part of the line at present held by the Irish Fusiliers. However, before handing over to us, the Fusiliers were to attack the Germans opposite them. The idea was for us then to move in and hold the ground gained by the Irish Battalion.

We prepared to move out of Cow Valley. Blankets were rolled and strapped horse-shoe fashion to valises. Every man was issued with a pick or spade. These were carried slotted between packs and backs – not as uncomfortable as it may sound. We were also issued with anti-tank mines – number 84 grenades, as they were called. These were intended to be dug into the ground before our new positions, in case we were counter attacked by tanks. We fused the mines by inserting a tubed detonator between the flat top of the mine casing and the slightly raised metal strip of the pressure plate, which had a downward facing 'V' notched into it. Under pressure the 'V' broke the tube and exploded the mine. Obviously, we kept the fuse and the mine seperated until the time came to actually lay them.

In single file, platoon by platoon, company by company, the Battalion moved out of the valley and headed for the front line, a piper leading each company. We shared the heavier burdens, the Brens, the Boyd's anti-tank rifle, the two-inch mortars, the packs of shells for it etc. A man would carry one or other of these for perhaps twenty minutes and then hand the load to the next man due to take it.

The hills about us were, appropriately enough I remember thinking, red with poppies. We marched in staggered formation either side of the road, both as a precaution against air attack and to leave the road itself clear for the lines of traffic proceeding to and from the front.

The thudding of the guns grew louder as we neared the line. I became increasingly apprehensive, wondering anxiously how I would stand up to the fire. The Company was halted in a sandy defile – 'wadis' we came to call such places later. We rested on the bank side. Suddenly we heard the crackle of small arms fire and then, as suddenly, the roar of an aeroplane. The plane was a German Me109 flying very low. It shot away, turned and then came our way. It roared above the wadi, barely two hundred feet above our heads. Everybody blazed away at the plane and suddenly it sprouted a thin trail of smoke, a wing dipped and the nest moment it crashed. Lieutenant Hutchinson, our platoon commander, waved his hands excitedly. 'We claim that,' he shouted, 'We claim that.' Certainly it looked as if it was our company which had brought down the plane but whether or not we were credited with the 'kill' I never found out.

6.

THE MIRAGE

AS A RESULT of the Irish attack the Germans, on our part of the front, had fallen back, but nobody was quite certain how far. Consequently, when the Fusiliers moved out after dark, it was decided we should advance some way in front of the positions they vacated.

Only an occasional gun fired as we went forward into the dark, the flashes briefly lighting up the hills about us. Eventually we came to a halt on a gradually sloping hillside and were ordered to dig in. Lieutenant Hutchinson took me forward about fifty yards in front of the rest of the platoon. I was to cover them with the Bren while they dug in. 'We don't know exactly where the enemy is,' he explained, 'but fire an occasional burst in that direction, just to let 'em know we're here and ready for them.' He waved his hand airily before him, then he was gone and I was left alone with the Bren. My first night in the front line; it was dark and I was both excited and frightened. I wished I knew how far away the Germans were – they might have been as much as half a mile away or as little as fifty yards, there seemed to be no planning at all.

A sound like a continuous ringing in the ears rose up from the ground below. It was the singing of countless thousands of crickets or grasshoppers – it sounded weird.

The artillery lads of both sides appeared to have gone to bed, not a gun fired. Apart from the noise made by the crickets, all was quiet. Time dragged by and I began to feel cold. Occasionally I heard the distant clink of a spade on stone or the faintest thud of a pick biting into the hard ground, as the platoon dug in behind me. The noises sounded to be very far away. As the time passed I grew colder. I remembered 'Hutchy's' order to fire a burst on the Bren now and again, but I held my fire. 'Supposing,'

I thought, 'Jerries are creeping towards us at this very moment; I would give my position away to no purpose. Bugger Hutchy.'

More time passed; it grew colder. A battery of guns suddenly erupted into life behind our lines. A moment or two afterwards I heard the shells go slithering through the sky, high above my head. I squeezed the trigger of the Bren and tracers streaked into the night in the direction of where I imagined the enemy to be. I gave a second longer burst, then, with pounding heart, wondering whatever had possessed me to do that, I quickly changed the magazine and lay perfectly still, listening and straining my eyes into the darkness.

The singing of the crickets had come to an abrupt end. I waited, hardly daring to breathe. Nothing moved, no sound broke the silence. After what seemed an eternity, a single cricket chirrupped, then several, and soon they were all back to full song. No German grenades had sailed through the dark to explode around my wildly imagining head. Just the same, I fired the Bren no more. I had done as I was ordered and that, I thought, was sufficient. I hadn't really bargained on being left alone on my very first night in the front line.

When Lieutenant Hutchinson arrived with my relief I was stiff with cold. I had lain there, I suppose, for an hour at the most but it had seemed to me to be half the night. I thought I had been forgotten. 'Everything all right, Framp?' 'Yes, sir,' I replied, wanting only to keep the palaver to a minimum and get back to the others and get warm.

My trench mate, a Staffordshire lad called Latham, had got about a couple of feet down with the foxhole he and I were to share. I took the spade from him and gladly set to work. The trench needed to be a couple of feet deeper still; the excavated earth I scattered around the top of the hole. By 'stand to', half an hour before first light, both of us were satisfied with the depth of the hole. We stood in it to await the dawn and about half an hour after that, the 'stand down'. It was unbelievably cold. At first light the guns of both sides suddenly and savagely opened fire upon each other. It was my first experience of the 'morning hate'.

No shells fell near us so we were able to to listen to the tremendous racket with a fair amount of detachment.

As soon as it was light enough we switched our attention from the noisy artillery battle to the much more rewarding business of readying the tommy-cookers. These were just large-sized jam tins with holes punched around the top. The bottom half we filled with sand and prepared them for action simply by soaking the sand with petrol poured from a jerry-can. In the same second as the order to 'stand down' was given, men flicked the match they'd just lit their previously readied cigarettes with into the cookers and on went the 'kettles'. These were also jam tins, minus the holes, and usually had wire loops attached to them for easier handling. No tea I have ever tasted was better than that which came out of those blackened and battered old tins. We guarded them as though they were gold.

The day began with a thick mist. As the sun got up this began to disperse, slowly at first but then, in a very short space of time, it was gone altogether. In the full light of day we were able to see much more of our surroundings. Our position overlooked a shallow valley, perhaps five hundred yards wide. It curved around us to the left and on the right the view ran out of ground at the crest of the hill some eighty or ninety yards distant.

Everything looked quiet and peaceful, until my eye was caught by the burst of several shells down in the valley, way over to the left. There was no sign of life down there. Indeed, apart from our own little patch of ground, everywhere else looked to be deserted. We wondered where the Germans were. Did we face this way or that to meet them, if and when they attacked us?

As the sun rose higher, a peculiar change began to come over our positions. The earth we had evacuated began to dry out and, as it did so, it turned almost pure white, like snow! We could not have marked the positions better if we had laid out on the ground the brightly coloured cloth sheets we carried in order to identify ourselves to friendly aircraft. This was also the explanation behind the ghostly appearance of the Irish Fusiliers.

It would not have mattered so much if we had dug in correctly on the reverse slope of the hill, but we hadn't. We had dug in on the forward slope – the slope, that is, in full view of the enemy, in our case the Germans on the other side of our valley and also, unbeknown to us, on the two hills either side of us. Completely ignorant of this fact and being the greenhorn troops we were, men were wandering about the hillside as if we were still playing at war back in Scotland.

I was dozing in the trench when the first German shells arrived. Suddenly I was jerked into full wakefulness by an ear-splitting shriek. A second or two later the shells exploded on the hillside. My blood froze in my veins. A second salvo screamed down upon us and the earth rocked with the violence of the explosions. Latham and I crouched as low as we possibly could in the trench. Explosions followed explosions in rapid succession. We were showered with clods of earth and small stones; dirt from the trench sides trickled down the backs of our collars as, each time, we ducked our heads. Neither of us dared to take a peep over the edge of the trench to see how the others were faring. Each deafening shriek convinced us that our own little hole in the ground was the sole target of the Germans.

Suddenly all was quiet once more. We waited, the quiet endured. Latham and I raised our heads and our eyes met. No doubt mine asked the question we were both too afraid to give voice to – was that it? Was it finished? I heard a voice calling and I peeked over the edge of the trench and saw the head and shoulders of Lieutenant Hutchinson looking out from his trench. 'Everything alright over there?' he called. I nodded my head, 'Yes, sir, I think so,' I answered.

The ground around us looked as if it had been freshly ploughed. Two men in the next trench to our own, had had a truly miraculous escape. A shell had fallen very close to their position. It had further exploded the 84 grenade, contained in one of the men's packs, placed alongside the trench. Under the shock of the double explosion the sides of the trench had collapsed, almost completely burying both men. However, apart from being badly shocked, in all other respects they were completely unharmed. This was my first experience of enemy shell fire and my worst fears, concerning my own feelings when the time came, had been confirmed – I'd been completely terrified!

The Germans shelled and mortered us, off and on, all that day. Every movement on the positions brought a fresh, fierce 'stonk' down on our heads. We were confined, every man, to his own trench. Night came as a blessed relief – we were able to stand upright and stretch our cramped limbs. The water ration was brought up and a hot meal – carried forward in insulated containers. The water was warm and heavily chlorinated. Each man was allowed to fill his bottle and that was his lot, for all purposes, for at least another twenty-four hours. Needless to say, nobody wasted any of that little on washing and shaving. The more heedful of the men sipped theirs sparingly, but one or two, out of sight of the NCO's, drank deeply of theirs. 'Who wants to die wi' a full water bottle?' they scoffed at us more cautious souls.

The hot meal was especially welcome, for though the days were warm, even hot, it turned bitterly cold at night. So much so that, in addition to our greatcoats, we wore blankets wrapped around our shoulders when on sentry.

Our company was very much on the alert that night. In view of the great attention paid to us by the enemy that day, we were convinced that we were going to be attacked that same night but the only thing of note which occurred turned out to be something of an anti-climax. A German officer crawled to within thirty yards of our right hand platoon and arrogantly called upon it to surrender. One of the men fired blindly in the direction of the voice and, by a piece of good luck, hit the German, wounding him severely. They brought him in the next morning after the 'stand down' order had been given.

As soon as it became light we discovered at first hand what 'the morning hate' was all about. The Germans commenced fiercely to 'stonk' us and the rest of that morning they plastered our hillside positions with gun and mortar fire at fairly frequent intervals, causing numerous casualties. They also sent over air bursts and these exploded above our heads with a terrific crack,

throwing shrapnel down into the trenches. A very large and jagged piece of shrapnel from one of these thudded into the side of
the trench between myself and Latham and dropped to the floor.
Curious, I picked it up, only to drop it instantly – it was red hot.
I tried not to think about the consequences of stopping a similar
lump!

In the intervals between the shelling we tried to get some
sleep, so to await the next 'stonk', call to duty or whatever!
Latham became restless and attempted to stretch his legs, impossibly, past mine. His constant writhing and fidgeting irritated me
and I snapped at him bad temperedly. There was a look of des-
peration on his face. 'It's no good, Charlie,' he said apologeti-
cally, 'I can't wait any longer, I'm going to have to do it here!' I
nodded my head dumbly. I didn't relish the prospect but I sympathised with him. On that exposed hillside in broad daylight it
was an awful long way to the latrine trench and none of the others would thank him for bringing about yet another burst of fire
down upon our heads. All things considered, it was definitely not
the time to cling to the social graces!

In the late afternoon I was dozing in the trench when suddenly I was jerked fully awake by the sound of men shouting. I
raised my head above the level of the trench and there beheld an
alarming sight. A section of men of our own platoon, fully
dressed and carrying all their gear, were running, hell for leather,
along the hillside, away from the positions. Corporal Murray, our
section leader, spotted me. 'We're getting out,' he called, 'get
dressed, we're next.' I needed no second telling, I wasn't going to
be left behind. Latham was fast asleep. I kicked his boots.
'C'mon Eddie, we're getting out', I called to him as I grabbed my
own equipment and commenced to throw it on. Latham hardly
stirred so I kicked at his boots savagely but still he didn't wake. I
bent down and grabbed the front of his battledress blouse with
both hands and shook him violently. 'C'mon,' I yelled desperately, 'we're getting out!' He just would not open his eyes. Again I
shook him, even more violently than before and at last his eyes
opened. Once I'd got through to him he moved like greased light-

ening. When Murray shouted to us to go we were both ready and out of the trench in a flash. The Germans woke up to the fact that we were abandoning the position almost too late. We did incur casualties but nowhere near as many as we had invited by leaving the comparative safety of our trenches in broad daylight. One of the chaps belonging to another platoon was hit by a bullet behind the knee as he ran. He didn't even know it until he reached the safety of the reverse slope of the hill!

Our Colonel was badly wounded on this day and Major Madden, the second-in-command, took over the Battalion command. 'D' Company went into Battalion reserve.

About a hundred yards below our new positions ran a stream. Its bed was wide but, as the rainy season was spent, or almost, the actual stream was confined to a narrow channel running along the centre. Here and there varying sized pools or ponds had formed. The water was badly discoloured and teeming with insect life and we were warned on no account to drink it. However, its use for washing had not been specifically forbidden so, at the first opportunity, I grabbed a mug, towel, soap and shaving gear and loped eagerly down the hillside to the stream. I chose a spot between the ponds where the water looked to be comparatively clear. I removed all my clothes, piled them on the bank and then sat down in the stream to take a much needed bath. The water was only a few inches deep but I managed to ladle it over my head and shoulders with the tin mug. There was no telling when next I should be able to take a bath so I ignored the myriads of insects and other life caught up in the mug each time I lifted it clear of the water.

I was in the middle of my bath and singing away to myself when I became aware of a tremendous racket going on around me. I glanced upwards to see a flight of half a dozen Stuka dive-bombers approaching. Flak was bursting all around them, they flew in the centre of a mass of little black clouds. Even as I spotted them one of the planes was hit – it broke formation and, with smoke pouring from it, turned and made its way back to the German rear. The others came steadily on – very soon they would arrive directly over the stream. I was not particularly bothered, flights of Stukas were not likely to be interested in a lone soldier, especially a naked one, sitting in the bed of a stream.

Suddenly, to my horror, the leading Stuka banked and began to dive straight towards me. I flattened myself quickly to the bed of the stream as the other planes followed the first. The increasing noise of the approaching planes became deafening – I never felt more naked in my life. One after another the Stukas screamed over my head. I neither saw nor heard the bombs coming down, I was frantically looking the other way with both hands clasped tightly over my ears.

There followed several thunderous explosions perhaps fifty, perhaps a hundred yards upstream of me. A miniature tidal wave of mud and water, mostly mud, suddenly swept round a bend in the course of the stream. It half carried, half rolled, me along with it. After the planes had gone and the firing had ceased, I climbed to my feet. I was covered from head to foot with slime and the water remaining in the stream was thick with mud and rotting vegetation. Luckily my clothes on the bank had escaped. I cleaned myself as best I could and after I had got the worst off and dried myself the towel was as mud itself. I left the stream much more in need of a bath than when I had arrived at it.

No soldier I ever met felt the least bit flattered by the attention the enemy particularly bestowed on him. I was no exception, which was just as well for, as I wearily climbed the hill back to my own position, several guns suddenly opened fire right behind me. The unexpected shock of the explosions so close caused me to dive for the ground once more. The guns were concealed in the river bed, they had been hidden from my view by the bend in the stream. It had been them, not me, the Stukas had been after. They were now barking their defiance – 'Yah, never touched me!' sort of thing.

Over to our right was a high mounded hill. It was very prominent and the Germans constantly shelled it. It may or may not have been occupied by one of our own companies – they were almost as isolated from us as were the other battalions of the brigade. Other than the fact that they were somewhere around, I rarely knew their exact locations. And that was true of all my front line experience. Other than the fact that they were somewhere on our left or right, we rarely made contact with them. We seemed to be permanently fighting the war on our own.

One day we watched the usual pounding of the hill and three German Me fighter bombers joined in. They flew low, one after the other, almost on a level with the crest of the hill, straight for it. A tremendous fire, most of it small arms and directed from the hill met them. The German planes flew steadily into it. Each one of the three was hit and brought down and two of these crashed into the hill. It looked like Kamikaze to me, long before I had even heard of the term. We were forced to admire the courage of the German pilots and the determination with which they had pressed home their attack.

Another morning, just after dawn, I casually glanced in the direction of the same hill and got the shock of my life – it had changed position! It now floated, completely isolated, high in the sky, like the island in Gulliver's Travels.

Even so, I could still make out its every detail, as well as the bright flashes of the shells bursting upon its slopes. I was thunderstruck, I had never before seen a mirage! As the sun got up, the mists slowly dispersed and, as they did so, the 'island' in the sky slowly sank until it eventually resumed its old position on the ground. In my ignorance I wondered what would have happened if German planes had attacked it while it was still in 'mirage' way up in the sky!

We lived on 'compo' rations. These came in wooden boxes about two thirds the size of an orange box and were meant to feed ten men for twenty four hours. As well as the bulk 'bully beef' and hard tack biscuits, they contained a few luxuries like cigarettes, sweets, jam, butter, tea and sugar etc. Occasionally a tin of steak and kidney pudding substituted for the 'bully'.

While we were in battalion reserve one man of each section was appointed 'cook'. This only meant he made the tea that day or, if water and fuel were plentiful, that he also heated up the occasional steak and kidney pudding.

It so happened that the day I was made 'cook' our section owned a large tin of rice. Every man in the section was smacking his lips in the anticipation of this unexpected treat. We decided that it would be nicer served hot so, accordingly, some way off, I made a fire and opened the tin. I had no sooner got this done when Corporal Murray appeared at my side. 'Forget that and get dressed,' he said, and his tone of voice was urgent. 'be ready to move out in five minutes, we're doing an attack.' My heart sank to my boots. I gazed sadly at the rice still in the tin. 'To hell with it,' I suddenly thought, 'that's not going to waste.' And with that my spoon was out and the next moment I was attacking the *rice*!

With one eye on the section I worked fast. The rice was sweet, cool and simply delicious. I ate the lot and threw away the tin. Hastily I made my way over to the trench, threw on my equipment and grabbed my rifle. I was ready! The NCOs were in conference with 'Hutchy'; the group broke up and corporal Murray rejoined the section. 'The attack's been postponed,' he announced. Then, turning to me, he said, 'Right, we'll have that rice now.' I felt my stomach turn over and I wished the ground would open up and swallow me. I almost wished the attack was still on. An hour later it was. I wouldn't go so far as to say that the news cheered me up but it almost did. The deadly hostility of the Germans I expected and braced myself to meet but that of the section I was totally unready for. I think right then they would have as readily shot me as any German. I marched to the start line for the attack with a much better heart than they did, I know. But then I was fortified by an eight man ration of rice pudding inside me.

We passed by a line of old trenches, the numerous shell holes around them and the litter of equipment and other debris, including a smashed rifle, told the story, somebody had had a rough time there. I wondered who and how long ago. Our attack was to be made upon the hill we ourselves had vacated several days ago. Apparently after we had gone, the Germans had moved on to it. We were now going to throw *them* off it. The attack was to be made in company strength. We were going to have the assistance of a couple of tanks and the support of our own three-inch mortars. Our start line was on the opposite side of the hill to the German positions. We reached it unobserved and spread out across the slope to await the arrival of the tanks and zero hour.

The evening sun was warm on the hillside, poppies bloomed everywhere. We lay down in the long grass. I had never before taken part in an attack and I wondered what it would be like and how I should behave. I felt very nervous. I took special note of the others. They all seemed to be their normal selves. We were by now a very bedraggled looking lot. We had been in the front line for not more than a week and we were filthy already. Many men had not shaved at all in that time. Clothes were thickly covered with dust and hung upon us like bags.

Our tanks were held up by a mine field. We would have to put in the attack without them, so we learned! Still being green-horn troops most of the men greeted the news with no more expression than a shrug of the shoulders. We waited longer, it was quiet upon our hillside but, in the distance, we could hear the irregular bark of artillery. Suddenly, with a heart-stopping shriek, a salvo of shells passed low over our heads and exploded on the hillside about halfway between us and the crest. There was a short pause and the next lot were dead on target. They homed in with the same deafening shriek and the rapid succession of explosions covered several of our section with dust and dirt. Men cursed savagely and loudly – it was obvious that it was our own artillery which was firing upon us, shell after shell screamed in and exploded amongst our ranks. We hugged the ground for dear life and then, as suddenly as it had started, the firing ceased.

We later received a message from the guilty battery – they were Americans. I remember the message well, it read: 'We apologise profusely and hope no one was hurt.' I don't remember whether or not we did suffer any casualties as a result of that 'stonk' but *they* would have done had they been within fist range of some of our lads, particularly my own section. I kept my silence but I sympathised with them, it just did not appear to be their day – nor was it yet finished.

The American 'stonk' upon us alerted the Germans to the fact that something was going off on the other side of 'their' hill. They promptly began to lay down a heavy mortar fire upon it and the shells rained down upon us once more. A little higher up the hill were a few old slit trenches. Someone discovered these and a number of men took cover in them but there were nowhere near enough holes to accomodate all of us. I was amongst the larger number who were unlucky. All we could do was to flatten ourselves to the ground right where we were and pray as the shells howled down from the sky and exploded around us. I pulled the stock of my rifle forward to give my head a bit of extra protection on one side – incidentally it was a trick which paid huge dividends at a later date. There was a rock sticking out of the ground right where I wanted to bury my face with each fresh shriek of approaching shells, I rooted it out and threw it to one side. Immediately, a whole army of huge red ants swarmed out of a hole previously hidden by the stone and proceeded to attack my face, neck and hands. The situation was impossible. I waited for a break in the shelling and when it came I instantly sprang to my feet and raced forward to 'find a better 'ole'. I heard the rapidly rising howl of more shells coming and was about to drop flat when I spotted, only a few yards further along, what appeared to be, on that God-forsaken hillside, a heaven sent gift in the shape of an unoccupied slit trench.

I had a few seconds left before the shells exploded. It would be touch and go but I could just make it. In the same second as I hurled myself frantically into the trench, the shells burst, the nearest not more than twenty or thirty yards away. Even as I was falling into the trench I realised to my horror why it was unoccupied. The smeared litter of paper in the bottom gave its secret away. It had been somebody's latrine trench and, by the look of it, for quite some time! I crashed into the middle of a million flies! They rose up in a solid black mass like a Texan oil gusher then, fiercely resentful of the gatecrasher into their party, they promptly began to resettle – all over me. I was covered in shit and flies. I struggled into a sitting position, debating the choice before me. I was already covered in the stuff. I had, in effect, paid the entry fee, there was no way I could recover it. An ear-splitting shriek, followed by a savage explosion close by, made up my mind for me, I would stay where I was. I did, for almost an hour, nauseated by the stench, tormented almost beyond endurance by the flies and bombarded by the Germans. I never in my whole life spent a nastier hour than that one!

To everyone's intense relief the attack was finally called off and a good job too. It had been dogged by bad luck right from the start.

It was impossible to obtain a change of clothing and I had to clean myself up as best I could by scraping with a jack knife and finally rubbing off with grass but the incidence of the latrine trench, following that of the rice pudding, was too much for my section mates. For several days afterwards they would not come near me nor let me near them. I wandered around in the centre of a permanent cloud of flies. Every time I approached the others they scattered, holding their noses in their fingers. Even my regular mate, Latham, dug himself in a separate trench away from me. I can't say I blamed him but just the same I felt very hurt and very much alone. Truly they had their revenge on me for the rice pudding!

To prevent enemy infiltration during the night hours we covered the gaps between company positions by placing standing patrols in them. These were usually of platoon size.

We moved into position as it got dark. The men were spaced out at intervals of ten, fifteen and even twenty or thirty yards between each man, so to cover the gap with a thin line of sentries.

We lay on the ground so as not to silhouette ourselves against the night sky. It was an utterly boring job, there was no relief, each man stayed in the one position until we all returned to our trenches at dawn. There was not the slightest chance of snatching a smoke, nor was there anyone to talk to, see or even hear. It was, too, bitterly cold. It was like lying out, all alone, in the middle of an empty prairie. The Corporal visited each man maybe once every half hour, to make sure he was still there and that he had not fallen asleep, which was very hard not to do despite the cold. His visits were welcome for, apart from the contact, he was the only one with a watch – between us we all but turned him solely into a mobile speaking clock, albeit an extremely bad-tempered one.

One night I had been lying out, bored stiff, frozen stiff and as usual longing for dawn when, in the early hours of the morning, my eyelids persisting in drooping despite the intense cold, I was suddenly jerked fully awake by what sounded like stealthy footsteps approaching from the direction of the enemy. The footsteps stopped and I strained my eyes into the darkness but nothing moved, everything was as still as the grave, no sound broke the silence, no guns fired anywhere at all. There was just myself, whoever it was out there and the great bowl of night. Then the footsteps recommenced, approaching slowly and deliberately and I could feel the hair prickling on the back of my neck. My eyeballs were nearly bursting with the strain of trying to pierce the darkness. Very slowly, inch by inch, I slid my rifle forward and slipped back the safety catch. The footsteps ceased, I waited! Whoever it was out there seemed to know I was there and, too, my exact position, otherwise why the excessive caution? I felt as though I was being stalked and wished desperately that Murray would come along.

Once more the footsteps recommenced. They sounded to be much nearer yet, strain my eyes as I might, I could see absolutely nothing. Very slowly I lifted my head a little higher and suddenly, from nowhere, I was struck in the face by a cold, wet, heavy object. So keyed up was I that I almost screamed with the surprise. The object fell wriggling to the ground in front of my face. It was a frog, a very large one, but still only a frog! It had been the thud of its body hitting the ground after each hop that I had mistaken for footsteps.

When Murray came to see me a little later I made no mention of the incident. I was, at least, too smart for that!

We took over a hillside position from some other crowd, I forget who. It had been too rocky to dig the usual slit trenches so they had built 'sangars'. These were small circles of rocks, built to the height of about three feet, with enough room inside to accomodate two men in the knees up sitting position.

We eyed the sangars suspiciously, they looked to be very poor protection against shell fire. It was our first experience of them though we later discovered that, as protection, they were almost every bit as good as slit trenches. A man could be safe in them from everything except a direct hit by a high explosive shell. Their main drawback, we discovered, was that unless you were extra careful with the blanket under which you sneaked a smoke in the forbidden hours of darkness, the light from the match could be spotted between chinks in the rocks and you would find yourself on a 'fizzer' before you could say 'Glasgay Toon'.

Smoking was our only luxury. As morale boosters, cigarettes were free and usually available in quantity. Given the long hours of boredom we smoked incessantly. Many a man who had not previously smoked became an addict under these circumstances. We took some stupid chances just to snatch a smoke.

On the very crest of the hill about forty yards above us we had an observation post. It consisted of a shallow depression in the ground and was only manned at night. When it came round to the turn of our section to man the OP, as soon as it got dark, Corporal Murray took me and another bloke, who seemed constantly to be on the verge of a nervous breakdown, to man the post. From there we could overlook the ground between us and the Germans. Not that there was anything to be seen, apart from the darkness. Fritz, like us, lived on the reverse slopes of his hills although, of course, patrols of both sides were always active in 'no man's land' after dark.

We reached the OP, set up the Bren gun, placed a few 36 grenades handy and settled ourlseves down for a long, cold, boring night's vigil. The time dragged by dead slow. The nervous breakdown chap jumped at every little sound – the unsympathetic Murray gave him a really severe roasting after he had spooked the two of us, totally unnecessarily, once or twice. About halfway through the night Murray suddenly announced that he was going to have a smoke. I was dying for one myself but the NB chap almost had hysterics. 'I'll report you!' he squealed. 'Aw, shut your snottering, man,' Murray replied. He removed his greatcoat and with my assistance, draped it over his head to conceal the flare of the match. The other bloke watched, his eyes dilated with fear. Murray had his smoke and then it was my turn. Like him I removed my greatcoat and draped it over my head. Unfortunately, as I jerked the match against the box, the overcoat fell to the ground. I sat there with the match flaring, in full view of the German positions, as if I was modelling for a new version of the Statue of Liberty or something! As I hastily blew out the match, the nervous breakdown chap gave a hoarse cry and fled down the hillside. Murray and I waited fearfully for the enemy reaction to our stupid carelessness for any nearby German patrol could not have failed to see the light. Murray hugged the Bren, I my rifle, but as time went by and nothing happened we relaxed once more. Maybe they were having a crafty smoke too. I didn't dare to ask the quick-tempered Corporal if I could now have my smoke. About half an hour later the other bloke came back. To our immense relief he had not gone all the way back to the platoon positions to report us. Murray gave him another bollocking and there the matter ended.

Some little way in front of our positions was a ruined Arab village which the Germans had used as a stores. Under cover of darkness several of our lads visited the village one night and brought back huge bundles of clothing, mainly vests, underpants and shirts. We were all badly in need of a change and as the German underwear was brand new we didn't hesitate. However, when we came to try the clothing on the sizes were enormous. We had heard about the Hermann Goering Guards, who were rumoured to be somewhere in Tunisia, but it was impossible to believe that even they could be so huge as to fit the clothes that we had found. The shirts hung on us like bell tents, the cuffs of the sleeves passed well below our knees! Nevertheless we set to work on the clothes. I hacked the sleeves of one of the shirts more to my size with a jack knife and changed it for my own. We looked an odd crew after the changes but as we weren't planning to go to any dinner dances or the like for some time, it didn't matter.

We got a glimpse of the true size of the enemy opposite us sooner than we expected. One morning, just after 'stand down', everyone was cooking breakfast, crouching beside our sangars, holding dixies containing strips of fatty bacon, over the cookers. The smell was beautiful, nobody had eyes for anything but the contents of the dixies. All of a sudden someone yelled out 'Germans!' at the top of his voice. Startled, I glanced towards the crest of the hill. A line of German soldiers had cleared the crest and were almost upon us. Cookers and dixies went flying right, left and centre as we all dived into the sangars and snatched up our weapons, whereupon the Germans raised their hands to surrender. It was a damn good job they did, they had almost left it too late. It was also a damn good job for us that they had come to surrender and not to fight for they had properly caught us unprepared. It transpired that they had been lying out in front of our positions waiting for daylight before they'd dared come in and give themselves up. I heard some time afterwards that they weren't Germans at all but Poles who had been conscripted into the German army. Be that as it may, at the time they'd worn German uniforms and after what they'd done to our breakfast they were lucky not to have been shot to pieces.

At that time, in North Africa, there was still a great deal of enemy air activity, as well as British and American.

Flights of Boston medium bombers regularly flew over our lines in tight formations, on their way to targets behind enemy lines – and flights of Stukas, Messerschmitts etc., flew the other way on similar missions.

One day we witnessed the simultaneous approach of a flight of Stukas, coming from the German and Italian rear, and a larger flight of Bostons, coming from ours. They looked to be flying at about the same height and to be almost on a collision course. They would meet almost immediately above our own positions –

and then what, we wondered? We didn't have long to wait for un-seen by us both flights were escorted by fighters, German and American.

The German fighters went for the Bostons, the bombers, still maintaining their tight formation and course, fired every gun they had got back at the fighters and the Stukas sailed majestically on, still keeping to their pre-set course. We watched spellbound.

From nowhere, about half a dozen American fighters sud-denly entered the fray and the sky above us was filled with diving, wheeling, screeching planes, all guns chattering.

We cheered the Yanks on. Suddenly one of the fighters started pouring smoke and we saw the pilot bale out. We cheered madly as the plane, dragging its plume of smoke behind it, headed for the ground just beyond the crest of our hill. The pilot himself landed behind our lines – we learned later it was one of the Yanks. Our aircraft recognition hadn't been so good.

7.

THE NIGHT ATTACK

THE YANKS are coming,' we yodelled to one another, and so they were, to relieve us. They were to take over our part of the line.

A couple of their officers came in advance of the main body to look over our positions. We eyed them curiously as our own Company Commander, Major Stewart, showed them around. They stood on the edges of the slit trenches, peering in and showering the occupants with dirt. They pointed this way and that way, all the time asking questions in loud voices. They nodded affably to anybody and everybody and even exchanged jokes with several of our men. I wondered what it would be like to be a soldier under their command – they didn't seem like officers, not like ours anyway, they were more like a couple of the boys. This was some time after the American débâcle at Kasserine Pass. I didn't know if these Yanks were of the same lot; if they were, then, judging by the two officers, their confidence was not in the least bit shaken by that shattering experience.

Our platoon was detailed to act as covering party for the relief which meant that we would be the last away. As soon as it got dark, we moved some way in front of the line of trenches and took up covering positions. We heard the Yanks coming a mile away. Every second man appeared to have his own jeep – engines revved and roared as though they were on manoeuvres 'somewhere out on the lone prairie' rather than conducting a front line relief in Africa only a few hundred yards from the Germans. 'Christ,' I thought, 'if Jerry doesn't hear that racket he must be stone deaf!'

Jerry heard alright and added to the racket by plastering the whole area with shells. We, out front, seemed to cop for most of the mortar fire. Robbed of our trenches we cursed the Yanks for bringing a totally unnecessary 'stonk' down upon our heads. After so long in the line nobody wanted to be hit now. We were ordered to spread out more but under that hail of fire nobody wanted to get up and move. Each man hugged the ground and waited for the others to spread out from *him.*

Corporal Murray crawled over to me, 'You, follow me,' he said. I did and we raced to the edge of a small shell hole which held two men. Shells were bursting fast and furiously around us and plenty close enough too. 'One of you two, come with me,' he bawled into the shell hole. Neither of the men moved. 'C'mon! One of you!' Murray barked impatiently. One of the two pushed the other. 'He means you,' he said. The other man pushed him back. 'No he doesn't, he means you,' he replied. The next moment the two of them were exchanging blows in the shell hole. Shells were bursting all around them and they were fist fighting in a hole! Murray swore out loud and jumped into the hole himself. He grabbed one of the men by the collar and almost threw him out. Nobody under fire laughs much, I didn't, but a cat might well have done!

At long last it was our turn to move out and we weren't a bit sorry. Jerry had got the message alright that something was going on behind our part of the line. His planes were now overhead, dropping flares by the dozen. The night was very dark so they were quite a help to us. We made full use of them to make faster progress, while at the same time keeping our ears cocked for the bombs to follow. The Yanks fired machine guns at the flares and tracers arched into the sky and bits still burning flew off the lights. Under different circumstances it would have been a really pretty sight to watch.

We were, after all, only exchanging one part of the line for another, one sector for another, the Beja sector for the Medjez-El-Bab sector. We had about twenty miles to march and had to be there by dawn.

We marched in great coats and were heavily laden. In addition, we had had no proper rest or sleep for weeks, It promised to be a tough march and so it turned out to be.

A mistake, or detour, added more miles to the march. A wind got up and became a howling gale. Heads down, we marched into the teeth of it. We leaned heavily against it to make progress. We passed through a town, probably Beja, where fires still burned from an air raid sometime previously. We had a timetable to keep so the pace was necessarily fast. Hour after hour we battled against the wind and the accumulated weariness of weeks. The less strong or most heavily burdened men dropped behind. Men fell themselves out of the line. or march to rest by the wayside, only to be ordered to their feet again by the next passing Officer or senior NCO.

Platoons became intermixed as the head of the one behind caught up with the tail end of the one in front. There was no easing of the pace nor was there any slackening in the gale force wind which blew into our faces constantly, filling our eyes with grit.

By the early hours of the morning the Bren gun on my shoulder felt as though it weighed a ton, both shoulders ached badly and my feet were as painful as if I was marching barefooted. Officers took to waiting by the roadside. 'Keep going, lads,' they encouraged, 'not much further now.' 'Only a few hundred yards now, lads.' One officer said cheerfully, as we passed him, 'breakfast's waiting.' A couple of miles further along another officer said exactly the same thing.

Dawn was breaking when, at last, we limped painfully into a wadi, situated between high banks, and came to a weary halt. Cooks waited for us beside their field kitchens – we had reached our destination.

Men struggled from their equipment and let it fall heavily to the ground then sank down gratefully beside it. Many closed their eyes and fell fast asleep in an instant.

'Breakfast up!' called the NCOs as they prodded and shook men into wakefulness once more. Sleepily, I undid the straps of my valise and reached into the tightly packed jumble inside for the dixies. I dragged them out and the 84 grenade came out with them, the handles of the dixies had somehow become entangled with the mine. They had slipped between the pressure plate and the casing of the main body of the mine. I tugged irritably at the dixies to free them. A man sitting beside me suddenly sprang to his feet. 'Look out!' he screamed frantically at me as he shot away, 'That bloody mine's still fused!' In an instant, forgetting their weariness, men scattered away from me in all directions. I studied the mine – it was too! It was still fused! I had forgotten to remove the tube of fulminate when I had retrieved the mine from the ground before my last position.

The handles of the dixies were pressed firmly against the fragile tube, the least disturbance of either could break the tube and explode the mine. All the breath left my body. I'd almost tugged myself, and the others too, into oblivion. Very, very carefully I removed the fuse. I had marched more then twenty miles with a time bomb ticking away on my back, set to go off with every jolt over every yard of the way. It was almost impossible to believe that it hadn't done so. I breathed a heartfelt prayer of thanks to the angel who had watched over me that night.

The area we now found ourselves in had been much fought over during the last few months. To our left was Banana Ridge, now held by the British. It had changed hands repeatedly since Christmas 1942. Beyond that was Long Stop Hill, held by the Germans. It also had changed hands several times during the some period of time. The fighting had been bloody, fierce and continuous. We were but the latest of many infantry battalions to become involved in it.

We dug ourselves in and waited. Every night the battalion carried out extensive patrol work over the ground between us and the Germans. The artillery of both sides was particularly active on this part of the front. We ourselves weren't subjected to a lot of attention by the enemy but, judging by the constantly recurring savage outbursts of gunfire someone, not too far away, was having a rough enough time of it!

We learned we were to attack that part of the German front which included Long Stop Hill – a nasty enough assignment. The Germans had been there a long while, they had had ample time to prepare and strengthen their defences. Our battalion objective was a village called Side Medienne.

On the day before the main attack our 'B' Company went

forward to test the defences. For them it was a day of disaster, almost every man was lost and, as a consequence, the battalion was reduced to three rifle companies.

The Germans had erected very thick and very extensive barbed wire barricades before their positions. Beneath these the ground was said to be thickly sown with mines, anti-personnel as well as anti-tank. It sounded a very formidable obstacle, our 'B' Company had never really been in with a chance of taking the position.

The battalion attack was to go in under cover of darkness. The plan was for the artillery to put a barrage down upon the German wire during the daylight hours when the wire could be seen, so as to blast gaps in it through which we could pass early that same night, before the Germans had time to repair the damage. The battalion attack was to be a silent affair with no artillery support *immediately* preceding it to warn the enemy of our approach.

All that day we listened to the almost non-stop crack and thunder of the divisional artillery and to the rush of the shells high over our heads as they streamed towards the enemy line – by comparison with ours the German guns seemed to be fairly quiet – no doubt they were saving their ammunition for the attack – which they surely knew must soon come.

Shortly after dark we tightened rifle slings, fixed bayonets, climbed from our trenches and moved silently forward to the attack. The intense artillery fire of the day had died down. Only a few guns fired and their flashes briefly illuminated the faces of the men about me. We, who had only heard about but had not seen the strength of the German barbed wire defences, hoped the artillery lads had made a good job of flattening them. The almost total loss of 'B' Company the previous day was very much to the fore of all our minds.

From time to time the Germans fired long bursts of tracers from their Spandaus warningly into the darkness before their positions. The rocketing streaks of light crackled viciously as they passed to one or other side of us. I prayed we wouldn't get stuck in the wire and become a helpless target for those deadly things. The nearer we got to them the more alert the enemy appeared to become. His Very lights shot upwards into the night sky with increasing frequency, each one briefly illuminating the ground before their positions with a wide moving circle of reddish light, as the flare arched through the sky.

Against the lights the sharply silhouetted figures of the helmeted men in front of me, their rifles and bayonettes held steady at the high port, assumed heroic proportions in my eyes as, each time, they waited, steady as rocks, for the lights to fall to earth, so to continue their relentless advance to close with the enemy. Foolishly, then, I imagined that only my own heart beat so wildly.

Silently we began to move uphill. We were nearly there and still undetected. Then a light arched into the sky and every man froze in his tracks. The next second all hell broke loose. We had been spotted and the Germans opened up a devastating fire upon us. The night was ripped apart by the flashes of explosions and streaks of tracers. Instinctively every man fell flat to the ground. Then Lieutenant Hutchinson raced amongst us. 'Forward!' he bawled above the bedlam of noise, 'Move forward!' I got to my feet and, with pounding heart, moved forward into a terrifying hail of fire. The man next to me dropped his rifle and fell to the ground screaming hysterically. He was clutching his stomach. I halted and gazed at him horror-stricken. 'Keep going!' a voice howled above the noise of the firing. We were either being mortared or grenaded, or both, by the Germans. As I began to move forward once more, a phosphorous shell or grenade exploded in front of me, its circle of fire reaching almost to my feet. That few seconds that I'd paused had saved me from a horrible death or injury.

By the light of the flashes of the constant explosions I saw the glint of the German wire. Men dropped flat to the ground before it.

'Get through the wire, get through the wire!' I heard Lieutenant Hutchinson's voice again above the bedlam of sound, now augmented by the cries and screams of wounded men. I began to scramble my way through the wire. Loose strands caught up first one leg, then the other. As quick as I freed one the other caught. Lines of tracer bullets from the German trenches shot by me. My brain was numbed with terror as if in a nightmare. Someone next to me was cursing savagely – he seemed to be inextricably caught up. I became desperate to clear the wire. Suddenly my helmet was jerked halfway round my head – a bullet had passed through the net and sand-bag camouflage where it tucked loosely under the rim. Then I was through! Others of the platoon had made it too. We dropped flat to the ground while the Germans – and everyone else it seemed – fired furiously over our heads.

Lieutenant Hutchinson appeared amongst us and once more he ordered us 'Forward!' Again I went forward – grenades were bursting everywhere, whether thrown by Germans or by our own men still behind us, I was unable to distinguish. Other platoon battles were going on all over the hill, it seemed as if the whole battalion, as well as the Germans, were firing into our little area of ground.

Several bursts of automatic fire came from a spot about twenty yards in front of me. Amidst a shower of exploding grenades I knelt down and pumped shot after shot into the position. I was still firing when Lieutenant Hutchinson appeared at my side. 'Who's that?' he cried.

'It's me sir, Framp,' I replied.

'Good man Framp,' he said breathlessly, 'stay there and I'll bring the rest of the platoon up to you.'

I was totally surprised – I'd thought the platoon *was* with me! I glanced quickly to either side – there was no one. Fire poured my way from all quarters, behind and before me. I'd properly got myself into a jam, right between two armies knocking hell out of each other for all they were worth and both of which would fire at any movement in front of them and ask questions afterwards!

With that sudden realization came panic. I hastily scrambled to my feet and made a crouching run to rejoin the others. Maybe if I'd stayed where I was I'd have been alright. As it was, a burst of tracers, fired from the German positions, shot by my ear. I heard a shout from McKenna, one of my own section. 'In here,' he bawled. He lay flattened in a shallow shell hole and I dived for the spot beside him. The stream of bullets followed me and I felt a terrific blow to my left arm, as if I'd been savagely struck by a cricket bat. I crashed to the ground and lay there panting for breath. 'I think I've been hit,' I eventually managed to say to McKenna. I moved my left arm up and down. 'No, I haven't,' I corrected myself, 'it must have been a blow from a stone thrown up that I felt.' Not many seconds later I knew I had indeed been hit for my hand suddenly filled with blood. I felt with the other hand and my battledress sleeve was sodden wet. The fierce exchange of fire continued for about another ten or fifteen minutes and then the firing from the German positions slackened – they appeared to be falling back. When I thought the firing was sufficiently quiet I set off to find the RAP (Regimental Aid Post) to get my wound dressed. I had no idea where it was, I assumed someone would tell me.

I was somewhere near the crest of the hill. A building close by had caught fire and by the fitful light of the flames and nursing my arm, I made my way over the uneven ground. Suddenly a Spandau swept the ground immediately in front of me with a vicious burst of fire and the next moment the firing broke out again, almost as fierce as before. It was totally unexpected. For the second time that night I'd landed myself between two opposing groups intent upon blasting each other off the face of the earth. By the light of the distant fire I saw, on the ground before me, the black outline of a slit trench. I scrambled into it, right on top of something bulky which quickly moved under my weight. It was a Jerry! I sprawled helplessly on top of him. Above us the lines of tracers going both ways swept viciously over the trench. I was unarmed, I'd left my rifle with McKenna. The German, however, when we'd finally disentangled ourselves, looked positively delighted to see me, as though I was an old friend who'd popped in as he was passing by. My face, I suppose registered my own surprise and alarm but he smiled reassuringly at me. He obviously wasn't going to fight, for which I was truly grateful. Apart from having no weapon, my arm was beginning to hurt. The German was big – almost big enough to fit the shirts we had found back at Beja! He also spoke very good English. 'Yesterday,' he said, 'we defeat one hundred British soldiers.' I thought about our 'B' Company. The German looked very smug, as if he'd defeated them all by himself, single-handed. I had a little think and then I replied, 'Yes, and today *you* prisoner.' I wasn't really sure if this was correct. It was quite on the cards that he was maybe thinking that I was going to make it a hundred and one for him! However, he didn't contradict me and I'd every faith in our own lads out there. I just hoped they would make no mistakes when eventually they appeared at the top of the trench.

Above the firing I suddenly heard the skirl of pipes and then there was a redoubled outburst of fire. The German intently listened along with me. It sounded very much as if our boys impatient to be done with the job had taken the bit between their teeth and were now coming in to finish it. And that's just how it was, too. I heard them calling excitedly to each other then, suddenly the hill was ours, all firing upon it ceased. I struggled from the trench, followed by the German, *my prisoner*. He seemed very cool and collected – I got the impression that he would have liked to have been formally introduced and to have shaken hands all round with the lads. I thought, 'Armholes to you, mate, I'm off,' and I left him there and went in search of the RAP once more.

As I, in company with several other walking wounded, followed the stretcher-bearers carrying a body, down the slope of the hill in the direction of the RAP a couple of short bursts of fire from a Bren gun, quite close, suddenly startled us. I heard several men screaming and then shouting – and then nothing. We continued on our way and I forgot the incident. We wanted to be off that hill before the German fire or counter-attack descended upon it – which it certainly would, once they were sure they'd lost it.

It wasn't until I returned to the Company, two or three months later, that I learned the true story behind that Bren gun fire and the screaming.

Several German prisoners were being escorted down the hill by a rifleman – it was in fact from him that I heard the story. Suddenly, despite the fact that they'd surrendered and were under escort, one of our Bren gunners opened fire on the group at point blank range. Two of the Germans fell to the ground, one dead and the other badly wounded, the others fled into the night screaming. The Bren gunner, having emptied his magazine, walked up to the German still writhing and screaming upon the ground, kicked his helmet off, reversed his Bren and cold-bloodedly stove his head in with the butt.

Evidently his own number two on the Bren had been badly wounded just previously. Not that that was an excuse for such a brutal action, not in my book anyway: we were all soldiers.

8.

THE MADONNA

THE RAP, when I found it, was some way below the crest of the hill. It was just a patch of ground commandeered by the MO and his staff. The area was thick with men standing and sitting around and almost as many more lying on the ground where the stretcher-bearers had lowered them, all waiting for first aid. The doctor dealt with the worst cases first, some of whom had suffered really dreadful wounds. Looking at them I realised how lucky I was, my wound appeared to be a clean through and through one, though it had, by now, become extremely painful and I was soaked with blood from shoulder to waist.

My arm was bandaged and put into a sling and dawn was breaking when I joined the steady stream of other walking wounded making their way back to the Casualty Clearing Station. We had taken the hill alright but it seemed to have cost us dear in casualties.

The CCS was a farmhouse about a mile back. I'm not sure if it wasn't the famous Cactus Farm. There I met many more of my Company, including our Company Commander and another of our officers. He told me he was disgusted with himself and he looked it too. He hadn't been wounded by the Germans, not directly anyway. He had fallen over in their wire and broken his arm. I thought about the chap caught up in the wire beside me, but his language, I felt sure, ruled out the possibility of his being an officer! Just the same, I made no mention of it to him.

Eight or ten of us were waiting to be examined by the doctor. We sat on benches and the doctor's room was on the other side of a curtained doorway. Suddenly the curtain was swished to one side and every man in the room instantly dived for the floor. The doctor in the doorway looked at us in amazement. It took several seconds for him to connect our behaviour with the noise made by the curtain as it was drawn back – it exactly resembled that made by an approaching high velocity shell!

I passed through field hospital and finally ended up at the 94th General Hospital situated in Algiers. I met a sailor there who told me that his had been one of the destroyers which had ferried us to Bone. On the return journey it had struck a mine and gone down with the loss of many of his mates.

While I was in this hospital the war in Africa came to an end. Rommel got away but he left behind 250 000 men who didn't which, I gathered, was as many as the Russians had captured at Stalingrad.

I was discharged from hospital after a week or two to a convalescent camp by the sea. It was like a holiday camp – I could have stayed there for the duration! We bathed in the Med. and loafed around the beaches all day and every day. It was perfect.

Then, all too soon for my liking, I was transferred to an IRTD (Infantry Reinforcement Training Depot). The IRTD was a completely different kettle of fish. Every soldier, to a man, hated the place. It was all red tape and bullshit. Veterans of many battles, from the First and the Eighth Armies, were reverted to basic training. Foot drill, arms drill, and all the rest of it. We hated every minute of it, we were put on charges for the most trivial offences.

Every man had the same ambition, to get the hell out of it and back to his own unit as quickly as possible. Which perhaps was the very purpose of all the bullshit and the pettifogging!

I rejoined the Battalion at Phillipville. I was very glad to be back – especially since some of the lads at the IRTD had been bundled off to units other than their own, which had caused a deep and bitter resentment amongst them.

Many old faces were sadly missing from the Company and from my platoon. Not all, however, due to enemy action, sickness had claimed a fair number also.

The Eighth Army and the Americans landed in Sicily. We waited on the opposite shore of the Med., wondering how long it would be before we were sent over. As it turned out, the armies there did quite well without us – they captured the whole island within a month of landing upon it.

About this time, the powers that be began to raid the depleted battalions of our division for reinforcements for the similarly depleted battalions in Sicily. They took men from all ranks, including officers. It was a bad time, men protested bitterly but there was nothing anybody could do about it. They'd have gone anywhere with the battalion, all the way to hell, but they didn't want to go anywhere without it. It was, in some ways, worse than losing men in battle. Draft by draft, the battalion was reduced to a mere skeleton. Mates, of years and battles shared, shook hands and parted, almost certainly never to meet again.

The Allies landed in Italy, broke out of the Salerno beachhead after terrible fighting and advanced steadily northward. As for us, the war seemed to have swept us into a backwater and forgotten all about us. Not that we were exactly busting a gut to get back into it, we were doing alright where we were, defending our property from constantly raiding Arabs and putting in a spot of pig and poultry farming on the side. Our pigs, two of them, were being fattened up for Hogmanay and the chickens and one lone duck were for fresh eggs every day. The pigs were doing fine, coming along very nicely, everybody passing the sty managed to spare a moment to glance over the sides to note their progress. The New Year was still three or four months away, they should have grown into real whoppers by the time it arrived.

The war seemed to be very far away during that period of our life but fate was catching up with us, faster than we knew. Our luck suddenly ran out altogether. Somebody in Whitehall back in England or wherever suddenly woke up to the fact that there was a lost legion, or part legion, somewhere in Africa! The first we knew about it was when an avalanche of reinforcements descended on us and we became a full strength battalion once again. Our idyllic pastoral existence of the past few months came to an abrupt and painful end.

We bade our pigs a sad farewell and sailed away to Egypt. We landed at Port Said and entrained for Port Tewfick. There we went under canvas.

The climate at that time of the year, November/December, was kind enough, like a sunny English summer. But our training schedule made it seem much hotter, the route marches in particular. There was a mountain, or very high hill, called Gebal Ataka and our CO, Colonel Madden, seemed to be obsessed with it. We were forever marching, like the Grand Old Duke of York's men, up and down that hill. We all became heartily sick of the sight of it, none more so than myself. With the new re-organisation of the Company I'd been made Company runner and, as such, given a bike. It was one of those massive iron things policemen used to ride before the war. I had to push it all the way to the hill, carry it up the hill and then all the way down again. I never got to ride it, only to clean it, push it and carry it. Nobody ever once thought to ask me whether or not I *could* ride the thing!

We did occasionally manage a night out in Tewfick – not that there was much to see or do there apart from the Suez Canal and a cinema with only half a roof. Shafto's it was called. Shafto's cinema was situated by a railway siding. A strange peculiarity of the wind there sent the smoke from the locos straight up and then straight down again into the cinema, every time. One moment you would be sitting watching Clark Gable wrapping himself around Betty Grable, or something like that, and thinking beautiful thoughts yourself, and the next you'd be in the thick of a wild reeling stampede for the exit as the place suddenly filled up with choking black clouds of engine smoke.

We celebrated Hogmanay in Egypt, with warm English beer and sweet Egyptian 'tatties'. It was a dull affair, nobody got even nearly drunk as I remember.

In the New Year I handed my bike in, thankfully never to see it again. We sailed for Italy and the war once more. Our ship was an old India trooper called the Cuba. Besides us it also cargoed a vast army of cockroaches.

A few days after leaving Port Said the Cuba docked at Naples and the battalion disembarked. Wiser, the cockroach army stayed put.

The harbour was littered with wrecks, most of which had

keeled over and showed a large extent of their sides above the water line. Many of these, we were told, had been scuttled by the Germans to delay the use of the port by the allies. The Americans had simply joined the wrecks together by a series of bridges. The end product of this piece of ingenuity provided them with several extra jetties for the unloading of their own ships.

Our first night in Italy was spent in a small village, about halfway between Naples and the Garigliano river, where the American Fifth Army was fighting, under terrible winter conditions, to maintain its advance.

We arrived in the village by lorry shortly after dark. Snow lightly covered the ground. All the houses in the village were built of stone and they looked almost as ancient as the Pyramids. Several also appeared to be very oddly designed inasmuch as they had the stairways to the upper rooms on the outside. Also built of stone, the stairways were completely unprotected and open to the weather.

By the light of flashing electric torches and swinging storm lanterns we were shown to our various quarters by members of the advance party. One of these unceremoniously flung open the door of a house. 'Six men in here,' he barked imperiously, holding his storm lamp high to light the way. Six of us Company HQ men trooped by him and entered the house. Inside upon a table a solitary candle flamed wildly in a metal holder. At the opposite end of the room a fire of damp twigs burned, protestingly, upon a large flat stone set in a large soot-blackened recess in the wall. Smoke from the fire wafted strongly into the room. In front of this, surrounded by several small, barefoot, tightly-clinging children, stood a woman. She, and they, gazed at us silently from wide, fear-filled eyes as we entered their home.

A battered and ancient-looking sideboard, a couple of chairs, equally battered and a couple of benches by the table which, like them, appeared to be home-made and by a not too skilful carpenter at that, comprised all the furniture there was in the room. A small square of old carpet in front of the fire represented the only covering on the stone-flagged floor. The house reeked of damp as well as smoke. There was in the room, however, just one touch of something other than grim necessity, just one item of extravagence. It was fastened to the wall above the fireplace and in the dancing light of the candle it eventually took on the form of a silver Madonna. It was my later experience of Italy that every peasant house, no matter how poor its inhabitants, had at least one of these prominently adorning its livingroom walls – as indeed every hamlet, every village, however small, however poor, appeared to have its quota of priests.

I was one of three detailed to sleep upstairs. We scrounged a storm lamp and I led the way up the stone stairway outside the house and pushed open the door at the top. Immediately our noses were met by a fearful stench. We looked in and there, in the light of the lamp, gazing placidly back at us, was a donkey. The room was filled with straw and donkey droppings. It was pretty obvious that the animal had been secreted there for some considerable time. Sleeping in the same room was out of the question. We closed the door on it and returned to the lower part of the house.

Donkeys and mules were worth their weight in gold to the armies in Italy. In many parts of that mountainous country they were the only means of transporting supplies to the front line troops. By dint of much sign language, vigorous head-shaking and repetitious use of the woman's very few words of English, we discovered that her soldier husband had gone missing about a year earlier. In his absence the family depended utterly upon the donkey's strength to cultivate their strip of land.

One of our Company HQ men appeared particularly touched by the family's obvious destitution – this was McOwett. A typically dour Scotsman and a family man himself, McOwett adopted the family for the period of our stay in the village. He scrounged tins of bully, packs of hard tack biscuits and whatever else was to be had for the scrounging from the cookhouse. He cajoled mates into parting with excess kit, khaki drill uniforms, spare shirts, underclothes etc., nothing came amiss to him. All of it he handed over to the astonished woman. A few days later we left the village for the front line. As we paraded in the streets, ready to move out, the women and children crowded in the doorways of the houses to watch us go. Gone from their eyes was the look of fear which had greeted our earlier sudden arrival in their midst. Their faces now, particularly those of the children, showed genuine friendliness and some, perhaps, even regret at our departure.

We had a long march to the front line and we were also exceptionally heavily burdened. To help us with the climb through the mountains beyond the Garigliano each of us had been issued with a five foot long staff.

Except for the snow on the hills, the country we marched through was very similar in appearance to Tunisia, ideal defensive country. I marvelled that any troops of any army would undertake to attack across it, even in summer, let alone winter. It was almost incredible to believe that the British and American troops of the Fifth Army had succeeded in taking so much of it in one of the worst winters there, we understood, for many, many years.

From their positions in the valley of the Garigliano, our guns blasted away at the Germans up in the hills. We passed through their lines, crossed the river by Bailey bridge and commenced the long climb up into the mountains. The only paths were goat tracks, which twisted and writhed agonisingly up and across the mountain slopes. It seemed as if we marched miles just to make a few hundred yards upward progress. Higher and higher we climbed and despite the intense cold very soon we were bathed in sweat and my legs ached cruelly from the effort involved. As we followed the endless zigs and zags of the trail we caught occasional glimpses of other little files of our burdened mates, toiling wearily up the mountain behind us. In the distance and still far below us they looked like files of tiny ants on the snow-splashed slopes.

Enemy shells began to fall either side of the track we followed. For most of our Company it was their first time under fire but so exhausted were they that they were completely indifferent to it. They barely flinched even when the shells fell quite close to the track.

High up on the mountain we moved off the track a little way in order to let a Company of the retiring Battalion go by. Like us, most of them also carried jerry cans but unlike ours, theirs contained no petrol or water – they were but returning the empties.

Our positions were on Mount Ornito and consisted of a chain of sangars strung across the mountain side just below the peak. The sangars were covered with groundsheets to keep out the snow. From our lofty peak we had a wonderful view of the village of 'Harrogate' in the valley far below. Looking down upon it, I gained an insight into the reason which impels men voluntarily to climb mountains. I also saw quite clearly, for the first time, the reason for the obsession with Gebel Ataker back in Egypt. Legs and backs needed to be thoroughly prepared to take on such climbs as the one we had just made and which were the common order of the day in Italy. It must have been sheer hell for the men, British and American, who had spent the entire winter attacking over these mountains. I didn't know the half of it then – but I was soon to learn.

It was bitterly cold on the mountain, blizzards were frequent and icy winds blew the snow through the unprotected openings into the sangars. No hot meals could be brought to us so our diet consisted of frozen bully and rock-hard biscuits. We wore leather jerkins over our great coats and, to further help us keep out the intense cold, we wrapped layers of sandbags around our legs. These we tied into place using strips of the same material. Weapons needed constant attention to prevent them from icing up or just becoming lost in the snow showers.

The Germans, over on the other side of the crest, some two hundred yards away, were rumoured to be suffering from the cold even more than we. One of our patrols reported finding a German position with a dead man in it. He wasn't even wearing an overcoat. There were no wound marks on him and it was readily believed that he'd died of exposure.

Tea was our life saver and, with all the snow about, water was no problem. During the hours of daylight, if petrol and tea rations allowed, we brewed up constantly. The jam tin we used for a kettle was seldom off the boil for very long, but, during the night hours no such means of combating the intense cold and the boredom were available to us. Then, we suffered in silence and longed for the dawn to break.

My sangar replaced one situated about a couple of yards away which had received a direct hit by an enemy shell. It had contained two men at the time, now it was just a mound of stones with an up-ended rifle stuck over it bearing a tin hat upon its stock. A blue-black hand poked out from the rocks and hung slackly down on the outside. Even though we were several thousand feet up and the wind blew fresh and cold, the sweet sickly smell of death hung heavily about the place.

When our padre discovered the grave he went off the deep end. 'Is this,' he asked angrily, 'how the Guards bury their dead?' He had the mound opened and the remains of the two men placed in blankets and carried down the mountain for a proper burial.

The bodies went but not so the smell, not completely – which wasn't surprising for, lying out in front of our positions were also the bodies of a large number of Germans, as many as fifty, it was said. Our mountain had been the scene of several fierce actions before we had taken it over. However, we now had the job of collecting the dead Germans for burial.

Every night parties were detailed for the purpose and every night, too, they were mortared by a grateful enemy – often with such uncanny accuracy and timing that it gave rise to the suspicion that the burial parties were working under enemy observation.

Some way over to our left front were the remains of an old cottage or shepherd's hut. It was suspected that the Germans might be using this at night as an advanced observation post. Accordingly, it was decided to send a platoon-sized fighting patrol to investigate and, if the suspicions proved to be founded, to wipe out the post. I was on guard duty when the patrol went out. That was one of the perks I enjoyed as Company runner – I was never detailed for patrols and that particular night I was especially thankful for the fact. It blew and snowed heavens hard. As

I watched the platoon assemble and then slip silently away into the night I didn't envy any man in it one little bit.

About half an hour later, a tremendous racket broke out before our Company lines. The three inch mortar platoon behind us joined in, to put down a fearful stonk upon some target somewhere. I wondered if the patrol had run into trouble, perhaps it had been ambushed itself. It was hard to make out just what was going on. Then, as suddenly as it had started, the firing stopped. I waited wonderingly. Perhaps twenty minutes later the patrol returned carrying several casualties, dead and wounded.

Their patrol had ended in a complete fiasco. Some little way from their objective the platoon officer had divided his patrol into two equal parts, the idea being to come at the suspected enemy post from two sides at once. There were no Germans at the ruined cottage. In the dark and driving snow, the two halves of the one patrol had crept towards their objective, from opposite directions as planned, and met – only each other! One man in one of the groups had mistaken the other party for Germans and promptly opened fire on it. Given no time to think, the second group had, as promptly, returned the fire. Several casualties were incurred before the awful truth was realised. I felt truly sorry for the men of that platoon but particularly for its officer. I would never want to feel as he must have done as he led his patrol back.

Of all the platoons which fought in Italy, it would be difficult, I think, to find a more cursed one than that. It appeared to be dogged by ill-luck. Within the first two or three months of its landing at Naples, almost all of its originals had gone, including its Officer, killed, wounded or captured.

The Germans on Mount Ornito had a particular refinement of front line warfare which I never encountered anywhere else, either before or afterwards. When the mood took them, they would fire onto our positions, at precisely measured intervals of time, usually a single mortar shell. The intervals between shells, be they of ten, twelve or even fifteen minutes, were always exactly the same, dead to the second.

In the dark and bitter cold of the early hours of one morning, after enduring several hours of this particular bit of front line nastiness, one of our men put a bullet through his foot. He had taken over the sentry duty from me only a matter of minutes previously. I heard the shot and went to find out from him what he had fired at. I found him sitting at the bottom of the sentry sangar, groaning horribly and clutching his foot.

After they'd taken him away, Major Coates, our Company Commander, questioned me closely about the incident. 'Do you,' he asked, 'think the man deliberately shot himself?' Truthfully, I thought he'd done just that. I knew he was worried about his widowed mother at home. I thought, too, that he'd allowed the stink of death and the upended rifle bearing the helmet upon its stock to prey on his mind. However, I supported his own story, I said I thought it was an accident. Major Coates looked at me very hard and very long – I think he believed it in the finish.

A couple of Germans appeared on our skyline one morning, bearing a stretcher with a body on it. I watched them walk right into our positions. The body was that of a British soldier, they'd thought we would prefer to bury it ourselves. Major Coates thanked them very much in their own language and then promptly made them prisoners. The two were obviously surprised. 'They've seen too much,' explained the Major, 'to allow them to go again.' However, as reward, he allowed them to carry the body down the mountain, under escort.

There too, we were regularly entertained, during the hours of daylight, by a little British spotter plane. The pilot's feats of daring and his deadly little games of 'peek-a-boo' and 'hide-and-seek' with the Germans were a delight to watch. He would fly very low over our positions near the mountain peak, then suddenly zoom upwards to hang for a few moments, it seemed by his propeller, right over the German positions. Then, as their small arms fire built up, he'd slip away, to one side or the other, circle behind our lines and then repeat the tactic – but never over the same spot twice. The Germans could never see him until, there he was, right over them, and they never knew from which direction he'd next make his appearance, so cleverly did he use the peak for cover and so expertly did he handle his craft.

On the very day we were to be relieved by a battalion of East Surreys I was taken ill. Under the circumstances there was no point in reporting sick, so I didn't, but the long journey down the mountain was almost as much of an ordeal as the climb up it had been. Eventually, after many miles of thoroughly exhausting march, we arrived at a spot below the mountains, where cooks waited to serve the first hot meal we'd had in goodness knows how long. After a short rest, we returned to the mountains – just where I don't remember.

In our new positions, high up on the mountain side, though not nearly as high, I think, as had been our former positions on Ornito, it was as bitterly cold and windswept. Sleet and snow showers were frequent but, in the long, narrow valley below us, there was no trace of snow. Down there, in sharp contrast to our snow-capped peak, it looked to be quite spring-like in the sunshine which bathed it, in the breaks between the storms.

From the far end of the valley, about a mile and a quarter away, a rutted track ran slightly off-centre towards a troop of three-point-seven guns sited below us. Beside the track, the sparkle of water here and there marked the path of a stream as it made its way from the mountain to the Garigliano. Nobody appeared to live in the valley – I remember no village or even an isolated cottage there.

I think part of it, at least, must have been under German observation, just where from I wasn't sure, but almost every time a truck serving the troop of artillery below us made its appearance on the road, the Germans chased it with shellfire.

The first time I witnessed this and we looked down upon the scene as from a balloon at a great height or, as I'd thought at the time, as God in His Heaven would see it. A truck entered the valley at the far end. It travelled slowly and bumpily along the track and it had covered about half the distance towards the guns when suddenly several founts of earth, which could only have been caused by shellfire, sprouted from the ground around it.

Immediately the truck halted, the door was flung open and the tiny ant-like figure of the driver bolted away from it, as fast as his legs could carry him. We, watching, thought he was being foolish. It seemed to us he would have been better advised to put his foot down on the accelerator and drive as quickly as possible towards the shelter of the mountain that we, and the guns below, enjoyed.

But that driver was no grandma to be taught by us how to suck eggs, he'd known what he was doing. After only about another half a dozen shells dropped in the vicinity of the truck the German gunners, without hitting it, switched their fire directly on to the three-point-sevens themselves. There were about six of these, each protected by a horseshoe-shaped breastwork built of turf and stones. The open ends behind the guns, their long barrels poking over the breastworks, appeared to be aimed directly at us, several hundred feet up.

The German shells burst amongst the British guns with astonishing accuracy – they were smack on target. It's never ceased to amaze me that guns sited several miles from their target and with never an actual glimpse of it, can be so accurately trained upon it, acting only on the information to be gained from maps and gun flashes observed at night.

The Germans maintained a steady rain of shells upon the guns which, so far that day, had remained silent. After enduring the fire for perhaps ten minutes, the British gunners suddenly decided they'd had enough. As we on our lofty perch watched, tiny figures burst from their protective coverings, scattered about the area, and raced towards the guns. We saw the long snouts lift and then, suddenly, belch flame and smoke. All the time the German shells were bursting steadily amongst them, they blasted back salvo for salvo. I wondered if their fire was as accurate as that of their tormentors. It was, in any case, a very remarkable display of cold courage. Witnessing it like that, from a position of complete safety myself, I was awed by it — how could such men fail to win their war? But the answer seemed to lie with the shell-fire, despite their own fire, still falling upon them. They were faced by like men. Suddenly it all seemed to be a dreadful misuse of wonderful human qualities on both sides, by both sides.

After a short time in battalion reserve we moved out of the line altogether to a village well behind the front. It was pretty much the same sort of village as the first one had been, stone houses, packed tightly together, surrounded by a stone wall and situated on a terraced hill top.

I liked the villagers of southern Italy. Their homes were shockingly poor, but despite this, they could be extraordinarily generous when the mood took them. I remember the time when two of us were trying to trade a tin of bully for eggs. We sauntered round the houses looking for a likely customer and eventually came to one occupied by a grizzled old boy and his wife. They invited us into their home which was, as usual, poor but clean. The couple were keen to trade so we ended up well satisfied with our side of the swap. For some time after the deal had been concluded we sat on a bench in their living room, just talking. We learned that the old couple had lost a son in the war. They listened quietly as we, in our turn, talked of our experiences. When the time came for us to take our departure, the old boy nodded to his wife and she disappeared through the back door to return a few seconds later carrying more eggs. These the old girl thrust into my hands and wouldn't take back, despite my protests. I was quite touched by their kindness.

The time came round for our next tour of duty in the line. The old men, women and children of the village – there were no young men, the Germans left none of them behind – looked on silently from the doorways of their homes as we shoulder slung packs and weapons ready to move off. No doubt they saw in us their own lost boys and menfolk. The war had gone on for a long time and the people of Italy were truly weary of it, it showed in all their eyes.

We were heading for a part of the line only a mile or two east of Cassino. We considered ourselves very lucky not to have been thrown into the centre of that particular cauldron. We'd heard much about the terrible fighting going on there – Monastery Hill, Castle Hill, Hangman's Hill, Snake's Head Ridge etc., were all familiar place names to us.

We trailed single file through a water-logged valley and by a village upon a hill, I remember the name of the village, one of the very few I do — it was called Aquafondata. Beyond the village was a pass through the mountains known as 'The Inferno'. Whether this was its proper Italian title or just a name bestowed upon it by the troops, I couldn't say. It was, however, very appropriately named.

The Germans knew its value to the Eighth Army as a supply route to the front line. Consequently, the exit end of it had come in for an awful lot of shelling. The trail, there and beyond, was blazed with the sweet, sickly smell of death, given off mostly by the bodies of mules. In our war, the bodies of men were never left lying for long.

Lacerated tree stumps and a few burnt out vehicles bore a mute testimony to the extent and accuracy of the German fire over a long period of hard fighting which, thereabouts, on the Allied side, had been conducted mostly by the Free French.

Still under cover of the pass, we came to a halt. We moved onto a hillside clear of the road, to await the coming of night. So far our progress had been uneventful, no enemy shells had come anywhere near to us but, as we waited, the Germans began to shell the area, not particularly heavily but steadily. The fire ranged up and down the road in front of us, seeking targets.

The shells were heavy calibre stuff and in the confines of the pass the crash of their explosions reverberated thunderously. I wished the battalion would get moving, 'The Inferno' was beginning to have a claustrophobic effect on me. I wanted nothing more than to be out of it.

We stayed, however, in the same position until well after dark, then we moved off to relieve a battalion of Goums (French Moroccan troops) in their front line position, a mile or so further on. We were utterly astonished to find the Goums had brought several women into the front line with them – their own, or Italian, I couldn't say. Apparently, even under these circumstances, they still considered it to be beneath their dignity as warriors to prepare their own meals. Even so, despite the presence of the women, they were a very dirty lot; they appeared to have shit wherever the inclination had taken them, it was all over the place. It was the same with their rubbish – tins, bottles, boxes etc., dropped apparently where they had last been used. The Goums had a reputation second to none as fighters but their house-keeping habits nauseated us.

Company HQ was in a stone cottage at the foot of one of two steep hills situated either side of a narrow road. The road passed through our Company positions and continued on into the German line, two or three hundred yards beyond.

One platoon was positioned on the crest of the hill above the cottage containing Company HQ, a second, which guarded the road, was reached along a marshy defile and the third platoon was sited over the other side of the road on a spur of the second hill.

I accompanied the last of the Goums to leave. I had a rendezvous to keep with a ration party at a crossroads about three quarters of a mile back as I had to guide it to our new positions. I reached the crossroads and settled myself comfortably on the grass verge beside the road to await the arrival of the party. It was very quiet on our part of the front, hardly a gun fired. Every now and again a group of soft-footed Goums passed by on their way to the rear. Time passed, I continued to wait patiently and the foot traffic ceased – there had been no other kind. There was now just me, the deserted crossroads and the night.

A shimmering in the sky to the west and the rumble of gun-fire told me that the fighting at Cassino raged on as fierce as ever. Suddenly, with heart-stopping abruptness a shell screamed in from nowhere and burst with a tremendous roar, not more than fifty yards away. A minute or so later the same thing happened again, but a little nearer. I considered my position. It looked very much as though the Germans were about to give the crossroads a pasting. I wouldn't be much use to the ration party dead or wounded. On the other hand, I daren't leave the crossroads, the company depended utterly on me.

Over on the other side of the road was a ruined cottage. It stood back from the verge about twenty feet. Its roof had gone and so had all its doors and windows but it still represented cover. I raced over to it and entered through the smashed door-way. I found a position in the chimney breast, sheltered on three sides by thick stone walls. I was also perfectly positioned to keep watch on the road through the greatly enlarged window openings in front of me. The German gun kept up a steady fire and every minute or so there would be a fearful shriek, followed by a tre-mendous crash as the shell exploded. The house shook with the force and pieces of stone fell down the chimney onto my helmet and shoulders. I began to grow anxious, it seemed to me to be only a matter of time before the house itself was hit. Several times, between shells, I moved quickly across to the window to scan the road better but nothing moved, there was no sign what-soever of the ration party.

Eventually the shelling ceased. I waited some time to make sure and then I returned to my former position. I hadn't been there more than five minutes when the party arrived. It was com-manded by the jumpiest officer I ever met. I got the impression that he had been waiting at a safe distance from the crossroads, for the shelling to cease before approaching it – not that I held that against him. However, he was now in a frantic hurry to com-plete his mission. He'd just one thought in his head and that was to get his supplies delivered and get back in the quickest possible time.

I couldn't go fast enough for him – he was constantly treading on my heels and whispering 'How much further now?' I got right sick of it and, to cut the story short, I ended up getting the party lost. I'd turned off the road too soon. The officer got himself into a right old lather when I confessed to it. However, I was fairly sure I wasn't all that far off course and I told him so. He calmed down at that and once again I led the way. We hadn't gone very much further when we came upon a notice board nailed to a stake in the ground. The officer and I bent our faces close to it. The board had just one word printed on it – 'MINUN!' I thought he was going to have hysterics. 'You fool, you fool!' he hissed several times rapidly. He really was in a dreadful state of nerves.

We retraced our steps – I was feeling very shame-faced. Eventually I was sure that I had found my bearings and, with growing confidence, I once more led the way.

Suddenly a challenge rang out from the darkness before me and it wasn't made in English! I froze in my tracks. The officer's hand was shaking as he laid it on my shoulder, his eyes round with alarm. 'You go forward and surrender,' he whispered in agitated tones, 'make them think you are alone.' I gazed at him in disbelief, but he meant it. The challenge came again. The officer roughly pushed me forward. Fearfully, I walked slowly towards the voice and there, sitting by the side of the track on a grassy bank, was a lone Goum! I was almost overcome with relief. I had never kissed a Goum before but I nearly did that one – I was home! 'Cigarette Johnny?' asked the Goum. I gave him several. What he was doing there so far behind his mates I had no idea. I had no idea either, then or now, exactly who the officer was who had pushed me forward into what he had believed to be the arms of the Germans. Of course, it may have been that, after his experiences of the previous half hour, he'd thought I would be of more service to the Army in some German Stalag!

The weather improved enormously. A great big Italian moon sailed smoothly through thin, fleecy clouds, high above the dark hills. Had it not been for the presence of the Germans opposite, I'd have whistled as I worked, or rather jaunted, between Company HQ and the platoons on my regular night-time errands. So quiet was it on our part of the front that it was sometimes hard to believe that several hundreds of armed men faced each other thereabouts at a distance apart of no more than two or three hundred yards. True, the Germans lobbed occasional shells into our positions and regularly machine-gunned the road during the night, just to let us know they hadn't gone away, but it was nothing.

When things were at their quietest, in the early hours of the mornings and when we stood sentry, we'd be reminded of the fact that there was a real war going on elsewhere by the shimmering in the sky and the rumble of artillery several miles to the west of us. There was the condition of our quiet, there were the two sides locked in bitter, bloody battle for the Via Caselina at Cassino, there was the commitment and the priorities of each side. We and the German soldiers facing us were committed to nothing more than holding operations.

In fact, apart from a very narrow escape which I had from a single, randomly fired mortar shell by the Germans, my clearest memory of that particular tour of front line duty is concerned, not with the activity of the enemy, but with that of a bird, a nightingale.

One night, when it was all quiet, after the usual hustle and bustle of early night was done, after the mule train bringing the rations had come and gone and the Germans had tired of machine gunning the road, I was posted on sentry duty.

There was a moon, it was an exceptionally beautiful night. Suddenly, out in 'no man's land', a nightingale began to sing. I was taken by surprise, that was the last sound I'd expected to hear coming from that particular quarter. However, having nothing better to do and having only once before heard a nightingale sing, I leant myself as comfortably as possible, upon the broken stone wall before me and concentrated my hearing, so as not to miss a single note of its song.

The clear, sweet notes floating upon the still air seemed, if anything, to intensify the extreme quietness which reigned over our part of the front. In the breaks between each snatch of song there came to my ears, more clearly than at any time previously, the low growling of the miles away guns of Cassino. When the nightingale sang the noise of the guns was lost, when it fell silent the low growling came rolling over the hills in perfect time to fill the breaks.

Eventually, far behind us, a spoilsport gun flashed and a second or two later I heard the shell go swishing through the air high over my head. It crashed to earth somewhere behind the German line. The song of the nightingale came to an abrupt end. I never heard it again.

98.

9.

OUT OF LINE ONCE MORE I was lucky enough to obtain a forty-eight hour's leave pass to visit Naples. I went along with my old 'mucker' of Africa days – Eddie Latham!

The leave turned out to be something of a disappointment. Everywhere we wanted to go in the city seemed to be out of bounds and strongly patrolled by military policemen. Where we were allowed to go, the prices of everything were geared to Yankee pay packets, which put us right out in the cold! Still, we enjoyed our break, what money we had was all spent on cheap wine and trashy souvenirs.

The battalion was bivouacked in a small but lovely valley. In places the snow still covered the mountain peaks but down in the valley you could feel, and see, spring coming. Though the nights were still hard with frost, the daytime sunshine warmed the hill slopes and produced a greening of new growth amongst the grey-brown of the old grasses.

A letter from home awaited me on my return to the camp. It contained bad news. My younger brother had been reported missing in action while serving with the Central Mediterranean Forces — which was in Italy. The news came as a bombshell to me. I'd no idea until then that he was even in Italy. The last I had heard of him he'd been stationed in Ulster.

In her letter, Mother begged me to find out what I could about the circumstances of his disappearance. I resolved to do just that. I hoped, for her sake, that he was a prisoner of war and not killed. But where to start? The front line in Italy was a hundred and fifty miles long, excluding Anzio. I enquired after his unit, the London Irish Rifles, everywhere I was able to get to. It didn't help not knowing which division it belonged to.

East/West travel, I discovered, was almost impossible in war-time Italy, all the traffic flowed north to south and vice versa; as it was I was turned back several times by military policemen.

Nobody I talked to anywhere knew anything of the whereabouts of the London Irish Rifles. The war in Italy seemed to have swallowed them without trace.

Eventually the time came for us to go back into the front line, into the roughest part of it, in the shattered town of Cassino itself. We couldn't fairly grumble, we had had a good run in the quieter sections while others had done the real fighting. The last battle at Cassino, fierce as it had been, had, in the end, resulted in little gain to the British. The Monastery still remained firmly in German possession. However, it was certain enough the battle there would flare up again when the Eighth Army was recouped.

Watched by the usual knot of silent women, we put on our battle gear and prepared to move out. As we marched from the valley my mood was sombre. I'd learned nothing of my brother and now, for the time being, there was nothing more that I could do, Cassino called.

The Via Caselina in Italy – we used to sing a song about it, the words I forget because they were in Italian but the tune was that of Lilli Marlene – was perhaps better known as Highway Six. It was the main road between Naples and Rome and it cut right through the heart of Cassino, hence the town's importance to both sides. The road approached Cassino across a valley and, for the last mile of the way, it ran as straight as a die. This stretch of road was known to us as 'the mad mile'.

The Germans had every inch of it covered by fire. Only under cover of darkness was it possible to use the route. Even then it was a hazardous enough journey. So close together were the two front lines in Cassino that, even at night, the British had to put down smoke in order to screen their activities from the eyes of the Germans.

Aided by the flashes of the guns behind us, we set off across the valley to relieve the battalion of Guardsmen waiting for us in the ruined town. As an aid to silence we wore gym shoes. Before us, streaks of brightly coloured tracers sliced through the darkness above the town and German flares constantly arched through the sky above the ruins.

We crossed a bridge where engineers were standing by. Every day the Germans smashed the bridge with shell fire and every night the engineers rebuilt it. A little way over to our right German shells began to fall. We saw the flashes of the bursts quite some time before we heard the sound of the explosions and the scream of their approach. It was very odd, as they didn't appear to be so distant from us, nor did they appear to be high velocity 88 millimetre shells.

As far as we could see in the darkness, every inch of the ground about us was ripped and torn by shellfire. On the outskirts of the town truly enormous craters began to open up in the ground around us. These were half filled with evil-smelling water which reflected the flickering sky above and the streaks of coloured tracers which traversed it. We skirted the craters with extreme caution. I glanced down into the yawning black holes – all kinds of objects littered the sharply sloping sides and poked from the still surfaces of the waters, a corrugated iron sheet, twisted and torn, a splintered wooden post, a rifle, encrusted with dirt, slabs of masonry. In one, butt in water, bipod still in firing position, lay a Bren gun. By its side a tin hat, on its back gaped blackly up at the sky. I shuddered to think of what might be completely submerged beneath the waters.

We came fully into the ruins. Every building was utterly shattered and irregular lines of broken walls poked through the mountainous heaps of rubble to give a rough indication of the former whereabouts of the streets. The air was thick with drifting smoke and filled with the hiss and pop of smoke shells, arrived and arriving.

Battalion headquarters was in the crypt of a former convent which was now just one more rubble heap. The company positions were a few hundred yards beyond it – 'D' Company's was astride Highway Six itself. As we were effecting the relief one of our men, Sergeant Wilson, was struck in the groin by a falling smoke canister. In spite of the terrible pain he was in, the man bit his lip and barely made a sound for the whole of the time he waited to be evacuated.

Company HQ was in the basement of what formerly must have been a fairly large house. It was situated immediately by the side of Highway Six. We reached our quarters through a small opening protected above by a strong brickwork arch. There was just enough room for a man to crawl under the arch and drop into the cellar and a similar sort of opening existed at the back.

Above the entrance to our cellar, poised like a giant boot over a beetle, loomed Monte Cassino. With the protective aid of a periscope we could see clearly to the top of it, right up to the monastery. So close was it, so threateningly did it tower over us that after the first eager look at it most of us preferred not to take another.

Our toilet area was in the rear part of the basement. It was partly screened from the rest of the room by a dividing wall with a huge hole in it. Goodness knows how many troops had used the place before us but it stank to high heaven. For that matter, all Cassino stank; after the ruins it was the next most noticeable thing about the place. The strong smell of putrefaction hung, like a cloud which had somehow got itself inextricably caught up on the jagged skyline of the ruins, heavily and permanently over the town. I've heard other people who served there, or say they did, say that they never smelt a thing. My answer to that is that they must have been entirely without a sense of smell.

After the first twenty-four hours, however, you ceased to notice smell. Only the component smells meant anything – smells of rotting garbage, of foul water, of human excretion, of burning, of drifting smoke and, even though both sides had removed their visible dead, of the dead bodies still buried beneath the rubble. Here and there the sweet, sickly smell of death seeped through the debris to hang cloyingly in the still air in the valleys between the rubble mountains. Every ruin, every space between ruins, every crater, every mound of rubble had its own smell.

As runner I was the only man to have free range over the Company area. All the other men stayed put in the same position

102.

until they were either relieved or carried out. It wasn't long before I came to know my whereabouts in the maze of ruins, even on the darkest of nights, by means of the smells alone. My nose became as keenly alerted to the smells of Cassino as did my eyes and ears to its dangers.

During the hours of daylight we looked out upon a dead world. Nothing stirred in the ruins. Even so, hidden eyes watched everything. They fastened themselves instantly upon the slightest movement so to bring down upon it, at once, a savage burst of fire. A rat, and there were plenty of those in Cassino, couldn't have moved during the hours of daylight, out in the open, without being observed by one or the other side.

Every day the guns of both sides methodically pounded some ruin or other they suspected of harbouring an enemy post. From their superior vantage points the Germans regularly fired long bursts on their machine guns through the broken windows and doorways of the ruins in the British sector.

Sitting as we were right under the noses of the Germans on Monastery Hill we, the Black Watch, were forbidden to reply to the fire but the West Kents, or whoever it was holding Castle Hill were under no such restrictions, they returned the German fire. It was quite a spectacular sight and a regular feature of night-time Cassino to see the brightly coloured streams of tracer bullets rocketing both ways between the Castle and the Monastery, as the two sides engaged each other in fierce and prolonged machine gun duels.

My own work commenced each night soon after dark. One night was pretty much the same as another. It usually began with the arrival, out of the smoke, of the ration parties at Company HQ. My job was then to guide the parties to the forward platoon positions, fanned out some hundred and fifty or sixty yards in front of us. It was no easy task – in the dark and dense smoke, every ruined building and every mound of rubble looked pretty much alike. It was the easiest thing in the world to lose men from the ration parties and it happened to me on a number of occasions.

The Germans knew quite well what was going off in the smoke in front of and below them. They were probably doing the same things themselves during the same time. They didn't, however, fire more heavily into the smoke than usual, mostly, I think, because it was still doubtful whether the fire would fall on the right spot at the right time but also because they had no wish to provoke the British artillery into replying in kind, which would have affected their own parties. It seemed to be understood that, as long as the parties of both sides went about their business quietly, there would be no special attention paid by either side to the known period of their activities.

But the members of the ration parties did not always appear to appreciate the finer points of front line ethics. Often, to begin with, they were either over-scared or not scared enough. They dropped flat to the ground or scrambled into cover at every general burst of rifle-grenade or machine gun fire. Or on the other hand, thay banged and jangled along like they were off on a picnic to the Monastery. In the first instance, I would be compelled to retrace my own steps to urge them on once more or search the surrounding ruins in the dark to find them. And, in the second instance, their noise would bring down upon our heads a veritable deluge of German rifle grenades and, occasionally, a short, sharp mortar stonk — which goings on, even though I was only a private soldier myself, sometimes set me to cursing them soundly.

My duties were seldom over much before dawn, when it became impossible to carry them out. The constant shelling of the ruins, by both sides, though light by full scale battle standards, went on steadily and monotonously. This brought me work too, as the German fire regularly caused breaks in the telephone wires connecting Company HQ with the platoons. My job was affected in two ways: firstly, sooner or later, I would have to take one of the two signallers attached to Company HQ out to find the break and then cover him with my rifle while he repaired it; secondly, many messages to the platoons, which normally would have been transmitted by phone, I had to deliver personally.

After the bustle of the activity of the early night hours and after the British had ceased laying down smoke, the early morning hours in the ruins could be eerily silent. Then the slightest noise could trigger off a German flare and bring down a rain of rifle grenades about your head. The Germans fired flares into the air constantly throughout the night. The deathly quiet did, however, have one advantage – it enabled a man to hear the pop of the pistol and the sudden hiss of the light as it shot skywards, which gave him just enough time to drop flat before the Very burst into full flame and lit up the whole area. But however careful I was not to make a sound, however alert I, myself, was for the slightest noise, there were times when I was caught, quite unprepared, by the lights. Then the only thing to do was freeze in your tracks and keep quite still. It was a truly nerve-racking business. I had stood in the light of the German flares before but never at as close range as this, in places it was no more than fifty yards. It was sheer bloody torture waiting out the time of the flare's flight through the air. Every fraction of a second of the time as I stood there, perhaps half-crouched, I awaited the vicious stream of machine gun bullets which, I was certain, must come to smash into my hopelessly unprotected body. I sometimes thought half the bloody German war effort went into the making of Very lights.

The German rifle grenades I became almost contemptuous of, I've had them popping off all around me only a matter of a few feet away and suffered no harm, not once but several times. However, their 'tatty-mashers' or stick grenades were a completely different kettle of fish. These exploded with a roar like that of a mortar shell.

One morning, just before dawn, in that deathly quiet hour which, in the front line, signals that the countdown has begun to the unleashing of the ritual 'morning hate', I was given a message to take to two of the forward platoons. I didn't like going out at that time one little bit, there was always the chance that I would still be out there when that fire came down, which thought tended to hurry me and, in the eerie silence of that place at that hour, hurry could be fatal.

I delivered the message to the first of the platoon officers and then foolishly, instead of retracing my route back part of the way and then going forward once more to the second platoon as I should have done, I decided to cut through the ruins directly towards it. No more than seventy or eighty yards separated the two platoons but it was all of it unknown territory. As my intended route was so close to the German line it also meant I should have to crawl across the open spaces between the broken buildings and the heaps of rubble. I set off and I'd got perhaps a little more than halfway when, to my horror, I suddenly realised I'd lost all sense of direction. I lay at the foot of an enormous mound of rubble, wondering what on earth I should do and cursing myself bitterly for letting windiness get the upper hand of me to the extent that it had driven me to take the short cut. In my position at the foot of the mound of rubble I could see almost nothing of my surroundings. I decided to do the only thing there was to do under the circumstances – climb the rubble heap to obtain a better view of the area!

All was quiet, no sound anywhere broke the silence. It was as if the whole world hung by a thread and was waiting for just one wrong move, one tiny little noise from me for it to come crashing down upon my head. Very, very carefully, despite my feverish impatience, I inched my way up the heap of rubble. I attempted the impossible, to climb a mountain of loose rubble without making a noise! A brick, or something, rolled away from under my foot, only a little way, but the noise it made sounded to my ears like a clap of thunder. In reality, I suppose, only ears very close and already alerted for just such tell-tale noises would have heard it but it was precisely those kind of ears which were most abundant in Cassino. The response from the Germans was electric. I heard a pop and a flare hissed by, startlingly close to my head. It came from a spot on the other side of the rubble heap not more than four or five yards from me – I'd almost blundered into German lines. The flare struck something projecting from one of the ruins and it fell, hissing and still burning brightly, to the ground behind me. Terrified I froze to the rubble heap.

Suddenly there was a tremendous explosion also behind me which was followed by another and another - the Germans were searching the area with hand grenades. They were overthrowing by far but nevertheless, if they kept it up, or I was to make any more noise, I'd be in really desperate trouble. My terror increased but there was nothing I could do, other than what I was already doing. The Germans threw several more grenades and one of these exploded much nearer to me than the others had done – it went off with a crack like the firing of a twenty-five pounder artillery piece. I felt the blast and in the same moment I was struck with terrific force by something which, at the time, I was convinced was shrapnel, just behind my right ear and I almost lost consciousness. Eventually the Germans desisted from their grenade throwing and the silence returned. Carefully I raised my hand to my ear and felt the very large lump behind it. It was bleeding badly and so hard was it that I was certain a piece of shrapnel had lodged itself in the wound.

For a long time I lay there unmoving, considering my predicament. I was terrified of making the slightest noise, which I risked doing if I moved. On the other hand, I certainly couldn't stay where I was, dawn couldn't be more than twenty minutes away at most. One good thing – I'd found my bearing, I now knew which way *not* to go!

Very, very carefully, more carefully than I'd ever done anything in my whole life before, even more carefully than when I had defused the mine at Medjez-el-Bab, I let myself down to the foot of the rubble heap and slowly began to crawl away in the opposite direction to that from which the flare and the grenades had come. I crawled around a ruined house and then I saw, on the top of a mound of rubble only a few yards away, a most welcome sight. It was the familiar outline of a knocked out Sherman tank silhouetted plainly against the sky. I had indeed strayed well off course for the tank was as far forward as our most advanced positions.

Dawn was breaking when at last I thankfully crawled under the brick archway and dropped down into our Company HQ basement. Joe, the stretcher-bearer, examined my 'wound', 'It's only a cut,' he said offhandedly and stuck a plaster on it.

Our 'right-wing' platoon was the one of the Ornito misfortune. I'd many good friends in it and they were always pleased to see me arrive at their positions. I was their only link with the outside world. The telephone belonged to the platoon officer so they relied on me to supply them with the latest rumours and other tit-bits of information I had gathered back at Company HQ. I also carried messages of a personal nature to mates in the other platoons and vice versa. My friend, Eddie Latham, was a member of this platoon and I usually had a jaw with him before I returned to HQ. One night, or rather morning, I had lingered with the platoon in this fashion, it was quiet as I made my way back, I'd travelled only a few yards when I became conscious of a faint, and unusual noise. Curious, I halted to listen. I heard it again – it had a distinct metallic quality. I couldn't judge how near or how far from me the source of the noise was. It was just a faint 'ping-ping', as if somebody, somewhere in the ruins was striking, very carefully, a chisel with a hammer! I'd used hammers and chisels enough myself as a bricklayer in civilian life and that's what it sounded like to me. But who would be using a hammer and chisel in those ghostly ruins and at that hour in the morning? My curiosity fully aroused, I continued to listen. The noise was repeated several times over. I was overcome by a feeling of deep disquiet but for the life of me I couldn't pinpoint the source of the noise. The hollow ruins and the extreme quiet of the place could, and often did, play tricks with sounds.

Eventually the noise ceased completely. Worried by what I'd heard, I continued on my way to Company HQ. That I ought to report the noise I knew but I was afraid of being thought over-imaginative. However, report it I did. I didn't mention the hammer and chisel connection – I should have done but I didn't. Captain Hutchinson questioned me carefully but, so unsure was I of myself and, I suppose, so vague were my answers that, after giving the matter some thought, he suggested that it may have been a tin sheet or something similar, swinging in the breeze. I had to agree that it may have been but for the fact that there was

108.

no wind. There the Captain let the matter go and, half ashamed, so did I!

The next night, when I took the ration party up to the same platoon, I'd forgotten all about the incident. Everything with the men was the same as before, I chatted in the usual half-whispers with several mates, including Latham, and then, as soon as the ration party had completed its delivery and collected whatever empties there were, I led it off into the night. I returned alone to the platoon once more, just before dawn. Everything was exactly as before.

The following evening I was resting in our Company HQ basement dug-out, awaiting my first assignment of the night. The ration parties weren't due for another hour, at least, yet. Captain Hutchinson sat at the table by the telephone. A storm lantern, placed alongside the telephone, provided all the light there was in the basement. The other members of Company HQ except for two sentries placed at the entrances, were still trying to catch up on a little sleep or were sitting talking in low voices amongst themselves. All told, there were about a dozen of us, including the signallers, the stretcher-bearers, spare runner, the two sentries, Sgt Major 'Davy' Davidson, Captain Hutchinson and, of course, myself.

The Germans had shelled the Company area a little while previously, not too heavily but enough to create the possibility of there being a break in one of the telephone wires. But, as time went by and no such break was reported, I was beginning to think my luck was in and that I wasn't going to be sent out on that particular jaunt that night. Suddenly the heavy curtain, the second of the two which screened the entrance, was agitated, forwards and upwards, and a wild-eyed figure tumbled from beneath it into our midst. I recognised him as one of the Ornito platoon. His startling appearance at Company HQ and his obvious state of agitation shocked all of us into an instant awareness that something was gravely amiss up front.

We listened, with growing alarm, as he told his story to Captain Hutchinson. It was short but stark in its implications. His platoon had been attacked and completely surprised by the Germans. He believed himself to be the only survivor, all the other men having been either killed or captured. The first warning they had received of the attack had been by way of a tremendous explosion which had wrecked the dug-out he shared with others of his section. Other loud explosions had quickly followed the first, and before they could react, the Germans had appeared at the wrecked dug-out entrance and commenced to toss grenades down into it. After the Germans had gone he'd managed to free himself from the wreckage and make his escape from a rear exit. He was certain the whole of the platoon positions were now in German hands. So ended his story!

Captain Hutchinson's first reaction was one of anger that a platoon under his command should have allowed itself to be so completely surprised and overwhelmed. He snatched up the phone to report the attack and its outcome to Battalion HQ. As he waited to be put through to the Colonel, he suddenly whirled round on us lot, still trying to grasp the full significance of this latest turn of events. 'Right, you lot,' he barked angrily, 'get dressed and get out.' Immediately there followed a mad scramble for the rear exit. 'Not that way,' howled Captain Hutchinson, even angrier than before, 'that way,' he gestured towards the front exit, *we're counter attacking.*' The mad scramble came to an abrupt halt, everyone gazed incredulously at everyone else. We could hardly believe our ears. Counter attacking? What with? He couldn't possibly be serious. Even if he took the full compliment of Company HQ, which was impractical to say the least, there'd be no more than ten of us and, out there waiting for us, was a whole battalion of German paratroopers, with every gun, mortar and machine gun on Monastery Mountain undoubtedly ready trained on our little company area, in anticipation of just such a hasty reaction on our part. All eyes were fixed on the captain. His face was grim, he meant it alright. His last words, before slamming the phone back on the receiver, were, 'I am now proceeding to counter attack with Company HQ.'

Six of us were selected for the attack. We were dished out

with grenades. I checked my tommy-gun and then, led by a truly mad captain, we crawled out into the night.

To our right front, long streams of coloured tracers flew thick and fast over the tops of the ruins between Castle Hill and the Monastery. The incredibly rapid 'Br-r-r-r-r-rp, Br-r-r-r-rp' of the German Spandaus sharply punctuated the steady tat-tat-tatting of British Brens. Before us burned a line of fires – incredibly in those constantly blasted and incendiaried ruins, the fires could always find something further to feed on.

We crawled rapidly towards the fires. As we had already guessed, they proved to be the positions of the lost platoon. Flames licked from the entrances of the dug-outs, infernos raged below. The Germans had gone – not surprisingly, nobody could occupy those positions, neither could anybody be left alive in them.

Captain Hutchinson, covered by us, scouted the positions looking for wounded or other survivors, but all he found was a dead German. One of our men, at least, had had time to get off a shot or burst of fire before going under. Of course, there may have been other Germans killed or wounded, which the enemy had taken back with them, we would never know.

Two things, however, were certain. One, the position was no longer tenable, and two, we should have been very hard put to man it even if it had been. Accordingly we returned to Company HQ dug-out.

Astonishingly, several more survivors of the platoon crawled into the positions of a neighbouring platoon the following night and nearly got themselves killed in the process, so keyed up and alert for trouble were the men of the second platoon following the attack upon the first. However, the men survived a shower of genades and succeeded in identifying themselves in time. Their story corroborated that of the first survivor – the sudden tremendous first explosion, followed immediately by the appearance of the grenade-throwing Germans, which had given them no time to recover from their initial shock. Eventually, like the first man, after the Germans had gone – the whole raid only took a few minutes – they had managed to extricate themselves from the ruins of their dug-out and then, under the command of a corporal, had taken up fresh positions in an adjoining ruin. There they had stayed until it eventually dawned on them that they would have been given up for lost. They had then decided to make their way through the sixty or seventy yards of ruins which separated their positions from those of the next platoon.

The fact that they hadn't seen the counter attacking party was not surprising. They'd been concentrating their attention almost entirely upon the German positions before them, ready to repel the next attack, and none of us of the counter attacking party had stood up in the light of the flames, nor had we heralded our arrival there with a blast of trumpets.

To have so completely surprised the platoon, the Germans would firstly have required to know the *exact* whereabouts of its dug-out entrances. The spine-chilling thought came to me that I myself may well have been instrumental in showing them these. It was distinctly possible. I had, after all, been seen when I'd frozen in the light of their flares but it had suited the purpose of the Germans better to allow me to carry on. My blood turned to ice at the mere thought of it. Once they had pinpointed the platoons positions, the rest wouldn't have been too difficult.

I thought again about the metallic noise that I had heard on the previous night to the attack. Could it have been caused by someone using a hammer and chisel? I thought so. Given the very close proximity of the two sides to each other, it would have been quite feasible for the Germans to have tunnelled under the ruins and break into the cellar adjoining the one occupied by the major part of the platoon. To do that they would almost certainly have needed to use tools. Most of the work involved could have been accomplished, quite safely, under cover of the constant noise made by the laying down of the nightly smokescreen. As for the tell-tale noises I had heard in the extreme quiet of the early morning hours, these may have been due either to German impatience to get the job done or, perhaps more likely, to some unnoticed break in the sound-proofing afforded them by the mountainous heaps of rubble.

Once through, it would have been simplicity itself to lay explosive charges against the last wall or walls separating them from the British platoon, with additional men poised above ground, to strike immediately the charges were exploded. Only twenty or thirty yards separated the two front lines at that point, the platoon would have had no chance to recover from the shock of the explosion before they were overwhelmed. Something like that, I think, did occur.

Some very odd stories come out of Cassino, arising out of the closeness of the two sides to each other, some funny, some not so funny. One soldier was said to have put his eye to a hole in a wall only to see, at the other side, another eye gazing right back at him. Still another was, one night, surprised to find himself joined by a German soldier in the latrine area, which he'd hitherto believed to have been the sole property of his own section! Nobody, at any time could be positively certain which of the ruined buildings within their view, were occupied and which were not, or by whom! Although on the maps of the time the front lines remained static and quiet, in reality all the time a game of hide and seek was being played out by the troops of both sides, within the town. Although no doubt the gains and losses so incurred were too small to merit adjustment to the divisional maps, nevertheless men lost their lives and many others were wounded in those deadly little encounters, as witness the fate of our own Ornito platoon.

After perhaps a week spent there, we were relieved by one of our own Companies. We then went into the battalion reserve positions on the town outskirts. There things were much more comfortable. We still had to avoid showing ourselves during the daylight hours but at least we could relax, talk in normal voices and, at night, move about naturally without bothering too much about the noise. It was good, too, to be rid of the nightly round of chores.

We were positioned close to the town's cemetery. This had been pretty much mashed up by shell fire but, during our time there, hardly a shell fell upon it. What German fire there was appeared to be concentrated almost entirely upon the first line infantry positions and the artillery lines further back.

As I stood sentry at night, gazing at the usual colourful firework display above the town and listening to the restless boom of artillery and the crump-crump-crump of mortars amongst the ruins, I was very glad to be in reserve for a while. I visualised the runners, further in the town, making their way through the maze of ruins and mountainous rubble heaps, alternately dashing and crawling through the smoke and the fire, and no doubt, like myself, soundly cursing the clumsiness of the ration parties, the slowness of the signallers in repairing the telephone wires and all the many other laxities which added to their work and the time spent by them to-ing and fro-ing between the platoons and Company HQ.

The time spent in reserve whizzed by and before we knew it it was time for another tour of duty in the first line. We took over several acres of ruins from our 'B' Company.

Major Coates resumed command of 'D' Company. Company HQ was, this time, above ground. It was located in the town's main post office. The building, which was modern, had been very strongly constructed of reinforced concrete. Its gaunt and broken shell towered prominently above the surrounding ruins. Inside, all the upper floors were in various stages of collapse. Over our Company HQ, which was on the ground floor, a large section of the floor above, still anchored firmly to one of the outer walls by a multitude of strong reinforcing bars, hung steeply downwards, its bottom edge resting upon a mountain of rubble on the ground floor. In the space created by the departure of the floor from its former position, held firmly in the iron grip of a writhing mass of broken reinforcing bars, gleamed a large unexploded bomb.

Its sleek, gleaming, deadly body hung down precariously but a few feet above our heads. It illicited from me an almost hypnotic response. It drew my eyes like a magnet. Whenever the building became rocked by nearby explosions, my eyes went irresistibly to the bomb. Should the bars, even for as little as a fraction of a second, relax their grip, the missile would fall plumb into our midst. It could hardly be expected not to explode a second time. I could have chosen better places for Company HQ, even in Cassino.

Major Coates used the services of the second runner to maintain contact with the platoons. I was, at one and the same time, both pleased and resentful. I wondered if perhaps he lacked confidence in me. I was, after all was said and done, the senior runner but, after the numerous narrow escapes of my first tour of duty in the ruins, so pleased was I to stay under cover all the time that I swallowed my pride and made no mention of my feelings to him. Of course, I was only being given a break from the duty. Furthermore, the opportunity was being taken to familiarise the second runner with the layout of the ruins. Everybody knew the lull in the fighting was only temporary, it might not be too long before we had to attack over those same ruins and it made good sense to have as many runners as possible familiar with them.

Before, and, as always, overlooking our new position, was a particularly active German machine gun post. Its crew appeared to have taken an extra strong dislike to the post office, they were constantly firing bursts through the windows and other openings on the side nearest to them.

The racket as the fire flew through the openings was terrific. It sounded as if the very barrel of the gun itself was poking through the window. Until we became accustomed to it the noise caused us to leap from our rest and snatch up our weapons, under the firm conviction that we were under immediate attack and the enemy was upon us.

During the night, sentries were posted at each of the windows. As soldiers on active service, they were supposed to stand boldly upright in the centre of the opening and look out but, being human also, they preferred to stand rather more to the side. The second officer in command was forever moving the men back into correct position but the moment he'd departed the sentries resumed their old positions. One sentry, at least, had cause to be thankful that he'd done this. Part of a burst of fire aimed at his window struck the side of it furthest away from him, causing chips of concrete to fly into his face and eyes. As it was he was blinded, but had he been standing in the correct position, he would undoubtedly have been killed outright.

There was nothing we could do about the German fire, no matter how provocative it became. We were still under strict orders not to reply to it. Sometimes men felt very strongly about it but all we could do was hurl obscenities at the Germans and even those in a voice not loud enough to be overheard by them. Nobody wanted to be a hero but we eventually reached the stage where we would have jumped at almost any chance to have paid that German crew back in its own coin.

Despite this denial of opportunity to use our weapons, imposed upon the battalion from above, it was fondly believed by us, certainly by myself, that if and when the occasion arose we would be able to muster a firepower, particularly in artillery, greatly superior to that of the enemy opposite us. However, an incident took place one night which caused me to seriously question that assumption.

One of the guns, *our* guns, laying smoke was firing short, its shells were dropping into our own Company area. In the time honoured military manner, the platoons complained to Company HQ – Company HQ complained to Battalion HQ – Battalion HQ complained to Brigade – Brigade complained to Division and Division got on to the artillery unit responsible, which of course all takes time – and still more time for the answer to get back again.

It was, however, impossible, without running an individual firing check upon each of the guns, to say exactly which one was at fault. Accordingly, all the guns were ordered to cease fire and then to recommence firing one by one until the culprit, as would be reported by us, was identified.

The guns ceased their fire, a comparative hush fell upon our part of the line and everybody waited for the first of the guns to recommence firing. While we waited, the silence seemed to grow and gather in intensity. Not for weeks had there been any change in the nightly smoke routine, everybody was uncomfortable and the very air seemed to become charged with menace. Suddenly a steadily rising howl, which quickly grew into a thunderous roar, shattered the silence and the next moment the whole area was deluged under a storm of bursting shells. The Germans had reacted with truly astonishing force to the silence. The stonk quickly grew in intensity until it became all but impossible to separate one explosion from another.

I cowered beneath my window. Smoke and dust billowed and blasted through the openings above my head to fill the whole building with stinking fumes. In the rapidly flickering light of the bursting shells I saw the shadowy outline of the officer second-in-command of the Company, I just can't remember his name, come stumbling blindly through the smoke towards us. 'Up! Up! On your feet! Watch your front!' he cried, without stopping, on his way to the next sentry in line. He thought we were being attacked! Heart pounding, I risked a quick peep through the window. Before my eyes, at the bottom of a thick, grey wall of smoke, yellow flashes leapt in a frenzied dance of death. I quickly lowered my head once more – no Germans could possibly attack us through that lot!

I never thought they were attacking us in any case. They were simply filling the gap created by our own short-sighted 'thirteen thousand yard snipers', as the artillery were called by the infantry in Italy.

The stonk lasted five, possibly ten, minutes, but it was enough. For the first time in Cassino we had been given a true glimpse of the enormous fire power at the disposal of our enemies also. Furthermore, such a lavish expenditure of shells on a merely 'suspect' area indicated that they were suffering from no shortage of ammunition.

The particular dislike for the post office shown by the German machine gun crew appeared to be catching. It spread to one of their mortar teams – their Nebelwerfer mortar teams. As every soldier who fought against the Germans knows, the Nebelwerfer was the very last word in mortars, better known perhaps as the

'Moaning Minnie' or the 'Sobbing Sisters'. It was an electrically operated weapon which fired six shells at one go and was reputed to be guaranteed to wipe out any infantry position up to a range of six hundred yards. The Germans opposite us possessed several of these super-deadly things.

I was guarding a rear entrance to the Post Office. It was a nice enough April morning: I was all alone, separated from the others by dividing walls. I could neither see nor hear another living soul. My view through the doorway took in several streets of silent ghostly ruins, nothing stirred anywhere, it was as if I was completely isolated in a dead world.

Suddenly there come to my ears the rapidly swelling roar of an approaching mortar shell. It exploded with tremendous force about twenty yards beyond my doorway. Splinters of steel hummed through the opening. The explosion had been plenty near enough to be frightening but not more so than usual. The Germans were inclined to toss the odd shell about like that, now and again, just for the hell of it. I resumed my former upright position by the doorway, quite prepared to dismiss that particular explosion from my mind as just one more amongst many.

Again I heard the gathering shriek of another approaching shell. This one exploded by the side of the Post Office furthest away from me. The detonation shook the building forcibly, causing pieces of rubble to fall from its upper parts and little avalanches of dust to trickle from the cracks in the broken walls. I began to get the wind up. It seemed very much as though the German mortar mortar crew was ranging on our building. The third shell left no doubt whatsoever in my mind, or in the minds of any of the others – that it was. A thunderous explosion over our heads brought chunks of masonry crashing about our ears and the place filled up with dust and smoke. They were no longer ranging, they had ranged!

In front of the steep incline of the collapsed first floor was a concrete stairway. Much of it was hidden in rubble but somebody had excavated the rubble from beneath the stairs to make a cubby-hole big enough to sleep two men. It was also, due to its position right in the heart of the building, plus the fact that it was surrounded and covered by such a large mass of rubble, an exceptionally well-protected spot – as near shell-proof as we could hope for. There was, however, a very large question mark hanging over it in the shape of the large unexploded bomb, suspended in the bars almost immediately above the entrance.

Evacuating the building, in broad daylight, was out of the question. We'd have been shot to pieces before we had gone ten yards. Bomb or no bomb, there was nothing else for it but under the stairs! The two men already there were almost crushed to death under the sudden avalanche of bodies which descended upon them as the howl of more explosives on the way rose higher and higher. Several legs, arms and bottoms were still not fully under the protection of the stairs when, with a roar like thunder the shells exploded, hurling huge chunks of masonry downwards and raising up clouds of choking, blinding dust. Now they had got the range, the Germans were loading all six barrels.

Into a space which was barely large enough to accomodate two men, eight or nine of us had packed ourselves. It was almost impossible to breathe, let alone move – not that anyone minded that, more bodies, more protection!

The Germans, for their part, went about the business of blasting us to kingdom come in quite a leisurely manner. Whole minutes at a time passed between salvoes. I spent the interval times trying desperately not to think about the bomb poised but a matter of feet above our heads, the situation was quite ghastly enough!

As the unearthly scream of each down-coming salvo swelled rapidly to reach such ear-splitting proportions that, even if you had screamed right along with it you would still scarcely have have been able to hear your own scream, I could feel the muscles in the wall of flesh about me tense up to receive the thunderous shocks about to follow.

On and on went the bombardment. It seemed it would never end. The long intervals between salvoes raised our hopes falsely several times. Eventually the ordeal did come to an end. We waited – ten, fifteen minutes went by and nothing happened. The men at the top began, slowly, to disengage themselves from the pile and one by one we struggled from the hole. All our gear, packs, blankets, weapons, etc., was buried beneath thick layers of dust and piles of new debris. I glanced upwards, miraculously, the unexploded bomb was still in the same position as before. I resisted an urge to reach up and pat it!

All of us were badly shaken but unharmed. It was a miracle of survival. Those of our Company mates who had witnessed the bombardment told us afterwards of the tremendous surprise they had felt upon learning that we were all still alive.

Some time, towards the end of April, we let our ruins in the town, rent free, to a battalion of Guards and we lot marched away for a rest. Company HQ was the last to leave and Major Coates and myself were the last of Company HQ. He wouldn't stop jawing to the Guards officers, consequently dawn was near breaking when we reached the town outskirts. I was feverish with impatience to be on and well clear of the town before full daylight came. It was then he stopped by the enormous crater where I had seen the Bren gun. It was still there. Major Coates spotted it and stood on the lip of the crater, looking down on the Bren. My anxious eyes were on the eastern sky. 'We could salvage that,' he said, ruminatingly: I didn't reply, I just groaned inwardly. Dawn was breaking as he climbed down into the hole and stood just above the water fiddling with the Bren. Eventually he reached it up to me. I grabbed it quickly, before he decided to clean the bloody thing.

The battalion was not done with Cassino, not by a long chalk it wasn't, but right then we didn't know it, nor would we much have cared if we had. In war, a week longer is longer than a long time, it's an eternity, and we could, unless something went especially badly wrong, look forward to at least that long away from front line duties.

The time we had spent so far in Cassino had, all of it, been in one of the 'quiet' periods, in one of the 'lulls' between battles. Even so, we had lost quite a high proportion of our Company strength, a sobering thought for later days.

10.

A Very Pistol Of My Very Own

WE ARRIVED AT A CAMP on the banks of the Volturno and immediately began practising river crossings. Our boats were small canvas affairs designed to hold eight men. One man held his paddle over the back end or stern of the boat and steered, six men paddled and the eighth manned the Bren gun, pointing it over the prow of the boat, towards the 'enemy' bank.

We practised the crossings by day and by night. Everything usually went fine until we got away from the bank but the Volturno flowed fast and the scene in mid-stream was often more reminiscent of a fairground dodgem set-up than an ordered river crossing by the horny-handed sons of a great maritime nation. Men paddled their boats furiously in opposite directions, steerers lost their paddles and everybody, literally everybody, shouted orders and bawled advice. We did however improve, to the point where our officers could be reasonably sure that most of us men, given enough time, could be trusted to arrive on the right bank of the river, not too far away from our designated landing points. As the powers that be appeared to be willing to settle for this level of efficiency, the boats were taken away from us. I personally had thoroughly enjoyed the exercises, despite the ducking I received on one occasion when our boat went down, after having the bottom ripped out of it by a submerged rock – debris from the stone bridge close by, blown up by the Germans in their retreat.

At last I received news of my brother. It came in a letter from home, dated weeks previously. He'd been found safe, if not altogether well, in a rear area hospital. He *had* been taken prisoner by the Germans, on the Anzio beachhead – small wonder I'd been unable to find his unit. However, he'd managed, along with a couple of his mates, to escape and find his way back to the Allied lines. There he'd been found to be suffering from trench feet and the effects of exposure. I was both pleased and sorry – pleased, of course, that he was alive and well, but sorry that he'd escaped from the Germans. I couldn't help but wish, for mother's sake, that he'd stayed a prisoner, then she would have been certain to see at least one of her boys come home after the war was over. As it was, it didn't look to be nearly over and all three of us, as rifle company infantry soldiers, were particularly vulnerable.

The German air force wasn't nearly as active in Italy as it had been in Africa but, occasionally, they made the odd sortie, if only to drop 'toilet paper' – i.e. propaganda leaflets – on us from great heights.

There was a Bailey bridge over the Volturno and Major Coates, ever obsessed with the war, thought that as we, Company HQ, were billeted right by it, we might as well mount a Bren gun at our end of the bridge, so to protect it from air attack. All you did for this was to hook the Bren on to the top of a steel tubular affair, something after the fashion of one of those old tripods photographers once used, only ours was higher. In the front line, the same Meccano-like contraption could be adapted for sighting the Bren on fixed lines. After we'd got it erected, not without the usual swearing, you could have as much difficulty with that contraption as you could have with an extra warped deck-chair on a windy beach, Major Coates inspected it and then wandered off, no doubt to find something else to 'defend'.

I was on anti-aircraft duty and the last thing I expected was an air attack – we hadn't seen a German plane for weeks.

Suddenly, with a roar like an express train hurtling non-stop through a station, a German plane appeared right above my head, no more than a couple of hundred feet up. I saw the single bomb it carried leaving the plane – it looked enormous, almost as large as the plane itself.

At the gallop, from nowhere, came 'Hutchy'. While I still gaped at the plane and the bomb open-mouthed, he seized the Bren and loosed off the entire mag. at the German plane, but it was then already too far away. I think the plane had gone, the bomb exploded and the mag. emptied before I'd even got my mouth shut again.

'Hutchy' lowered the Bren and I thought, 'Jesus Christ, now for it, hands in pockets, day-dreaming on duty, he'll never let that go!' But he did. As he passed me he just grinned: 'That was a close thing, Framp.' He meant the bomb, it had only just missed the bridge. That was just like 'Hutchy'. I breathed a sigh of relief and thanked my lucky stars it hadn't been Major Coates himself, he'd have bawled me out at the very least. Major Coates had been a solicitor before the war and a territorial soldier, he was one of the battalion's old guard, a real disciplinarian, a brave and competent officer, but no 'Hutchy'. He never grinned at you nor you at him.

About this time, two men came up before him on Company orders. They'd been caught dozing on sentry duty, on our very first night out of the line. Company Office was in a kind of barn with a part upper floor above. I and the two signallers were on the upper part and we could hear every word spoken below.

Nobody could roast a man like Major Coates could and all without using one swear word or repeating himself. He told the two that in the last war they'd have been shot and if he had his way they'd be shot in this one, and so on and on.

I squirmed for the two men. The upshot of it was he sent them to appear before the Colonel. The two were sentenced by him to stand guard every single night, in addition to all their daily duties, until such time as we went back into the line proper.

Incidently, when we did return to the front line, the two men were almost immediately killed, a direct hit on their trench. The odds are they would both, mercifully, have been fast asleep.

The whole battalion was paraded to hear an address by Lt Colonel Madden. We sat on the ground in the form of a large square and the Colonel stood in the middle. He informed us of the purpose of our recent training on the river. It was intended to prepare us for the crossing of the Rapido, which was to take place very soon, a mile or so west of Cassino. Our Division, the Fourth, had been selected to smash through the defences of the German Gustav Line and bring the bloody four month's long battle for Cassino and Monastery Hill to an all time end.

The Colonel pulled no punches. He told us, in plain language, what we were in for. The Rapido was no-man's-water, it flowed between the two front lines. The perfect anti-tank ditch, its current was swift and strong and every yard was covered by German fire. It was also under clear observation from the Monastery. We already knew previous attempts to cross it had ended in disaster and since then the Germans had had ample time to further strengthen their defences.

The Division was intended to cross the river by boats under cover of an enormous artillery barrage and establish a bridge head on the German bank. The engineers, then, under cover of night, would build a bridge over the river to allow tanks to cross. Our own brigade, the Twelfth, which also included a battalion of Royal West Kents and one of the Royal Fusiliers, was planned to cross with tanks and, with their support, break out of the bridge head in the direction of Cassino, so to come at the town and the Monastery from behind. A tall order, a very tall order, but the Colonel at least, judging by the expression on his face and the enthusiastic tones in which he couched his address, had no doubts about the successful outcome of the task entrusted to us.

He held a 'sticky bomb' high in the air. This looked like an enormous toffee apple on a short stick. 'Don't be afraid,' he bawled, flourishing the bomb, 'when the Germans counter-attack and the tanks come rolling over your trenches, all you have to do is stick one of these,' – again he flourished the bomb, 'up its ass as it passes, ten seconds later your tank is blown to blazes.' He made it all sound so simple, everybody had to grin.

After the battalion briefing by the Colonel came the Company briefing, given by Company Commanders. For this purpose, Major Coates had managed to obtain a blackboard from somewhere. We sat cross-legged before it while he drew various coloured lines and squiggly shapes upon it. It appeared, after we'd crossed the river, we had a green line, a blue line and a red line to attack. Each coloured line represented the successive lines of the German defences. Nobody seemed to be very interested, now they knew the general plan, who the hell cared about details?   It wouldn't matter a monkey's what bloody colour line a man 'bought it' at, it would all be the same to him, so appeared to be the general attitude.

The Major went on to describe the role of the tanks in the coming battle. Each Company was to have three Sherman tanks in support. When we, the infantry, were held up by too strong a German fire, one of our men would crawl forward to within Very pistol range of the enemy machine gun post, or whatever it was causing the hold-up, and drop a red flare onto it. With the target so identified and pinpointed for them, the tanks would then do their bit.

My ears pricked up at this. There was a VC going there for somebody – the posthumous kind. For a start, whoever was given the task of pinpointing the target had first to get within Very pistol range, over ground allegedly impassibly swept by enemy fire – that alone was one hell of an undertaking. Secondly, even if he made it safely, the moment he fired the flare, he'd give his whereabouts away to the enemy. The thought had already occurred to me that the ranges of Very pistols and German 'tatty-masher' grenades, thrown by a strong arm, were about equal. He'd be a very lucky man if he got to fire a second flare, should the first one miss or the tanks be slow to react to his signal. Certainly, I thought, such a responsible job would be entrusted only to an officer or senior NCO, they being more likely to be possessed of the stuff candidates for VCs needed to be possessed of.

We were breaking comp preparatory to taking up positions nearer to the Rapido. 'Framp,' called Major Coates.

'Yes, sir,' I replied, dutifully and promptly.

'Go to the stores and draw a Very pistol and cartridges,' he commanded. I scooted away and returned a few minutes later with the Very pistol in a leather holster attached to a shoulder strap and the necessary cartridges. The Major was busy talking. I waited respectfully for him to finish speaking and then, 'I've drawn the pistol and cartridges, sir,' I informed him, bursting with curiosity to hear the name of the super-soldier I was to hand them over to. His eyes dropped disinterestedly to the articles in my hands. 'Oh good,' he replied lightly and then turned upon his heel and wandered off to attend to some other business. I gazed after him stupidly, then I felt my stomach lurch. It was all too clear, the Very pistol and cartridges were mine, I'd won first prize, a Very pistol of my very own, exactly what I'd always never wanted!

It was now into May and the weather had improved by leaps and bounds. It was shirt sleeves and denim trouser order for the battle. We carried a minimum of equipment and a maximum of ammo., including several hand grenades fastened to our belts by the pins, bent over, of course.

As we moved, in single file, up to our assembly area, we met a team of Red Cross workers. They handed to each man, as he passed them, a sandbag containing a few luxuries – an orange, a few sweets, a few cigarettes and, what I enjoyed best of all, a packet of dates. We thanked them politely as we took the parcels, it was like receiving a goodbye gift. The Red Cross women handed the gifts over without fuss but with encouraging smiles for each and every one of us. Close by, I remember, was a Salvation Army mobile canteen, the military police had prevented its going any nearer the front. The chap in charge of it was maintaining a furious argument with the redcaps. Most of our lads hated their guts and some jeered at the redcaps as we passed by. This front line area was their own ground, they didn't fear arrest there.

The attack was due to commence an hour or two after dark. Our Company lined a grassy bank, we didn't expect to move into the attack ourselves until dawn. It would take that long for the other two brigades of our division to establish themselves on the German side of the river and for the engineers to build their bridges.

The weather was fine and the front quiet. When night closed in only an occasional gun flash here and there lit the sky. We'd nothing to do for the time being but wait. There was a subdued air about the Company, indeed about the whole of the front. All around us thousands upon thousands of other men waited, too, for it to begin. I was glad we hadn't been chosen to carry out the initial crossing.

I pictured the lads of our other brigades at that very moment, crouched by their boats, ready to dash for the river. The moment the British barrage came down the Germans would react and it would be they, poor devils, who would cop it first and worst. One of our officers began the countdown to zero hour. All in the same second every gun on the entire front opened fire. It was as if the very world itself had suddenly ripped apart. As far to the east and west as we could see ran an unbroken line of flashing white fire. The crashes of hundreds upon hundreds of guns combined to produce a thunder of stupendous dimensions, it was scarcely possible to believe it was the work of men, it seemed it must shake the very stars out of the heavens. I gazed upon the scene with awe. Never, in my wildest imaginings, had I thought to see and hear such a mighty unleashing of naked terror. Germans or no, my heart went out as much to the poor devils on the receiving end as it did to those of our own boys advancing, naked of cover, into a rapidly rising storm of fire, as the German line flamed into counter action.

No call came for us to move forward that night. Disturbing rumours began to reach us, the spearhead brigades had been cut to ribbons by the German fire during the night. Only a small bridge head existed on the other side of the river and the Germans were furiously counter attacking. Owing to the intense German fire, the engineers had been unable to build their bridge, the situation was desperate! But the troops in the bridge head held out. For a day and a night they held out against everything the enemy could chuck at them and then, by morning, the second day, the bridge was completed and we, who had waited anxiously all that time, listening to the ceaseless thunder of artillery, were ordered forward across the bridge and into the battle.

It was then that a million to one chance encounter occurred to me. We were moving forward, fairly fast, along a narrow road, a steady rain of German shells falling around us. Other troops, waiting to cross the bridge, had taken cover in the many holes and craters on our left, just who they were I didn't know. Suddenly one of these raised himself and waved a hand excitedly. 'Hey, Charlie!' he bawled. At the sound of my name I turned my head towards his. He'd be about twenty yards away from me. At first I didn't recognise him, my eyesight was never the best, it was also slightly misty and one face under a tin hat looked pretty much like another. I waved a reply, 'Hello,' I called back, without stopping. A moment or two later recognition hit me, it was 'young Norman' from my home town, Scunthorpe! He and I, as well as being friends, had worked for the same firm as apprentice bricklayers. 'Norman!' I hollered back, debating quickly, dare I break ranks to shake his hand and exchange a quick few words? I decided to postpone our meeting, I'd see him later. I'd already come to the conclusion that the troops in the shell holes must be of our own battalion. I gave him a last look back and waved my hand and at that very moment the ground beside Norman suddenly erupted high into the air as a heavy shell exploded and that was the last I ever saw of him. I learned, a long time afterwards, that he'd been killed that same morning and I thought about the shell that had burst beside him.

Norman's unit, I eventually discovered, was the 2nd Battalion Royal Fusiliers, one of the three which made up our Brigade.

We raced by a Bren carrier which was on fire, its cargo of small arms ammunition exploding in all directions. We passed a number of bodies — their faces, where visible, were already taking on a waxen appearance. The bridge was hidden by smoke but the Germans knew, roughly, its whereabouts and deluged the area with fire. We ran a gauntlet of bursting shells and then we were on the bridge. As we raced off at the other end, we passed still more bodies lying scattered on the ground. One of the men was still alive. He lay spread-eagled on his back, snoring frantically, blood bubbles forming and bursting in rapid succession around his mouth. The din of battle reached new heights as we raced by a line of slit trenches, many only partly dug. The ground about them was torn by shell fire, a litter of abandoned and broken equipment surrounded the trenches. I saw Lt Colonel Madden walking along through the fire, swinging his stick as though he was out for a country stroll. Then we met our tanks, we had still several hundred yards to go to our Company start line. Rounding a very sharp bend in the road, one of the tanks tippled into a ditch. Major Coates swore at the crew but they were unable to extricate their vehicle and we carried on without it. I felt an iron band of fear clamp itself tightly about my chest.

Our Company objective was a group of farm buildings, or rather, what remained of them. It was a strong position, we'd been told, and the Germans were well dug in. I didn't know whether it represented blue line, red line or what, nor did I care. We couldn't see it but fire from it ripped through the mist towards us. That morning the mist was our friend. As we moved steadily forward, through the shellfire, the strangest thing happened to me. The band of fear which had clamped itself tightly round my chest suddenly relaxed its grip. I felt a tremendous upsurge of spirits. I felt something I'd never felt before – I can only describe it as an exultation, perhaps the exultation of battle. It may sound boastful but that's how I felt just then. I walked forward boldly and confidently, I amazed myself. The crackle of small arms fire and the repeated 'Br-r-r-r-rp, Br-r-r-r-rp,' of Spandaus before us grew louder. We took to the ditches in order to deploy ourselves for the final assault across the two hundred yards or so of fire-swept ground remaining between us and our objective.

Company HQ crawled single file along a ditch, bullets cracking and zipping above our heads. A constant hail of shells howled down and exploded around us as the Germans, well aware of our coming, frantically shelled and mortared the area. I was struck forcibly on the head by a huge clod of earth thrown up by a very near miss on the ditch. We'd come to a halt and I waited patiently for the man in front of me to move on. He didn't, so after a minute or two I ventured to ask him: 'What are we waiting for?' He didn't answer and something about his reluctance to answer aroused my suspicions. I crawled right up to him and repeated the question. He gestured towards the man in front of him, indicating that he was waiting for him to move first. I looked

at the man in front – he lay still, too still. I crawled up to him –
he was dead. I was certain the other man had guessed it but had
decided not to make sure, in order to stay longer in the protection
of the ditch. I cursed him soundly – he could have lost us touch
with the others of HQ.

I took the lead and led the way forward once more. I quite
surprised myself for the second time that day, by this assumption
of responsibility. That kind of thing I'd always been more than
content to leave to others. Nor had I been at the whisky bottle –
such front line luxuries as that weren't for the likes of us. I'd
never ever sought promotion, it had never occured to me: nor, I
think, had such a preposterous idea ever occurred to my superi-
ors. I was a born private, tailor-made for the rank.   I knew it,
they knew it, and I was quite happy, confident in the final victory,
to leave the actual conduct of the war in such capable hands as
those of Lance-Corporal Smith, Sergeant Major Davison and, of
course, Major Coates.

We lined a ditch, the company now deployed before its objective, ready to make the final assault across the hundred or so
yards of ground which remained between us and it.

The noise was deafening, a terrible artillery fire was falling on
the German positions. I could see the scores of yellow and orange
flashes flickering and dancing in the grey wall of smoke which
marked them. The moment the fire lifted we would attack. I saw
the bright gleam of polished steel, describing the movement from
scabbards to rifle muzzles, all along the ditch, as the platoons
either side of us fixed bayonets.

Our tank, mysteriously we seemed to have got down to one,
had meanwhile coyly taken cover behind a broken hedge, perhaps
twenty yards to our rear. Major Coates had argued himself
hoarse getting it even to accompany us that far. We believed, certainly I did, that the tank should be in the front, so as to frighten
the life out of the German infantry and cause them either to surrender, or bolt, before we reached them. the tank commander, on
the other hand, appeared to believe that we, the infantry, should
go first, so as to cause the German anti-tank gunners to surren-

der, or bolt, before he reached them.

I sometimes thought tanks were more bother than they were worth. I'd known occasions previously, back in Africa, when they'd appeared on our company positions and kicked up such a racket that they'd brought down on us, it seemed, half the German artillery fire on that part of the front. They'd then withdraw and leave us to enjoy it all by ourselves.

The British barrage on the German positions in front of us abruptly lifted. I saw the platoon men scramble, 1916 fashion, from the ditches and move forward in an extended line with rifles held at high port. For the time being Company HQ stayed put in the ditch. Despite the British shelling, a gathering storm of small arms fire shot out from the Germans positions. I gazed after our lads, their outlines blurred in the mist and the smoke of the battle so that I couldn't tell who was who, but they all looked equally magnificent as they walked steadily forward into the German fire. I felt almost like a traitor to them as I crouched in the comparative safety of the ditch. No one who has ever witnessed a sight such as I witnessed then could ever fail to be deeply impressed by it. It was a truly magnificent display of courage and discipline and I felt proud to be one of them.

The crackle of German small-arms fire seemed to redouble in intensity. Long bursts of Spandau fire ripped through the mist into the steadily advancing ranks of our boys. We were incurring casualties fast, the stretcher-bearers – Smithy, Dolly, Joe – were wanted everywhere at once. Our left hand platoon, the one of the 'Ornito' misfortune, was eventually driven to the ground by the fierce German fire. Major Coates despatched me after it to find out the exact cause of their trouble. I moved along the ditch for about twenty-five yards and then climbed from it onto a road which ran obliquely towards the German positions. Short stretches of high hedge, plus the mist, screened the road, or much of it, from the German view, or so I thought. I walked boldly upright towards the platoon which had taken cover in the ditches either side of the road, about eighty yards further along. In the road, between the groups, lay several bodies, all our lads.

One I recognised as a special friend, Dick Biley. He lay perfectly still with blood pouring from a wound in his neck. I gazed down at him with horror. 'Is he dead?' I asked a man in the ditch. 'No, but you bloody well will be if you stand there any longer, what the hell do you think got them?' he rapped back at me. I hastily jumped into the ditch alongside him.

I found the platoon officer a few yards further along the ditch. He took me forward a further few yards to a spot where the ditch ended and cautiously lifted his head above the ground. He pointed to a low mound of stone rubble about seventy yards away. 'There's a Spandau there, covering the road. Tell Major Coates I need a tank to destroy it before we can move,' he said. I nodded my head and made my way back, this time sticking to the ditch. The bodies had been lifted from the road and carried into the shelter of the ditch. I'd time to spare them no more than a quick glance but I resolved to tell the stretcher-bearers of Dick's whereabouts.

I delivered the platoon officer's message to Major Coates and he immediately despatched me with a message for the tank commander. The tank was to move forward to a position where it could see the target and open fire upon it. I scooted off quickly, before he remembered the bit about the Very pistol. I'd slung it behind me when I'd reported back to him, so as not to jog his memory too obviously.

I reached the tank which was still in the same position as before, behind the hedge. At the rear of the tank was attached a telephone, to allow anyone on the outside to communicate with those inside. I picked up the phone and pressed the buzzer. No answer. I tried again, same thing. I was still trying when Major Coates lifted his head from a ditch a few yards away. He gestured impatiently towards the turret of the tank, which I took to mean I should climb up there and try to get in touch with the crew through the closed hatch. I'd already started to lift one foot to place it on the track of the tank when it suddenly dawned on me that up there, above the hedge, I might possibly be in full view of the Germans. I hastily lowered it again, they'd never believe the

British Army were fielding ten foot high soldiers, they would guess at once that I was standing on the tank they so desperately wanted to locate – they must have heard it earlier. I felt the iron hand of fear grip my chest once more – the rest seemed to have done it good, it gripped tighter than before. Perhaps I had misunderstood the Major's gestures, his words anyway, at that distance, were mostly lost to my ears in the tremendous racket of noise going on all round us. In any case, I was sure the telephone was in working order, the trouble was with someone, or something, inside the tank. Major Coates angrily left the ditch. I told him I was sure the phone was functioning properly. He tried it himself several times and eventually slammed it back into position and walked to the front of the tank. He rapped on the driver's vision slit with his stick and I banged on the side with my tommy-gun. The situation was becoming both difficult and farcical. The Major stood slightly forward and immediately beneath the long barrel of the tank's 75 mm gun and pointed his stick repeatedly along the road in the direction of the pinned down platoon. The meaning of his gesture should have been perfectly clear to anyone inside the tank seeing it – he wanted the tank to move in that direction. But the tank commander, if he saw, misunderstood. There was a tremendous crash and a flash of flame burst from the mouth of the gun, just above the Major's head. He reeled to one side , clutching both hands to his ears. I beat wildly on the tank side with my tommy-gun once more – the damn fool inside couldn't even see what he was firing at. The Major recovered himself, white with shock and anger, and we eventually got the tank moving. The Major led the way and I followed him fearfully, wondering if I was about to be called upon to do my Very pistol trick.

We rounded a slight bend in the road and there we beheld a wonderful sight. Before us the platoon had left the ditches and now stood boldly upright on the road. In their midst stood about a score of German prisoners and others, hands on heads, were streaming along the road towards them, one man carrying a mate on his back. Some of the others were wounded also and most looked to be frightened to death. But one of the last Germans to come in, even though his hands were upon his head, put on a show of defiance. One or two of our lads, further forward, still lay in the ditch covering the Germans as they came in and waving them by. As this particular German passed each one he commenced to spit upon them. I saw one of the lads in the ditch angrily jerk his rifle up at the German – it was enough. Someone said he was the Sergeant-Major – I could well believe it, he looked to be a nasty enough piece of work. Accordingly, as he'd been so sluggish in getting himself onto parade with the others, he was given several extra prods with the points of bayonets, as the Germans were herded into line by the remaining lads of the 'Ornito' platoon for wristwatch inspection.

Even though the Germans on our particular objective had surrendered, the battle raged on with unabated fury on either side of us. The entire bridge-head, every part of it, it seemed, was deluged under a storm of exploding shells, British and German. Between explosions there came to my ears the crackle of Spandau fire and the steadier note of British Brens replying – somebody close by was still at it.

My company had suffered grievously, casualties lay everywhere and the stretcher-bearers were overwhelmed with work. I was ordered to assist them. I was more than glad to, working was better than just lying under that awful storm of fire with nothing better to do than think about it. Under fire, officers, in one respect anyway, had the best of it, they'd nearly always something else to think about: a problem of attack or defence to solve, or maybe just concentrating on setting an example, gave their minds something else to dwell on other than the immediate prospect of coming to a sudden, bloody end!

My front line ear was perfectly tuned and so too was the man's at the other end of the stretcher. We both knew the shell was going to be close and we lowered our burden quickly, but not quickly enough. I'd time only to throw up an arm before the shell exploded. Thirty feet in front of us a fountain of earth and smoke abruptly shot into the air. A second later a searing pain

134.

shot through my left arm as shrapnel smashed into it just below the elbow. The arm was bent, I could neither straighten it nor bend it more without causing myself the most excruciating pain. It was impossible for me to continue helping the stretcher-bearers but at least the instinctively upflung arm had certainly saved my face from injury and perhaps myself from death.

The RAP was in the corner of a field. The ground about it was thickly covered with wounded men awaiting attention or evacuation. The MO, even more so than the stretcher-bearers, was overwhelmed with work. My arm – the same arm as I'd previously been wounded in – was bandaged and placed in a sling and I was instructed to find my own way to the casualty clearing station over on the other side of the river. For the second time in the war I joined the ranks of the walking wounded. Fifty yards out I looked back to see several shells burst horrifyingly apparently on and around the RAP. For a moment I debated whether to return but there would have been nothing I could do for anybody so I continued on my way.

The bridge was about half a mile away but such was the intensity of the German fire that every yard was fraught with peril. It was going to be run a few yards and then drop flat, run a few yards more and then drop flat again, all the way to the bridge. Fortunately the land was criss-crossed with innumerable ditches – if the morning mist had been our best friend that day, the ditches ran it a close second. Where these ran in the right direction, I stuck to them.

I came across a first aid post at a junction of ditches. Several packs, all empty and bearing the Red Cross sign littered the banks about the post. Two men, wearing the armbands of medical orderlies, stood in the ditch staring expressionlessly before them and listening dully to the incessant din of the battle. They barely seemed to notice me. I passed them by without a word.

Maybe sixty or seventy yards further on I hastily threw myself into the bottom of a ditch as the rapidly rising shriek of what sounded like a whole salvo of shells swelled to an ear-splitting crescendo. The shells exploded with a roar a few yards beyond the hedge which followed the ditch.

At once I scrambled to my feet to be off. As I did so, through a gap in the hedge there came stumbling a blood-stained khaki figure. The man toppled into the ditch at my feet. I gazed down upon him with a mixture of horror and instant compassion which rooted me to the spot. A black shrapnel hole, the size of a two shilling piece, in the man's face, drooled blood. Red stains, rapidly spreading, glistened on his tunic. His eyes filled with pain and a look of mute appeal lifted to meet mine.

His voice was little more than a whisper as he uttered those words I had heard so many times that day – 'stretcher-bearers!' But there was nothing I could do for him – I had no field dressings! His eyes pleaded – I remembered the two medical orderlies, but they were seventy yards back, seventy yards in the wrong direction, twice seventy was a hundred and forty. An extra hundred and forty yards through that dreadful fire, but I knew I had to go. I turned about and made my way back the way I'd come.

When I reached the medical station – whose it was I had no idea – I told the two men there about the man in the ditch. They raised bleak eyes to mine. 'Nothing we can do mate,' one replied in a low, toneless voice, 'we've no dressings left, nothing at all.'

'And there's wounded all over the place,' the second man added in a similar voice. I gazed despairingly at the two. There was a finality about the flat spoken words which numbed my brain. The strain of it all was beginning to be too much for me and I felt my self control would snap at any moment. I turned away from them and once more made my way along the ditch. When I came to the wounded man he was lying perfectly still his eyes closed. I think he was dead but I didn't try to find out for sure, just in case he wasn't. I couldn't bear to think of those eyes opening to see, not the help he so desperately needed, but only my useless self. I stayed with him for perhaps a couple of minutes then, despairingly, I went on my way.

I was nearing the bridge – it was still hidden in smoke. I followed a line of slit trenches, the same ones we'd passed by earlier that day. One, I noticed, still contained a body. A drift of smoke revealed the hazy outlines of the bridge about a hundred yards away. I was nearly there when a howl of shells, rising to a shriek, caused me to throw myself frantically into the nearest trench. It was nowhere near completed, not more than a foot deep, and there wasn't room to get the whole of my body below ground level, nor was there time to find another hole. Instinctively I thrust my feet out of the trench — better they be exposed than the other end of me. The shells burst, showering me with dirt. Immediately I sprang to my feet, the bridge and safety were very close now, two or three more dashes and, with luck, I'd be there.

It was then that I heard a voice hailing me. I turned and saw a head sticking out of a trench and a hand waved over the head. For a few moments I hesitated, every instinct in my body frantically urging me to ignore the man in the hole and sprint for the bridge while the going was good. The man called again. I went over to him and with him, in the bottom of the trench, was slumped a second man. He looked to be extremely badly injured but he was, however, still conscious. The first man wore a sling, he'd been wounded in the left arm, like me. 'Do you think,' he asked, that you and I could carry him across the bridge?' – he nodded towards his mate. I glanced down at the wounded man – his eyes were rigidly fixed on mine, awaiting my answer.

I lifted my eyes to the bridge, a moment ago so near and now, suddenly so far. Here and there, shell bursts leapt and danced in the smoke about it. I pondered the question – what should I, how could I, answer? The bridge occupied a position right at the heart of the German barrage, more than anything they wanted that bridge. Alone, unless my luck was to completely desert me, I stood a very good chance of making it to the other side. With these two, it would be a snail's pace over every yard of the way, and I'd already been hit because I'd tried not to lower a man too hastily to the ground. I felt the weight of their combined gaze upon me.

In their slit trench, I reasoned, they'd be safe from everything except a direct hit, the risk would be far greater to them if they were to desert it. Only men able to move rapidly should attempt to make, and cross, the bridge under such fire. The German fire must, in any case, eventually slacken. Then they could attempt the journey with a much greater prospect of success. But also, I very well understood how they felt. Anything was preferable to just sitting under that awful fire. I raised my eyes to meet the questioning gaze of the lightly wounded man. I explained my reasoning to him. He nodded his head slowly, whether in agreement or resignation, it was hard to tell. 'I'll tell you what,' I blurted out with sudden inspiration, 'there's sure to be a stretcher party somewhere near the bridge, I'll get them to come and pick him up!' Both men nodded their heads gravely.

I crossed the bridge alone. I found no medical team but I did inform a group of soldiers – engineers, I think they were – of the whereabouts of the two wounded men. They promised to inform the next medical team or ambulance crossing the bridge.

A quarter of a mile beyond the bridge, near to the spot where I'd last set eyes on Norman, I rested on a grassy bank. The Germans were still shelling the area. It seemed to me, sometimes, that they'd more guns than we had. I watched several shells burst in the field on the other side of the road. The heavy detonations flung great fountains of earth and smoke into the air. I was in no danger, they were plenty far enough away and by comparison with the fire in the bridgehead over on the other side of the river, the fire here was almost as nothing. A company of infantry, making fast time towards the bridge, trotted by in lines, three abreast. As the shells screamed over their heads they dropped flat to the ground. They were in no real danger, their ears weren't yet properly tuned. I smugly waved them to their feet but I suppose my own appearance, complete with bloodied sling, wouldn't have given them too much confidence in my judgement

I wondered who they were – West Kents? Fusiliers? Bedfords? Surreys? Whoever they were, they rose to their feet and continued at a jog trot towards the bridge. The British were now pouring men by the thousands into the bridge head and I was but one of many hundreds of casualties who retraced their route that day.

As I rested on the bank, watching still more troops making rapid time towards the bridge, I became assailed by a feeling of guilt. I thought of the two lads I'd left at the other side of the river and the face of the severely wounded man persisted in rising before my eyes. No matter how vehemently I told myself I'd done the right thing, the thought came inexorably back to me – really, had I chickened?

To the twenty-one year old young man who was then myself – perhaps 'boy' might yet be an apter description of him – reared from his earliest days on a diet of 'derring-do and warriorship', consequent upon the events of the First World War and, later, those of the Civil War in Spain, it seemed I had.

Man or boy, I was already becoming experienced enough to appreciate that funk in battle always, at the time, presents itself as 'common-sense' – and I was troubled.

Looking back on the event and with the knowledge acquired much later, that so formidable are the defences of the ego that it's almost impossible to breach them alone. I believe that though funk may have been the dominant partner at the time, 'common sense' was its sensible ally.

I'd done the right thing. They *were* safer in their slit trench, safe from everything except a direct hit. I didn't know it then but not so many more months of the war were to elapse before I was to find myself again in a like situation – but then I was to be the gravely wounded man.

At the casualty clearing station I was given a drink of fruit juice, whereupon I immediately became sick and I was quite ill for several days.

11.

THE LANDING STRIP

I ENDED UP at a base hospital in Bari, where the shrapnel bullet was removed from my arm. It had embedded itself in the bone but not broken it and it was painful only for a short time.

There were many German prisoners also in the hospital and as far as I could see thay were treated and cared for in exactly the same manner as we were. Other than the fact that we less severely wounded British soldiers had to sit on a chair in the wards which contained them, just to keep an eye on them, you couldn't have told the difference between the wards, theirs and ours.

I was one of those detailed for this duty, perhaps a couple or three times in all. I remember the first time I got the job, I was sitting on the chair at the end of the ward, arm in sling, interestedly looking over my charges. Most were only slightly wounded and many of these sat upright on their beds, apparently quite happy with their lot. After a while I became aware that the casual conversations they'd been conducting amongst themselves had ceased. A silence had fallen on the ward.

I looked up and every damn German in the place had his eyes firmly riveted on me – that is, all except those too badly wounded or too ill to do so. I thought they were going to try something but they neither moved nor spoke, just sat there staring and staring at me. At least a couple of dozen pairs of eyes were riveted upon me. There was no other Britisher in the ward, not even a nurse, only me. I felt uncomfortable. I tried to stare calmly right back at them but I couldn't, there were too many. After what seemed an eternity, a nurse came into the ward. I was very relieved, it broke the spell. It had lasted no more than ten or fifteen minutes at most but, as they'd intended, I'd felt very, very uncomfortable while it had lasted. I suppose they thought they were conducting some sort of psychological warfare on me. How that helped their war I'll never know.

The next time I got the job they tried a different approach. I was always amazed at the number of Germans who could speak good English and this bunch ran true to form, several of them could. While I sat there several German aircraft attacked the shipping in the harbour and one of them flew right by the hospital. All the Jerries in the ward shouted and cheered like mad, you'd have thought they'd just won the war.

After the planes had gone and the ack-ack had ceased, one of the Germans, a tall, well built, blond-haired bloke of about thirty years – as I got to know them better I put him down as their main ring-leader – turned to me and informed me, in very good English, that those planes had flown from their aerodromes in Africa. The surprise must have shown on my face — not surprise that they were still flying planes from North Africa but surprise that anybody could be dim enough to believe it! Or dim enough to think I could be made to believe it!

The blond-haired bloke then went on to inform me that fighting was still going on in Africa and that the Allies were retreating there. When I shook my head, they all began shouting together, 'Yes, yes, yes! Fighting still in Africa!'

One of the other guards, if that's what you could call us, told me of an experience he had with them. A nurse had propped one of the more severely wounded Germans up and was giving him a drink from a tin basin. Suddenly the German raised his hand and dashed the basin from her grasp, spilling its contents. It went rolling across the floor.

With no other thought in his mind but to retrieve the basin, the guard rose to his feet and made towards it. Immediately about ten of the lightly wounded Germans leapt from their beds and formed a line between him and it. There they stood, arms folded across their chests, defying him to advance another step. The nurse retrieved the situation, she rose and got it herself.

I don't think British soldiers in the same circumstances would have behaved in the same way. Warring, to them, was for the front line. It seemed ridiculous to carry it on in a place like a hospital ward, especially since they were all being so well cared for. It was our considered joint opinion that a mental hospital would have been a more appropriate place for them!

I'd been transferred to a convalescent camp at Tranti a day before I heard the news of the capture of Rome. We didn't find the news so greatly exciting. The fall of Cassino and the capture of the Monastery by the Poles, two or three weeks earlier, had, in our eyes, been the real achievement.

A few days later we learned of the invasion of France – D Day. That *did* excite us, we were certain the war would not last much longer now. Most of us inmates of the convalescent camp were pretty well convinced that, with a little bit of luck, we'd never see any more front line fighting.

Up until then it had seemed that we in the Med. had been fighting the war alone, a feeling very much encouraged by the Germans. They'd regularly bombarded the front line areas with propaganda leaflets, depicting the Yanks, back in England, sleeping with the wives of the British soldiers absent in Italy. 'Is this what you're fighting for?' they asked.

There was plenty of substance in this. A popular cartoon of the time – I can't remember now if it was German or British in origin – showed a British soldier, returned home on leave, opening the door of his house to a very smartly dressed Yank bearing flowers. 'Is our wife in?' asks the Yank. All very cunning but sadly, in many cases, all very true.

Some of my fondest memories of the war concern the 'characters' I met. The British Army abounded with them and the transit camps, between the base hospitals and the front line battalions in Italy, were particularly fertile areas in which to find them.

Men from almost every infantry regiment engaged in the fighting in Italy came together in these. For a few days, occasionally for a few weeks – strangers to each other – they briefly shared the same tent, the same mess table, before being all too quickly whisked away, back to their own front line units. Every man Jack of them had a story to tell and yarning was our favourite pastime.

Nobody cared how obscene, how crude or how impossible the story, as long as it was well timed and told. I still chuckle over some of the tales I listened to in those now long-departed and forgotten camps. But my prize for the best goes to the tall, lanky, beak-nosed fusilier I found myself teamed with, amongst others, in the convalescent camp at Trani.

Eight of us shared a table, four on each side. The cooks had come up with something nobody, for sure, recognised. Some said it was toad-in-the-hole, some said pizza and still others this or that. No matter, everybody polished it off and the general verdict was that 'it' wasn't bad, whatever 'it' had been.

The beak-nosed fusilier – he spoke with a southern accent – was sitting on the other side of the table from myself. He glanced at his neighbour and then asked abruptly: 'Ave you ever tasted human flesh?'

'Human flesh? Course I bloddy ain't!' answered the neighbour and then, sensing that the question wasn't altogether idly asked, 'Why? 'Ev you?'

'Ah don't know,' said the fusilier.

'Wot the bloddy 'ell d'yer mean, y' don't know?'

'Wot ah say! Ah don't know – ah'll tell you the story, then you can tell me whether ah 'ave or ah 'aven't.'

Beak-nose had captured the interest of the entire table now.

'It was like this,' he began, 'we'd jus' come out the line an' they gave us this job of making a landing strip for one of them little artillery spotter airplanes. It only meant shifting a few rocks, filling a few holes in and takin' the bumps out. Our own pioneer sergeant was in charge of the job, a fat-arsed, bossy little sod. 'E was allus throwin' 'is weight abaht, even 'is own platoon couldn't stand 'im. 'Owever, when we'd got that part of the job done 'e ordered us all to stand clear. There was abaht 'alf a dozen trees at one end of the strip 'e wanted dahn. 'E was goin' to do this with gun cotton, 'jus' blow 'em dahn. We all stood clear abaht 'undred yards from the trees while 'e got 'is stuff together, gun cotton, detonators and the rest of it.

'Anyway, while 'e stood there examinin' these trees, up wanders a bloody great pig, an' 'afore you could say 'Jack Robinson', starts eatin' the sergeant's pile o' gun cotton and detonators. By the time we got 'im to understand what was goin' on, the bloody pig 'ad near eat the lot. Well, 'e run up to the pig an' fetched it a bloody great kick, an' that was it – there was an effin' great flash an' a bloody great bang an' the two of 'em 'ad gone – pig an' sergeant an' all.'

The next thing we knew, something come flyin' through the air an' plonked down right beside us, it was the arse end of the pig. "Ere, we're not gonna waste that," one of our lads said, "that's fresh killed meat."

'Well, neither did we, we got the cooks to make us some bread an' cook the 'ams and ah can tell you mates, it tasted jus' be-ootiful, best meat ah've ever 'ad in all me life!'

'Well, a couple of days after, we was talking to some of our 'B' Company lads and we told 'em abaht the 'ams jus' to make 'em jealous. Well, ah could see, by the way they looked at each other, somethin' was very wrong. Then they told us jus' the same thing 'ad 'appened to them and they'd snaffled the arse end of the pig an' eat it.

'Well, pigs only 'ave one arse end, same as us. There was no daht abaht it, mates – one of us lot 'ad gone and eaten that fat-arsed Sergeant's fat arse!'

144.

12.

THE MEETING

CAUGHT IN THE STEEL GRIP of a vast and mighty war machine, over which such lowly forms of military life as us had not the slightest shred of influence, we were passed back stage by stage, camp by camp, closer and ever closer to the front line and the ever hungry guns. We knew quite well what lay in store for us at our journey's end, who better than us?

We were not the 'stiff upper lip' type. Indeed, if anybody of our service had come that, he would have been regarded with suspicion by the others. We freely and without shame confessed our fear to each other – 'Jesus Christ, mate, ah was shittin' myself, ah can tell yer,' was the usual way of putting it. Ours wasn't to set an example, ours was but to follow where they, the other type, the officers, led. Officers above battalion level and often, too, a fair sprinkling of those below it, were generally considered to be a load of 'chinless wonders'. But still we followed! Perhaps those such as myself, a little less unwillingly – after all we'd volunteered for it and, also, we were generally younger and still unmarried.

Sometime early in July I arrived at an Infantry Reinforcement Training Depot. Other than the fact that it was north of Cassino, through which we passed on our way to it, I've no idea now just where it was.

God, how we hated those places and the staff who ran them – most, if not all, of whom we were sure had never, themselves, either fired or seen a shot fired in anger. The bullshit began immediately you arrived at the place. You were put on charges for the least little infringement of the rules. The saluting drill, foot drills, arms drills, OPT, white-washing, blancoing and polishing were endless. Any ideas you may have entertained that as veterans you were above such basic training were knocked right out of your head at once. You reverted right back to rooky status and were chased from reveille to lights out.

How long did I stay there? Maybe ten days, perhaps a fortnight, I can't remember now but the day came when a number of us were loaded into a couple of trucks. We were on our way to the Divisional Camp, the last before we rejoined our own units. We weren't sorry — anything was preferable to that hateful camp.

I can only remember staying one night at the Divisional Camp. Then we dozen or so Black Watch types were exclusively bundled on to yet another truck under strict orders not to stop until it had delivered us safely into the waiting arms of the Battalion Regimental Sergeant Major.

I had had little contact with him, his rule was confined almost exclusively to the Battalion HQ Company, in front line areas anyway, which, in Italy, was the whole of the time.

I was lucky in one more respect, the battalion was in reserve. 'D' Company was bivouacked in a grassy meadow at the foot of a hill. As I entered the company area almost the first man I saw was Company Sergeant Major Davy Davison. He was washing from a canvas bucket on a trestle and blowing and snorting like a surfacing bull whale. He hadn't seen me. I came up behind him just as he started drying. 'Hullo, Sergeant Major,' I said softly. Still vigorously rubbing his face, he turned towards me. When he saw who it was, the delight which came over his face was, I'm sure, absolutely genuine. He downed the towel and grabbed my hand and proceeded to pump it vigorously. I've always been a little embarrassed in such circumstances but the glow of pleasure I felt then far outweighed it. Sergeant Major Davison made me feel as though I'd come home again after a long, long absence. It was a wonderful feeling!

In the ten weeks I'd been away the Company had seen much hard fighting but most of the Company HQ lads had survived. Joe, Dolly and Smithy were there to welcome me back. But McOwett had gone – missing, I believe – Major Coates had been killed and our pipe-major, too.

They told me that after the fighting at Cassino, 'D' Company had become so reduced in numbers that it had been disbanded and its survivers re-distributed amongst other companies. It had only just been re-formed shortly before my return after the battalion had received a fresh draft of reinforcements.

Major Callander was now commanding 'D' Company – he hadn't served in our company before. He didn't know me but I knew him, he was one of the old-timers with the battalion. I'd often seen him at Battalion HQ and other places during our travels. He was later to be killed during the attack upon the Gothic line over on the other side of Italy.

But, right now, we were marching through Tuscany and I'd been restored to my old job as Company runner. The Germans were retreating steadily northwards and, upon our part of the front, falling back upon Florence and the line of the Arno river.

Tuscany was a beautiful place – purple hills, winding roads, lovely villages. Everywhere the land was rich and fertile, all its orchards and vineyards were in full fruit and also mostly booby-trapped by the retreating Tedesci! Always the villagers and farmers warned us of the booby-traps in their orchards. Even when there were no booby-traps, they still warned us! We didn't doubt they'd just as considerately warned the retreating 'Teds' of British or American unexploded bombs in the same places.

The Germans were expert booby-trappers, they left many nasty surprises for us behind them. One particularly nasty device was known to us as the 'debollocker'. The usual place for this was just inside doorways and the weight of a man's foot triggered it off. A fraction of a second later it fired a small charge, straight up, hence its name!

The Germans also very heavily mined the roads and verges. Tanks and other vehicular traffic could never ignore the danger. But infantry could and did, we were always acutely conscious of the danger when we were in the lead, way out in front of the engineers who lifted the mines. The favourite anti-personnel mines of the Germans was the 'schu' mine. Its casing was made of wood to defeat the metal detectors. If a man trod on one of these, there was no escaping the loss of a foot at least – nasty, vicious things they were. Their second anti-infantry mine was the dreaded 'S' mine. It was triggered off either by a trip-wire or by a three-pronged plunger. Either way the effect was lethal. Instantly upon contact, the jam-tin shaped container leapt from its metal case buried an inch or so beneath the ground surface and exploded with a tremendous crack at about the height of a man's head, scattering its tightly packed shrapnel bullets over a tremendously wide area. It had the capability of decimating a whole platoon.

The Germans even booby-trapped their own mines by putting other explosive charges beneath them, so that as the first one was lifted, it triggered off the one below.

Even so, booby-traps or no booby-traps, mines or no mines, we followed in the wake of their retreat, always we were there. In my memory's eye I can still see the little files of our lads, widely spaced on either side of the road, helmets angled, rifles slung, tin mugs swinging from packs, plodding patiently on, mile after dusty mile along the alternately sunlit and then starlit roads of Tuscany. Never any rest, always pressing and jollying the Germans further and ever further back.

About every sixth man in the files carried, as well as the white enamelled mug swinging from his pack strap, a usually well-blackened and battered old jam tin. This was his section's brew tin and easily its most prized possession. If the length of time of a halt appeared to justify it, none of the weapons they carried were ever faster swung into action than those old tins.

The older hands had learned always to carry a little fuel, either petrol or sticks, so that they were never caught out by shortage, either of kindling or of time. Within a few minutes of a halt being signalled, little fires appeared all along the line. Always a matchstick minus the head was dropped into the brew tin. It was said this prevented the water from becoming 'smoked'. Whether or no, it was part of the ritual and therefore duly observed.

Another trick of those same older hands – if you looked closely you could pick them out by the way their equipment hung

148.

– was to load only one Bren gun mag. into their pouches. The rest of the room there was given over to cigarettes. This not only ensured them a superior supply of smokes but also very considerably lightened their load on the long, hot thirsty marches. Some carried extra water-bottles, often German, and these as likely contained wine as water, or maybe the section's emergency petrol supply, filched from some lorry or tank parked in the 'safe area' behind.

Still on the subject, if you were a young second lieutenant, new out from England or the back areas – and there were plenty of those as the casualty rate amongst platoon officers was fearful – and you'd checked the contents of the packs of these same old sweats, you would have been horrified to discover that in scarcely any way at all did they conform to regulations.

No spare shirt, no groundsheet, and, sometimes, not even the 84 anti-tank grenade. Lost? Dumped! In favour of extra rations – maybe tea and sugar, maybe half a dozen eggs, maybe bread, and too, the extra socks, always extra socks! If you didn't know before, you bloody soon learned that 'you couldn't 'ave too many socks – the bloody roads are red 'ot.'

'Groundsheet? 'Oo needs an effin' groundsheet? 'cept for playin' cards on, then yer c'n allus borrer one off the new boys. If yer've got yer gas-cape mate, yer don't need an effin' groundsheet; wrapped in that yer c'n drag yer pack and rifle in with yer an' sleep all night by the roadside in pissin' rain as dry 'n snug as a bug in a rug.'

'Spare shirt? This bugger ah'm wearin' 'll do me 'til we get pulled back, then yer c'n allus snaffle another at the de-lousing camp.'

'Eighty-four grenade? Ah lugged that bloody thing all way from Cassino an' only used it once and then all it did is blow up one of we own effin' Bren carriers. 'Sides, Jerry's not comin' this effin' way, 'e's goin' yon! Fuckin' new boy, what does 'e know abaht it?'

The accents in which these earthy sentiments were expressed were, by now, nearly all English. Long gone was the time when the battalion had been composed solely of Scots lads. Ever since Dunkirk, more than four years previously, it had been receiving drafts of 'new boys' and each successive draft contained a greater and greater proportion of 'Sassenachs'. Every county, from Kent to Cornwall and from Cornwall to Northumberland, was represented. Very, very few of the old Scots originals now remained with the battalion, the long, long trail of its travels through Belgium, France, North Africa and now Italy, was marked by their graves.

Every now and again, the Germans set up an ambush for us. We'd be trudging along in the night, each man sleepily following the swinging white mug just in front of him when, suddenly, there'd be a streak of light skywards and the next moment, a German flare would burst into full glare right over our heads, to be followed immediately by long bursts of machine gun fire. Tracers streaked from out of the inky darkness before us and crackled viciously as they shot by. Instantly, too, our weariness dropped from us and we'd scatter into the cover either side of the road, praying, as we did so, that that particular area wasn't mined.

Company HQ usually followed the leading platoon, with the other two platoons following behind us. Major Callander, calling for me to follow him, would then either crawl or run, half-crouched, to confer with the officer of the leading platoon to decide upon their plan of attack. Almost always, by the time they'd done this and got it into motion, the Germans had departed, swiftly and silently – on bicycles.

Occasionally the Germans positioned a mortar behind the machine gun and then they gave us a short, sharp stonking as well; sometimes they fired on us from longer range with their artillery but, almost always, as we seriously deployed for attack, they pulled back.

The inhabitants of the villages and hamlets scattered along the roads welcomed us warmly – even rapturously – when we appeared in their streets. Some overdid it – not the women, the men! One bloke I had to theaten with my tommy gun in order to bring the hugging and kissing to a stop. I'd sat on a pile of hay in a farmyard – we were only snatching a breather before moving on – and suddenly the hay beneath me began to rock violently. Alarmed, I sprang to my feet and whirled about upon it but, before I could do anything, the hay parted and out sprang a dirty, old man. Then, greatly to the delight of the rest of Company HQ lads, he threw his arms about me and proceeded to plant firm, juicy, whiskery kisses on both my cheeks. Nor did he stop it, until he felt the barrel of my tommy gun rammed into his belly!

Our officers were forever studying maps and looking through field glasses at the country ahead. Occasionally they were joined by the 'bloke' with the red hat. They would then stand in a group by the roadside, pointing this way and that and talking earnestly amongst themselves. I never tried to overhear what they were saying, I knew they were cooking up something for us but I wasn't particularly interested. Whatever it was we'd find out soon enough. While they talked, we rested, and the longer they talked, the longer we rested and that was all we cared.

We were standing on a high hill. Major Callander passed his field glasses to me. 'Take a look down there,' he said, with a pleased expression on his face. Wonderingly, I put the glasses to my eyes – he'd never before bothered to do a thing like that. A wide valley stretched before us. Two or three miles away was a river and on the banks of the river gleamed the buildings of what appeared to be a large town: 'What do you see?' enquired the Major. I wasn't too sure about what I was supposed to see. 'A town by a river,' I replied hesitantly.

'That town on the river, Framp,' he grinned delightedly, taking the glasses back, 'is Florence. Within two or three days we shall be in it.' Which remark just goes to show how wrong a man can be. We, that is, Major Callander, myself and the rest of the battalion, never did get to enter Florence. Before the Major's 'two or three days' were up it was snatched from us, not by the Germans but by the British – a change of plan!

However, before that came to pass, they found us a real job of work to do. Between us and the Arno, laying in wait for us, was an estimated couple of thousand Germans. We were ordered to bundle them over to the other side of the river. Our colonel protested against the order, his battalion, he argued, was too greatly understrength and too exhausted, it had been continually fighting and marching for more than three months, ever since Cassino, it was worn out! Brigade replied sympathetically but firmly, the attack must be made. However, we received the promise that after we had completed the attack we would be withdrawn from the line and sent back to enjoy a long rest and that was that.

The Germans shelled the area from time to time, with guns sited over on the far side of the river, just to let us know they were ready and waiting for us. It was to be a night attack, nobody had any illusions about it – the Germans were deployed before us in strength, it was going to be a hard fight. Night came and we prepared to attack but almost at the last moment the attack was postponed for one hour.

We waited and smoked and fretted, nobody wanted to talk. I'd never seen the lads at such low ebb, many were, quite clearly, almost at the end of their tether. If you happened to catch a man's eye he jerked it away again moodily. In similar circumstances, not so long ago, it would have been the signal to exchange wry, encouraging smiles, but not now, not any more. At almost the last minute the attack was called off altogether. This was due to the fact that Florence was to be declared an open city, and the further fact that the Germans had decided, off their own bat, to cross to the other side of the river.

We were relieved by a South African division. A few miles behind the line we were all put through an American de-lousing centre, which was contained in several marquees. We stripped off before entering the marquee and while we showered and shaved, our clothes were treated in one of the other marquees to kill off any vermin they contained. Which, really, was quite a joke, as we were booked into the biggest bug home in all Italy, namely the lunatic alylum at Foligno – our billet to be for the next week or two.

We were 'admitted' to the asylum the following evening. The patients had gone but they had left their friends behind, millions of them, bed-bugs! And they were starving! When we awoke the next morning, every man Jack of us was bitten from head to toe. We looked as if we'd all contracted galloping scarlet fever. The building was hastily evacuated and the 'Corps of De-buggers' was called in to deal with the situation.

They did a first rate job, every last bug was killed by them. About twenty-four hours later we were re-admitted to the asylum and the following morning, most of our men awoke with tears in their eyes. The tears had nothing to do with the tremendous slaughter of the bugs which had occurred there; rather they were due to the extremely powerful stuff the de-buggers had used to fumigate the place! We cried all the way to breakfast.

Now commenced the long rest we'd been promised. The entire Fourth Infantry Division was concentrated in the area. Leave began – and where else but in Rome? In my company, I was included in the first batch to be given leave passes. I felt a bit of a fraud. I'd been back with the company barely a month after enjoying ten weeks in the back areas, whilst most of the lads, during all that time, had been continuously involved in the fighting. But who was I to argue? And so, in the company of Joe, Dolly, and Smithy, the stretcher-bearers, it was away to Rome.

Population-wise, it resembled New York more than an Italian city. There were Yanks everywhere, millions of 'em. I'm sure they outnumbered the actual Romans. Be that as it may, we now set about the serious business of enjoying ourselves. We ignored the numerous small boys who constantly tugged at our sleeves with cries of 'Sister! Johnny'.

Nearly all of us had quite a bit of accumulated back pay but, even so, the usual thing had occurred, the prices of everything, from booze to souvenirs to women, had become geared to the Yankee pay packets. Our little party at least, therefore, forgot about the women and concentrated on the booze firstly, eats secondly and souvenir hunting lastly. We all had our photos taken, to send home. After Dolly had shown us his, the rest of us were privately agreed that his wife would have a sound case for sending it right back again.

Of course we saw the sights. We visited the Coliseum and I stood in the amphitheatre and tried to recapture the sights and sounds of the old Roman crowds of 2000 years ago baying for blood. We looked into dungeons and dens where they'd kept the lions and the gladiators too. The place was honeycombed with dark recesses, holes, and corners, the floors of which were covered with a profusion of French letters – which sight prompted one of our lads to remark, 'Oh well, when in Rome . . .'

We returned to Foligno broke but reasonably contented with our leave. Not long after our return, the same bunch of us, through Sergeant Major Davison, managed to wangle a forty-eight hour pass to visit Perugia. A great little man was CSM Davison, we Company HQ lads were the apple of his eye, nobody was as privileged as we were. Mind, it was woe betide you if you presumed on that!

Such men – and our Company had at least its fair share of them, the stretcher-bearers for instance – had each of them earned an MM several times over, and there wasn't a man in the Company who had served with it any length of time who wouldn't have readily agreed. No enemy fire, however fierce, had yet prevented them from doing their job. They were the backbone of the battalion and, too, such battalions were the backbone of the British fighting forces on land; never mind your so-called 'élite' commando and airborne units – not that I wish to take any credit away from those units where they've earned it.

Why the British Army was so grudging with its medals I'll never know. The German army, not to mention the Americans, was much readier, in this respect, to acknowledge a man's worth.

Perugia was crammed with Eighth Army soldiers, every regiment in it appeared to be represented as they strolled along the pavements and jostled each other at the entrances to the cafés. Almost the first ones I identified wore the bright green plume of the London Irish Rifles. Excitedly I made my way over to them, wondering if they could possibly be of my brother's battalion. Not only were they of his battalion, they were of his company, and they knew him well.

Their camp, they informed me, was only a mile or two out of town. With that I was on my way. When I found Donald he was on cookhouse jankers. His eyes widened and his jaw dropped with surprise when I suddenly walked in on him. Together we went to see his Company Commander who turned out to be a real decent sort. The moment he learned of our relationship he cancelled the jankers and presented my brother with a pass to absent himself from the camp until midnight.

The occasion called for drinks and to the occasion we rose, in almost every cafe in Perugia! Neither of us got drunk, not hopelessly so at any rate. At only the second or third attempt I managed, late that evening, to get him onto the right side of the tailboard of the lorry which was to take him back to camp. However, before we parted, we had talked quite a lot. His division was the Fifty-sixth, the famous Black Cat Division, mine was the Fourth and there were also other divisions in the area. We were both of us seasoned enough to guess that such a manning of divisions portended something big – which could only be a full-scale offensive upon the German Gothic Line.

We'd heard more and more about this line as the war in Italy had swept further and further north. It was reputed to be every bit as formidable, in its defensive capabilities, as had been the Gustav Line. Big brother-like, I solemnly urged Donald, when the time came, to take good care of himself, whereupon he burst into such merry laughter that I was ashamed I'd so openly revealed my concern. As we finally gripped hands over the tailboard of the lorry, neither of us guessed that, before the war in Italy had done with us, it would bring us together yet again, albeit the next time under circumstances vastly different.

As all good things must come to an end, so did our long rest. For us it was back to the front line. My brother's division had already disappeared from the area.

The Eighth Army, as we had correctly anticipated, had launched a massive offensive upon the Gothic Line and the fighting going on there was as bloody and fierce as any so far in Italy. In the area of the Gemano and the Corriano Ridges, men were dying in hundreds and bleeding in thousands every day.

Our assembly area was situated several miles behind the Line, in the hills east of San Marino and south-west of Rimini. At night we could hear the rumble of the front line artillery and see the reflections of the gun flashes on the rain clouds – the northern horizon flamed unceasingly. My brother's division, I knew, was already committed to the fighting and before long so should we be.

Our division was under the command of the Canadians. Our particular rôle, we gathered, was to exploit the breakthrough which was expected to be made by the Canadian armour. In the event, the breakthrough didn't come – the Gothic Line, like the Gustav Line before it, was evidently proving to be a much tougher nut to crack than had been anticipated. For several days we kicked our heels behind the Line. It rained quite a lot during that time, then the weather took a turn for the better.

To while away the long hours waiting to move into the front line proper, the lads played cards much of the time. At times like these nobody greatly valued the money they carried in their pockets and consequently the gambling was reckless and the stakes, by our usual standards, high. Mostly we played a game called Moogie which was popular amongst the lads of the 6th battalion Black Watch. A number of us had got a game going. It was a fine evening, our last, we believed, before being committed to battle. We sat on the short grass out in the open – the spot we'd chosen was hidden from the eyes of the officers, not that they'd have put a stop to the gambling, they rarely did unless it was too. blatantly exposed to their notice. When we'd been playing for perhaps a couple of hours, I lifted my eyes from the cards lying on the groundsheet spread over the grass which served as a table and beheld, over the shoulders of the players opposite me, a most peculiar spectacular sunset. Above the jagged peaks of San Marino, the whole sky flamed with colour, the sudden sight of it quite took my breath away. I promptly lost all interest in the cards – I had, in any case, for some time past become increasingly bored with the game. I played my hand out and then withdrew from the school. I rose to my feet and wandered off. Over the rise of the hill, two or three hundred yards away, out of sight and sound of the noisy card players, I found myself a secluded spot behind a hay-stack, of which there were a number scattered about the hill slopes.

There I settled myself down, back to the stack, to enjoy the sunset, the magnificent view of the mountains and, by way of a change for a private, a little privacy.

I lit a cigarette, it was very quiet and peaceful just there. As I continued to gaze at the truly extraordinary, colourful sunset and the beautiful scenery before me, there came to my ears, like the muttering of distant thunder, the low rumble of the guns.

My thoughts went to my brother Donald, perhaps no more than eight or ten miles from me, at that very moment quite possibly stumbling and scrambling up or across some rain-sodden slope, under a hail of mortar fire and another horizontal one of equally vicious small arms fire.

My thoughts went out too to my other brother in France, how was he faring? Would the war never end? It seemed it had lasted forever and would last forever. And myself, how long would my luck hold? So far, by infantry standards, it had been good, bloody good – twice wounded, each time cleanly and each time, too, in the left arm. It wasn't possible for an infantryman to ask for better luck than that, somebody up there was looking out for me alright. On the other hand, there was another way of looking at it. 'Yes, yer bugger, I've just missed yer twice, I'll not miss the third time.'

I recalled the nightmare I'd had the previous night, I wasn't sure that I hadn't had the same one several times. I wasn't the only one to have them, I'd often heard others muttering and moaning in their sleep, and nearly every night the lad from Somerset, in Company HQ, woke up almost screaming, and when you went to wake him for his turn on 'stag', he damn near jumped out of his skin, frightening you as well.

In this nightmare of my own there was this soldier in battle kit, lying prostrate and still on the ground and, though he was fully dressed, I could see the red-rimmed, blue-black shrapnel holes in his body. He was dead – yet he couldn't be, for in there was myself, kicking and screaming frantically to get out of him. The recollection of this nightmare filled me with foreboding, it seemed to be prophetic, to be some kind of premonition.

How many dozens of times in my youth had I listened to mother going on about her 'second sight', as either this or that occurrence had 'broken' her dream. She firmly believed in such things. I suddenly became very afraid, not the physically afraid kind of thing you feel all the time under fire, but a deep-down, icy, bone-chilling afraid, which seemed to seep into every corner of my body. At that moment I felt very alone and very helpless.

I'd never been religious, though I suppose I'd always had some kind of vague notion about God, about 'something' up there somewhere – though it had always seemed to me to be too complex and much too distant for me ever to be able to understand. I hadn't ever really given much thought to such things. The only religious education I'd had had consisted solely of Bible readings, given by a bald-headed, gimlet-eyed, 'silly ow'd sod' during 'Scripture' lessons at school.

True, mother had tried to get us three boys to attend lessons at the Salvation Army hut down the street on Sunday afternoons, so that she could then have her rest in quiet. But we very rarely went, we'd much preferred bird-nesting or just simply potting at rats and rabbits with home-made catapults in the fields.

However, so afraid had I become that at that moment, on that hillside, in that sunset, I said a prayer. Not for myself, I was still trying desperately to scoff at my 'premonition'. I said a prayer for 'Ernie and Donald', that they would be safely delivered from the war and back to mother.

13.

Drum Fire

THE NEXT DAY we broke camp. Our time had come, our entry into the battle, raging as ferociously as ever a few miles away, was to be no longer delayed. Watched by the usual knot of silent villagers – old men, women and so-solemn, wide-eyed children – we put on our equipment, slung rifles – in my case, tommy-gun, – fastened grenades to our belts and then, led by the pipers, set off to take our place in the battalion line of march.

As I followed the eternal jogging pack and swinging mug of the man in front of me, I became once more filled with foreboding. More than at any time previously, I dreaded that which lay up ahead. With each marching step the conviction grew stronger within me – this time I wasn't going to make it!

Old Infantrymen – I know, I've swapped experiences with many of them since the war – will recognise and sympathise with the state of my mind at this time. It was in no way exceptional or different from that of many, many thousands of other men who had previously survived wounds and other battles. For there's nothing like a bullet wound or a shrapnel wound to knock the idea out of a man's head, once and for all, that he's somehow different, that mutilation or death are rather more for others than himself.

Prolonged combat drains all men – that is, all but a few supermen I've heard of but never met – of their reserves of courage and resolve. Some completely, some only partially, some sooner, some later, but the process, once begun, progresses with each fresh exposure to fire. Thus does a man eventually have to fight two wars, one without and one within. And frightful as may be the one without, it is almost as nothing compared to the frightfulness of the one within, for that one he fights alone. Therein lies true bravery.

From way up front, the brave, melancholy sound of the pipes came back to me. Who was that piper – 'Old Jock' Fleming? Memory fails me but I do remember the time back in Scotland once, out on the march, one of the lads had somehow managed to stick a french letter over the end of one of the drones. We'd marched quite some way before 'Old Jock', suspecting something was amiss with his beloved pipes, discovered it.

Nearer and nearer we marched towards the ever rumbling guns. I glanced along the lines of men marching on either side of the road. Everything looked to be just the same as it had always been ever since I'd joined the battalion an eternity ago, but it wasn't. There'd been a time once when I'd known every man Jock in the Company but now, even as reduced in numbers as it was, I could put names to barely a third of them.

The 'new' boys? They marched well . They managed, too, to smile, even to share a joke and to laugh defiantly occasionally, as they marched. None of them were, I think, so new that they didn't have an idea of what lay in store for them up ahead.

The old hands, they marched differently, not all that noticeably until you studied them closer, somehow rounder shouldered, very slightly stooped and with that kind of lope in their stride which was born of many, many hundreds of marching miles. They smiled not near as much, if at all, their expressionless gaze appeared to be fixed solely upon the rhythmically moving boots of the man in front of them, each one lost in his own thoughts.

Before us, further out into the roadway, the wiry figure of CSM Davison accompanied Major Callander. They only moved to the side of the road when forced to do so by passing traffic. In the seven or eight weeks I'd been his runner, I'd come to like Major Callander – in my book he was another 'Hutchy'.

Over on the other side of the road, and slightly behind, Sergeant Hancock, 'Hank', marched at the head of his platoon. We'd been privates together, back in Scotland, but his promotion had separated us. Blond, compactly built, his face wore the same relaxed expression it always wore. He'd seen every action with the Company and never suffered a scratch! Such astounding luck I

160.

could scarcely believe. If I had cause to worry about my own luck running out, how much greater cause had he to worry about his!

We were approaching a village – a number of its roofs had been holed by shellfire but the village itself appeared to have escaped the worst ravages of the war thereabouts. The main street of the village and also its side streets and courts were choc-a-bloc with military vehicles parked nose to tail, no doubt awaiting orders to move up nearer the front. The crews stood by their vehicles, hands in pockets, solemnly watching us go by.

Beyond the village the rumble of guns became much more clearly defined, you could begin to pick out, roughly, the individual battery positions, each time they blasted the enemy.

We passed more trucks at a standstill by the roadside. Their drivers, too, hands in pockets, watched solemnly as we went by. I could tell by the looks on their faces that they weren't envying us one little bit, but I was them. God, what wouldn't I have given to be one of them just then. We squeezed up tight to the trucks to allow an ambulance to pass by. The rumble of guns had become a thunder.

Now we passed through a regiment of tanks – Churchills – which were scattered about in the fields, either by the side of the road, parked hard by isolated cottages, under trees, by hedges, all screened from the enemy air observation by means of camouflage netting, tree branches or whatever else they'd been able to press into service, to break up the angular outlines of the vehicles. Their crews, too, spared a little time from their brewing up, to watch us go by.

The sickly sweet smell of death assailed my nostrils. It became stronger and by the roadside, a little way ahead, we discovered its source. Two gigantic white oxen lay dead, one of which was almost completely disembowelled. Its guts, crawling with flies, spilled onto the grass. God, if shellfire could do that to their great hulks, what hope was there for our puny selves?

We had entered the gun lines and there was never a moment without its ear-shattering explosions, either to one side or the other of us.

We were marching by a high hedge when suddenly, without the slightest warning, a battery of guns concealed somewhere behind it, blasted off. The shock of the detonations, so close, caused me to jump almost clean out of my equipment. We were momentarily deafened. I felt the iron clamp of fear about my chest – 'Please God, don't let me crack!'

One blessing, the German counter battery fire appeared to be extremely light hereabouts. No doubt all their guns at the moment were ranged on the more immediate menace of the infantry attacks going in on our flanks – poor bloody infantry.

On we marched, the band about my chest tightening by the hundred yards. Again the sweet smell of death. A little way up a track, running from the road, a soldier stood, looking away from us. Beside him, on the grassy side of the track, lay a row of khaki-clad bodies. How many? I didn't see, the hedge suddenly blocked the view.

Now we ourselves had left the road and were moving along a tree-lined track. Behind us the guns appeared to be working themselves up into a still greater frenzy. Their shells streamed over our heads, it seemed by the hundred.

We came to a wide, shallow stream, crossed by stepping stones. Somewhere over on its other side, was the start line for our attack. In the air above us I heard the sudden rush of German shells but they were too high to be of menace to us.

Company HQ was crossing the stream. One of the stretcher-bearers lost his footing on the slippery stones and to save himself from completely over-balancing, he jettisoned his end of the stretcher, thus immediately causing his mate, carrying the other end of it, exactly the same trouble.

In such seemingly innocuous little incidents, which may even appear to be funny at the time to those watching, can the grim hand of fate later be discerned, especially so in war. Such a one was this.

The two retrieved their stretcher, shouldered it once more and we continued on our way. A thirty or forty yard gap had, meanwhile, opened up between us and the rest of the Company

162.

HQ file. We still weren't deployed for the attack when the stretcher-bearers decided to up-end their stretcher to drain it of more water. Goodness knows why, but I, too, stopped with them. The following platoon began to file past us.

It was at that moment that the German artillery found us. I don't think any war screams ever uttered by the most savage and blood-thirsty warriors in the entire history of warfare, could ever have had even near the same capacity to strike such instant terror into the hearts of men as does the sudden ear-splitting shriek of shells by the mass, as they hurtle unstoppably to earth amongst them.

When the shells were 'yours', definitely 'yours', you had two, possibly three, seconds, depending on the velocity of the shells and the angle of their approach, to hit the ground. For experienced soldiers this was barely sufficient, for the inexperienced it wasn't enough.

It's one thing to undergo the ordeal of shellfire in trenches but quite another to endure the same fire out in the open. In the first instance, a soldier of even little experience, can fortify himself with the knowledge that he's pretty safe from everything except a direct hit, and even then he would almost certainly have a mate to share the misfortune with during its actual occurrence.

Out in the open, no such props exist – any one of the shells falling within half a hundred yards of a man may be the one with his 'number on it'. And, as for the reassurance to be derived from the presence of the mate, flattened to the ground two or three yards away, he might just as well be on another planet.

Caught out in the open, on the receiving end of concentrated artillery fire, a man's world becomes reduced to that little patch of it actually occupied by his own body. If the 'stonk' or barrage be prolonged more than a few minutes – and under such circumstances minutes become hours – it shrinks still further. Limbs become expendable if they can be utilized, in even the smallest way, to protect the vital parts. Deeper and deeper a man withdraws into himself, until finally all that exists of him is a bursting heart, gripped in a fist of terror and protected by – just nothing.

And, too, just nothing else exists in the whole, wide world but it and the heaving, howling, exploding hell of flying earth and steel, raging over and all around it.

I can well believe that, under such circumstances, in the greatly prolonged artillery barrages of the First World War, death itself became an angel of mercy – self-inflicted or otherwise!

In the same fraction of a second that I hit the ground, the shells exploded. I felt something strike, with the force of a thunderbolt, my right leg. I thought it had been torn off. I'm sure I must have screamed out with the pain and shock but if I did I don't remember it. I do remember the dreadful piercing screams of the others, one of which was abruptly cut off in mid-scream as more shells fell amongst us and another which subsided to a spluttering gurgle. Someone was choking – or drowning – in his own blood.

In an almost impenetrable grey fog of smoke and fumes, the incessant screams of stricken men and the howls, shrieks and explosions of shells, rapidly merged to produce a single, unbroken cacophony of utter terror.

Patchily, through the smoke and flying earth, I saw a figure scrambling towards me. It was Joe. It was an extraordinary feat of bravery. No man, even partly elevated above the prone position, could really expect to survive that terrible fire unscathed. No more than two or three yards from me, Joe was blasted sideways in another explosion of shells. I heard his scream – his leg had been almost completely shattered.

I was hit again, in several places, almost simultaneously, with the same thunderbolt force as before. I felt the dreadful searing pain of shrapnel as it struck home to my shoulder, my back and my other leg. The fire continued to pour down upon us and I frantically clawed the ground in a futile attempt to find myself even the least scrap of extra cover.

From nowhere, a body either hurled itself or was hurled across mine. It rested on me, it seemed with all the weight of a steamroller. It was unmoving – dead or unconscious, I don't know. Crazily, I fought to extricate myself from beneath its suffocating weight but the only part of my body which would respond were my arms. I paused from my struggles in despair and fresh explosives showered the two of us with earth. I was struck in the face by a ricocheting stone or piece of shrapnel and it lodged in the flesh of my cheek. I felt the blood run down my jaw, then the salty taste of it in my mouth.

By now I was literally soaked in blood from head to foot. I could feel the warm stickiness of it spreading over me under my clothes. Whoever lay across me added his to mine, I felt it trickling down my neck. My hands were black with dirt and several nails were broken and bleeding.

How long did it last? Ten minutes? Fifteen? Thirty? I've no idea, it was an eternity.

How many guns had fired upon us? One battery, two, several? Again, I have no idea, it really makes little difference what number, it was enough! A couple of thousand guns, firing on a twenty mile long front, are only as deadly to the men they fire at as the several which are actually ranged upon them – all the rest are only background.

I was never able to personally view the full extent of the carnage wrought within our ranks. I never rose under my own power from that spot again, but I heard, much later, that such was the extent that it had caused the postponement of our attack.

I recall the growing feeling of wonderment and the scarcely daring to believe flood of relief with which I greeted the abrupt lifting of the fire. As the smoke slowly dispersed, so quiet did it seem in contrast that it seemed you could have heard a pin drop.

In response to my groans, someone removed the body resting on mine, but that was all. All those able to rise and move away, did so. Some, the walking wounded, back to the RAP to have their wounds dressed; the unwounded, forward – the attack wasn't yet postponed. We who were unable to move, were left where we lay to be picked up later.

Dolly, the only stretcher-bearer still unwounded out of the four, stayed to dress the worst of our wounds, then he too moved off. I remember begging him not to go but to stay with me, in such a state was I – shades of the Rapido bridge head.

Slightly to my right and a little way in front, a figure lay quite still, face to the ground. Behind me someone was groaning horribly and I heard other groans. I couldn't see Joe. I learned much later, from him himself, that when the fire had lifted, he'd crawled away to find a safer spot, in case it should return, but such was the impediment of his leg that to be rid of it, he'd used his jack-knife to cut through the tendon and the few remaining shreds of flesh which still attached it to the rest of his body.

The German fire was now directed upon an area of ground somewhere to my left, I felt the ground quivering beneath me. What time it was, I don't know. I believe it was early evening, the sun was going down, that much I do know. As I watched the lone figure of Dolly finally depart, I felt myself overcome by a feeling of nausea to the point of swooning. I fought desperately against it, if the stretcher-bearers came while I was unconscious I would be left for dead. Once, twice on the point of passing out I recovered myself. Then, suddenly, with startling clarity, the 'truth' hit me, the 'premonition', the 'nightmare' this was it exactly! I was dying. I felt the hot gush of tears come to my eyes and roll down my cheeks. The sky before me flared with coloured lights, like the sunset of the previous evening, and then faded rapidly into total blackness.

It was dusk. I came round to the feel of hands removing my equipment. I was lifted onto a stretcher. The journey to the RAP was a nightmare, the Germans were shelling the area, not heavily but steadily and persistently. Several times my stretcher was hastily lowered to the ground, to the accompaniment of a howl of shells, as the stretcher-bearers hastily scrambled for cover.

I remember several German-helmeted faces peering down at me – prisoners, pressed into service by the medical team.

At the RAP my wounds were redressed and then I was put on to one of two stretchers, one above the other borne on a Bren-carrier. A German prisoner accompanied us, sitting on the side facing us. He was very young and very dirty. With each fresh lurch of the carrier I felt the jagged lumps of shrapnel inside me bite still deeper into my flesh. The British fire raged on unceasingly, its thunder never stopped.

I was lying on a table or slab – in the yellow light a white-coated figure loomed over me. From the next table a face grinned my way – it was Smithy's.

I'd suffered seven shrapnel wounds in all, the holes ranging in size from the largest, which you could have put a couple of clenched fists into, to the smallest, no larger than might have accepted your little finger. I'd lost a near fatal amount of blood and, too ill to be moved, I stayed at the Casualty Clearing Station, which was Canadian, four more days and nights, during which time a battery of guns positioned, it seemed, almost immediately behind the marquee I occupied, constantly and deafeningly blasted its shells off at the enemy, right over our heads.

Many of the men in the marquee with me had suffered indescribably hideous wounds. There was no point in moving them on, they were already written off. I felt very, very lucky when I compared mine with theirs. Amongst his other wounds, the poor chap on my right had been struck in the windpipe. They'd reconnected his air passage by means of a tube of some sort and it constantly filled with blood. Those who were nearest him had then to holler for the orderly, to prevent him from choking to death.

On the other side of me was a chap who had lost an arm and a large slice of his shoulder. His groans were terrible to hear. Of course, all were heavily sedated with morphia, but they still writhed and groaned with the pain. One or two had their hands tied to their beds to prevent them tearing their dressings away, to get at the pain.

I make no apology for dwelling on such harrowing scenes. I do so in the belief that I'm 'doing my bit', not only towards 'outlawing' war, but, more pointedly even if belatedly, towards pricking the consciences of those who have influence in such matters, with regard to the circumstances in which very many war pensioners live today.

In no way do I refer to myself or my circumstances. I'm alright, Jack. I recovered very well from my wounds and, further, I consider life has been very good to me since those terrible times.

The nation's method of awarding war pensions is unfair – twenty per cent for the loss of an eye, forty per cent for the loss of an arm, fifty per cent for this, sixty per cent for that, may have the merit of fairness when applied to purely professional soldiers where equal disability may be deemed to imply equal set-back to career prospects. But the same standard applied to the largely civilian armies of the two world wars, be they Kitchener's men or militiamen, can be seen to be manifestly unfair, and the man most discriminated against by it was the skilled manual worker.

A clerk or a teacher, for example, who has suffered the loss of an arm may quite possibly, be able to resume his career from the point where he left off and indeed find his pension quite a useful little supplement to his salary. But to a fitter, a carpenter, or a bricklayer, the same loss spells almost total disaster. I met a plasterer, a few years after the war, who had suffered just that injury as a consequence of his war service. He was still bravely trying to carry on his trade. None of the local builders would employ him so he had become self-employed.

I wonder, did 'they' threaten to stop the payment of his war pension on the grounds that he was retarding his own recovery by persisting with such folly? I myself once had such a warning from the Ministry of War Pensions.

Another time, much more recently, I had the experience of applying for a job, only to be told, without so much as a medical examination or a trial period of work, that I was considered to be unsuitable because, due to my war wounds (which I had to declare on the application form), I wouldn't be able to do much bending. This was confided to me by the Manager's secretary. I know I could have 'eaten' the job.

Today, 1985, in these times of very heavy unemployment and when many thousands of war veterans have still not reached retiring age, another blow awaits the unemployed war pensioners amongst them. At their age, their only prospect of work, in almost all their cases, lies with the Manpower Services

Commission. But its rules state that the prospective employee must be in receipt of a state benefit at the time of his (or her) application for employment. War pensions don't count.

The rub is, if one is needed, that in very many cases it is precisely because a man is in receipt of a war pension that his income becomes tipped, be it ever so slightly, above the poverty line qualifying level for Social Security benefit. Thus, he suffers a double disqualification, from benefit and consequently from employment.

Eventually I was transferred, first by field ambulance and then by air, to a base hospital in Southern Italy.

No solid food had passed my lips for three weeks and I had lost stones in weight. Perhaps a month after I had been wounded, my brother Donald found me. By his own account, he'd passed my bed twice before he definitely recognised me. He'd been wounded too, in the leg. He informed me that Ernie, our eldest brother, had also been wounded, in the arm, in France. The three of us had been wounded almost at the same time. The local paper later featured a small article on the 'coincidence'.

I was well on the mend now and after he'd gone I fell to thinking about my 'premonition' and the prayer I'd made as I'd watched the sun go down over San Marino. The 'premonition' had been fulfilled, albeit not as finally as I'd feared at the time. And, too, my prayer had been as completely answered as makes no difference – both my brothers, as a direct result of their wounds, were physically down-graded and neither saw front line service again. They were well and truly delivered safely back to mother, at the war's end.

And, just to complete the coincidence, before she knew anything at all about the happenings to her boys, mother dreamt one night of myself being helped through our own front door at home by a stranger. In the dream, I was minus a leg. Well, I didn't lose the leg, a last minute change of mind by the doctors saved it, though it would never be the same again. But mother did, several months later, come to witness my being helped through the front door with my leg completely encased in plaster, and so another of her dreams was 'broken'.

We were going home. The kindly old Major in charge of the base hospital came to say goodbye to us as we were loaded into the waiting fleet of ambulances. He had a letter for me and he read it out. It was from GHQ, Middle East, and was to inform me that as I'd been wounded for the third time, I was to be immediately repatriated to England and furthermore, I should not again be asked to undertake service in the front line. Both the Major and I laughed heartily. It was funny, I was going home in any case, and I should never again be fit enough for front line duty.

Our ship, HM Hospital Ship *Abar*, steamed into the harbour at Liverpool a couple of days before Christmas 1944.

Every other ship in the harbour saluted us with mighty and prolonged blasts of their fog horns. We were given priority for docking. As the stretchers bearing us were carried from the *Abar* to be put aboard the hospital train awaiting us at the quayside, the nurses of the *Abar*, who had lined either side of the short route, softly sang 'Silent Night' for us.

Nobody's war ever ended on a softer, sweeter note.

PART THREE

THE WORKER

And then hard by the factory gates
loud speaking came the Party candidates,
on matters great and small,
of the iniquity of the State
and of the corruption of the Town Hall
and tho' each I heard out to the end
that perhaps of these I'd learn the mend,
it seemed on only this they were agreed,
when the gates were opened,
their depart to take with unseemly speed.

C. Framp

PART THREE

THE WORKER

14.

THE 'PREFAB'

I WAS STILL IN HOSPITAL when Hitler became no more and the German war, after six long years of blood, toil, tears and sweat, came to its final, bloody end.

I was still in hospital, though not the same one, when the war with Japan came to an even bloodier end in a double hell blast of atom bombs – thus compelling its leaders – and its men-folk who, like their German counterparts, had allowed themselves to be reduced to the level of robots by those same so-called leaders – to witness, also like their German allies, the ultimate horror of the retribution for their own crimes and their own folly falling upon their own innocent women and children. Truly a monumental betrayal of trust by them.

I was discharged from hospital in April 1946 – as a civilian, I'd been discharged from the Army the previous year – but I would still be an outpatient for several years to come, to undergo physiotherapy treatment three times a week and occasionally, when the skin grafts failed to hold up, to have my wounds dressed.

On May 15th, 1946, I was married. I'd met Jean while I'd been in hospital – she was, bless your life, the daughter of the Army Recruiting Sergeant at Scunthorpe – Regimental Sergeant Major Wright, late of the Sherwood Foresters. It's our joke I did all my courting in bed.

She was a brave lass to marry me – a more calculating one wouldn't have. I'd no job, no immediate prospects of one and no home to take her to. Neither had I any money apart from a meagre war pension.

Mother came to the rescue as far as the home was concerned – she offered to let us have her own front room until such time as we could find something better.

The house was badly over-crowded – my elder brother Ernie had returned home after his de-mob and so had my sister with her one child – her husband had been killed in the war, shot down over the Med., 'no known grave'. My younger sister still lived at home and my younger brother Donald was expected home after his de-mob.

The house by this time had had water and electricity laid on but it still had no bathroom or inside toilet. We had to take our baths in the scullery using water heated on the old coal-fired copper and take our turns through the week. Even then we almost always had to share the bath water with at least one other person.

With the mass exodus of men from the forces in 1945 and 1946, the pressure on what civilian accomodation was available for them was enormous – in Scunthorpe it seemed every second house was home to two families, occasionally more.

A movement which began at Scunthorpe in 1946 soon spread all over the country. People, almost all of them returned ex-servicemen, 'squatted' in the rapidly emptying military camps up and down the country, British, American and Canadian, and resisted all attempts by the authorities, both military and civilian, to evict them. It was very reminiscent of Churchill's order during the blitz forbidding the people of London to use the underground tube stations as shelters – and it met with the same response from the people, 'Up yours too, mate!'

I obtained a job with the Redbourn steelworks of Richard Thomas and Baldwins Ltd, – or rather Dad obtained it for me. It was in the department of the works in which he himself worked – the Bricklayers' Department – he'd been forgiven his sins of the 1920s against the steel bosses and given a re-start in 1940. I was given the job of re-lining and repairing the huge one hundred ton capacity steel ladles in the melting shop. The job was the lightest the Bricklayers' Department had to offer – it was intermittent work which involved no climbing or heavy lifting and I was very glad to have found such a job since I was not anywhere near fit enough to tackle work on the building sites.

Although I'd been born and reared in the shadow of the steel-works, I knew little enough about them apart from the fact that the work generally was dirty, demanding and dangerous.

The huge areas of blast-furnaces, coke-ovens, melting shops, rolling mills, loco sheds and all the rest of the plant conglomeration which goes to make up a steelworks were the homes of many kinds of dangers. Roaring, spitting, fire-breathing dragons lurked behind every other corner waiting to pounce upon the unwary – over the generations their victims had been many, some of whom had disappeared without trace. Their fates could only be guessed at and talked of in whispers – there is blood on the steel too.

The melting shop of Richard Thomas and Baldwin Ltd in which I commenced work in 1946 and which housed the company's seven open hearth furnaces was an enormous building – more than a furlong in length, a hundred yards in width and about seventy feet in height. It was flanked by a row of seven one hundred and twenty feet tall brick chimneys, one for each furnace, which pumped a steady stream of dust, smoke and other pollutants into the atmosphere. The melting shop was also a bedlam of noise, smoke and dust in which men communicated with each other as much by signs as by shouts.

To stand on its stage side and look along the row of squat, ugly, hissing, roaring furnaces leaking fumes and smoke from half a hundred doors and other apertures and to see before them the sweating furnace hands bathed red by the fiery light of the furnaces on the one side and trailing long black shadows behind them on the other as they hurled the contents of their shovels deep into the fiery hearts of the furnaces, was to obtain a living picture of Hell itself.

Jean became pregnant in the first couple of months of our marriage – which fact when I learned of it alarmed me. That wasn't how we'd planned things at all. We worked out the probable date of the birth – it fell on All Fools day in 1947.

It's a matter of history now that the winter of 1947 was the worst on record – and I believe still is for the amount of snow it delivered, it snowed almost non-stop for about six weeks until in places it covered the tops of the telegraph poles.

When you opened the door to the street in the mornings, the night's fresh fall of snow fell into the houses and you couldn't close the door again until you had removed it. It was the devil's own business getting about and especially to work, the main roads in the town were being kept open for four-wheeled traffic but the steelworkers abandoned their cycles in their thousands and either walked to work or travelled on the buses – which services performed miracles in getting the men to their destinations. Many men from the outlying villages, once they'd got to work, stayed there, sleeping in the cabins and eating in the works canteens, some for as long as a fortnight during the worst of the weather.

Fortunately when the thaw began, about halfway through March, it was mercifully slow. Even so, there was much serious flooding reported all over the country. On 28th March, Jean walked with mother to the crest of the hill overlooking the Trent valley – a distance of about half a mile from the house – to view the flood waters sweeping along the valley floor, forcing many people to abandon their homes and seek refuge in Scunthorpe.

On 29th March our first child was born – a girl, born in the same house as I myself had been almost twenty-five years earlier. There was little prospect of our being able to obtain a house of our own in the foreseeable future. We had no money to buy and thousands of families, many with several children, shared the housing list with us. It seemed, so far, that my life was but a repeat of my own father's after his return from the First World War.

The spring and summer which followed that dreadful winter of 1947 were as warm and sunny as any the British people might reasonably hope to enjoy in their own land!

As far as the country itself had been affected by the winter, the building trade had suffered the worst setbacks. The frosts, the snows and the floods which followed them had set it back a long way and at a time when the need for houses had never been greater.

Sometime in the spring of that year I met a bricklayer I'd

known briefly before the war. He told me that he and a mate were about to start sub-contracting brickwork from one of the more prominent local builders – who also happened to be the town's MP.

The brickwork was all council house work on one of the new estates they were creating in town. He told me they had been offered £150 for the completed brickwork of each pair of houses and he asked my opinion of the price. It sounded to me like a fortune!

He then told me that he and his mate needed one other brickie to make up the two and one gang and asked me if I was interested in joining them. I most definitely was – it sounded to me like an opportunity to make some real money. I was still attending the hospital three times weekly but I was pretty certain I could handle the job.

I gave in my notice at Redbourn. There was quite a bit of head-shaking from dad and a few others – they thought I was taking too much of a chance on the leg by leaving the light job which I had for the uncertainties of the building trade and the pressures of piecework conditions, but I wouldn't listen. A month later I was wishing I had done, my leg swelled up like a balloon and pained me pretty badly. I went along to my own doctor's one evening after work and he lanced it there and then. The poison which gushed from it had to be seen to be believed.

Since being discharged from the hospital the previous year, my war pension had been reduced from a hundred per cent payment to seventy per cent. While I was off work I was able to claim the hundred per cent once more for the length of time that I was unable to work, and then it reverted to the seventy per cent level.

One hundred per cent or seventy per cent, it was still only a pittance and nowhere near adequately compensated me for the loss of my wages – I lingered no longer than was absolutely necessary at home.

Within a fortnight I was back at work and within another fortnight I was off again – same trouble, same doctor, same treatment and the same unbelievable quantity of poison gushing out of the incision made by the doctor as before.

This time, acting on the doctor's advice, I stayed away from work for a longer period of time – maybe a month – and I felt very guilty about it all. I felt I was not only failing Jean and the baby but my two mates at work as well. Which of course I was, though they were both very decent about it and very patient.

Once more I returned to work – I think I managed to remain at work a little longer this time, I don't remember for sure, and then the whole miserable business began all over again and I knew I was beat. I couldn't fairly expect mates to tolerate that kind of attendance indefinitely, as decent as they were. I told them to find themselves another mate and I would find myself another job when I recovered, which they did.

It was during this time, while I was off work and feeling pretty miserable about the whole thing, that I received a letter from the Ministry of Pensions threatening to cut me off without a penny unless I gave up my attempt to follow the trade of brick-layer. By so doing I was, so they said, retarding my own recovery. They made no suggestion regarding an alternative means of my earning a living nor did they offer me any training which might have allowed me to consider the possibility of switching trades. As it was, I knew nothing but bricklaying. I'd no office qualifica-tions, I'd have been as out of place in that environment as a flying fish in a budgie cage! I didn't dare risk forfeiting the pension – pittance though it was, it was the only sure income which I had.

One evening in October, or about then, I was babysitting at home – Jean had gone to the pictures with mother, it was only a tanner in those days – there came a knock on the door. I an-swered it to see, standing on the step, my ex-boss from Red-bourn. I invited him in and then he told me he'd heard of my pre-dicament from dad and he was there to offer me my former job back and though it was still a bricklaying job, he would himself write to the Ministry of Pensions explaining the nature of the work and his own confidence in my ability to do the job, seeing as I'd already done it. If then the Ministry made any difficulties over the matter, he would enlist the aid of our local MP, who was also the builder I'd been working for, to sort out the whole sorry business. If in my life I've come across more than a few second and third rate people, I've also come across some first rate people and Albert Pogson stands high on their list.

He was the turning point in my life. After his visit I never really looked back. The leg healed and settled down to the job it had been designed to do – keep me off my backside. I've had little bother with it since – the muck and the poison which had come out of it would have had to have done sooner or later, it was just unfortunate that it chose that particular time. The worst effect of it was that it robbed me of confidence for quite a few years afterwards. I tended, because of it, to treat myself as more of an invalid than I was – but that also I outgrew eventually.

In those days, the late 1940s, families went out walking on the fine summer evenings much more than they do in these days of cars, television sets and videos. Jean would put the baby in the pram and then the three of us would set off for our walk and you could bet that no matter in which direction we went – north, south, east, or west – the walk would eventually take us through one of the new housing estates in the making.

Jean just loved looking through the windows of the completed but as yet unoccupied houses, hoping against hope that one would soon be hers. Nor was she – nor, to be wholly truthful, were we – alone in this. All over the estates other couples were doing the same thing, some of them accompanied by as many as three children. Like ourselves, they too were hoping one would soon be theirs – of course they were.

One day in August 1948 it happened! The magic letter informing us that we had been granted the tenancy of a house was popped through the letter box. Jean was over the moon with delight. The tenancy we'd been granted was for one of the prefabricated bungalows which we'd watched going up all over the town. We would have preferred one of the traditional brick built houses but they were reserved for the larger families and rightly so. After two years of living in one room, our bungalow seemed like a mansion to us!

Nor did I, as dad had before us, have to cash in my pension in order to furnish it, because furniture, like almost everything else in short supply, was still rationed. You were allowed a certain number of 'dockets' with which you could buy the utility furniture in the shops, the prices of which were also controlled. You could, of course, if you had that kind of money, always buy second hand furniture and get ripped off for it. This was the heyday of the second hand dealers, of the profiteers and the racketeers anxious not to miss the opportunity afforded them by the almost desperate needs of the returned ex-servicemen. They made little enough out of me!

I think that perhaps of the sixty-five years of my life so far, that first year following our move into the little pre-fab bungalow was the happiest. The trauma of the war years was behind me. I had Jean beside me, a perfectly sound and beautiful baby, a house of my own – and with a bathroom, the first I'd ever had in my life – and a good secure job which was also well within my capacity to hold down.

Occasionally as I lay in bed at night with Jean's head resting peacefully in the crook of my arm and the baby sleeping soundly in her cot in the corner of the room, watching the play of the red light from the steelworks beyond the window on the drawn curtains and listening to the low rumble of the distant mills which sounded to me just then to be as reassuring in their way as the once similar low rumble of guns in the distance had been menacing in theirs, it seemed to me that I had just about all a man could reasonably ask in life. Never, I thought, could the skies above our little pre-fab have glowed rosier.

1949 was a memorable year for us – it brought one death and one birth to the family. It was also the year the American bombers returned to Britain – which did nothing at all for my peace of mind nor, in my opinion, for that of the rest of the world.

Jean's father was killed in a motor-cycle accident. At the time of his death he was still the Army Recruiting Segeant for Scunthorpe. The accident happened in the September, so he never got to see his second grand-daughter born in the November

180.

– for another girl it was.

Churchill, whose mother had been an American, was, it seemed to me, himself suffering a crisis of identity. From my point of view he seemed to spend far too much time over there whooping up the cold war. I was afraid that in Truman he'd a too ready disciple. I feared for the future of my family but I only became seriously worried about the turn of world events when, with the connivance of a Labour Government in Britain, the American bombers returned to this country. I for one felt betrayed.

There were wild calls emanating chiefly from the United States, which itself had never been bombed, for a pre-emptive strike at the Russians while the balance of nuclear power still lay heavily weighted in the West's favour.

I considered emigrating to Australia where my family would be safe but Jean, whose temperament was always less volatile than my own, would have none of it so we stayed put in Scunthorpe.

We did, however, move house – now we had two children we qualified for a larger house – for one of the traditional brick built houses on the new Lincoln Gardens Estate which Jean had always wanted and which she now meant to have and never mind your atom bombs and your Australia. We moved there in January 1950.

That year also the Communist Armies in China won the final victory over their Nationalist rivals for power and China, for the first time, became united under a single regime – in the historic words of Mao Tse-Tung, 'China stood up'.

A year later in Scunthorpe – to use the same metaphor – the steelworks stood up, they became 'ours'. They, and all the rest of of the crude steel making industry, were taken into public ownership. On the day of the take-over, flags flew from the high points of the mills and melting shops and other building to celebrate the occasion – but they flew over largely empty scrap yards. The previous owners had allowed the stocks of scrap metal and other raw materials, needed to sustain production to run down to dangerously low levels which, in view of the generous terms of compensation paid to them for the loss of their works, was generally considered to be a bit of a dirty trick

In 1951 the Korean War broke out, which war, although it was fought in that luckless country, was basically a war between Communist China on the one side and Capitalist America on the other

If the first rule of war is 'Never invade Russia', then surely the second must be 'Include the British'! No war, large or small, near or far, however costly or however unnecessary, seems to be complete without them and the Korean War, which was about as far away as you can have a war without leaving the planet, was to prove to be no exception. In no time at all a British contingent had appeared over there to support their American allies. Both forces were ostensibly a part of a larger United Nations force, but in practice that august body lent no more to that particular war effort than its name.

The war was started – men fought, men suffered, men died – and then the war was ended without the loss in action of a single national leader on either side, which fact was hailed as a victory by both sides, or appeared to be – neither had anything else to cheer about.

In March 1954 our third and last child was born – a boy, which seemed to round off the family nicely. Jean said: 'Three's enough'. I didn't argue, so enough it became!

15.

IN LATE 1954 or perhaps early 1955 I joined the newly formed branch of the Labour Party on the estate. I really don't know why – while I'd always been interested in politics on a national level I'd never been able to get particularly worked up over local issues. It's always seemed to me that as long as the country itself is reasonably well governed, the nitty gritty issues of local politics, though they may be more immediate, are also much less urgent and may, therefore, for the most part anyway, be left in the hands of those who feel they should be left in their hands and goodness knows there's never any lack of them – I wasn't going to muscle in on their territory.

I went along to a few meetings, though I doubt if it was ever noticed – I never uttered a word at them, acting on the principle that it's better to keep your mouth shut and be thought a fool than it is to open it and remove all doubt. I kept mine closed and my attendances at the meetings became less and less until they ceased completely. In effect I faded away and I doubt also whether anybody noticed that.

One evening I was sitting in the local pub enjoying a pint when a bloke of about my own age sat down beside me. He was a stranger in the place but he seemed to be friendly and soon we fell into conversation. He told me that he was a Communist, which surprised me – I'd thought the species was extinct, in Scunthorpe at least. I liked his conversation and evidently he liked mine for he invited me to join his party. This invitation I refused but I did accept his other invitation to go along to a meeting he had organised for the following Sunday evening on the subject of 'Peace', which really did interest me, nothing more so. The meeting was to be held at the Trades and Labour Club which I knew well from my frequent attendances there at our own trades union branch meetings.

Came the Sunday evening and along I went to the meeting – and while I hadn't expected to find great crowds of people there, it was something of a shock to discover there were only about a dozen people there all told, and half of those I discovered later were themselves Party members.

At the time the cold war had become so intensely cold that it had, so to speak, created two new poles in the world, an east and a west, and buried everything between the two under a political and cultural ice-cap of such enormity that it seemed to many, if not most people, it would only ever be removed again by the application upon it of a force of comparable enormity, such as the hydrogen bomb.

The shockingly low interest in the meeting brought home to me, more than anything I heard said at the meeting itself, just how desperately urgent had become the peace message.

The subject of the meeting was 'Peace' – not disarmament, either eastern or western, unilateral or otherwise. Peaceful co-existence was the theme and it made absolute sense to me. After the hysterical nonsense of 'better dead than red' that one heard on all sides in Britain and the USA of the time, it was to me as a soothing balm upon a fevered brow to listen once again to rational argument. And if it made sense to me then I was sure it would to others too – the alternative was utterly unthinkable.

Following that meeting and after I'd had time to think about it, I joined the Communist Party. I became a peace-monger in a country which appeared to me to be dangerously overful of war-mongers. That there would be little I could do to effect events I was only too well aware, but that seemed to me no good reason for not doing what little I could to help the peace and to bring about a better understanding between east and west.

To be a Communist Party member in Britain in the 1950s was to gain an idea of what it must have been like to be a Christian in pagan Rome or perhaps a dissident in modern Russia – you were a political pariah, an outcast, an untouchable, or that is what the media and particularly the popular press would have you be. It was as Aneurin Bevan once said – in some countries it's imprisonment, in others it's exile, but in Britain the method chosen to deal with political dissidents is character assassination and the media went to town on the character of the British Communist Party – and by implication upon the character of its members. You were traitors, you were Russian agents or, at the very least, dupes.

My family had proved in two world wars and in others before them where its loyalty and its patriotism lay. My father and brothers and myself had all served in the Army during the two wars – nor did we have to be conscripted in either – and all of us had been in at the sharp end as infantrymen. We had all shed blood as the result of enemy action – our patriotism wasn't just mouth and flag-waving or running with the pack – but none of us had ever been asked to make war on women and children nor to put our own women and children in the firing line and that is what we were being asked to go along with now. I wanted no part of it – and neither would I have any part of it. If I was going to make war I determined that it would be on the war-mongers and the hate-mongers themselves.

Although I helped to organise public meetings on the subject of 'Peace', I myself never spoke at them. I lacked the confidence and, as I saw it, the education. But I did take my message to work with me and to my trade union branch meetings and other places where I was known personally.

The reaction of most ordinary working men to the cold war might be best summed up by the old adage, 'eat, drink and be merry for tomorrow you may die'. Whenever I spoke about it they'd listen politely enough, perhaps even nod their heads from time to time in agreement with me and then they'd prefer to change the subject. They didn't really want to think about it. It was their opinion generally that there was nothing they could do to change things, therefore it made more sense to make the best of life while you were still able to – which sheep-like attitude often made me angry.

Of course, in such a political climate I aroused much hostility too. In the almost exclusively trades union and steelworks environment in which I spoke this came almost exclusively from the local trades union hierarchy, one or two of whom were also local councillors.

But I was never afraid of them. I was for the most part as well known to our joint trades union audience as they were themselves and I like to think in many cases better respected. One or two of them were well known for the steelworks bosses' yes-men and the thorough going opportunists that they were. Their kind are to be found everywhere, wherever there's an establishment band-wagon rolling, be it capitalist, socialist, facist, industrial corporation, trades union or whatever, there you'd find them clambering aboard for the ride and every one of them more Catholic than the Pope.

I never counted for much in the Communist Party or, for that matter, out of it, but there was a place where I did count for much and that was at home. There I was dad, husband and breadwinner – the great protector and provider – and that counted for much with me – in fact everything!

It also counted for everything with Jean. Her family was her world, her all. She never got worked up by what Kennedy or Kruschev were saying to each other, or whether Castro was winning or losing his Cuban revolution, nor did she care a toss whether the Pope was on our side or not. She was usually more interested in the weather – would it or would it not stay fine for the wash? Not that she was blind to, or totally uninterested in the larger world – far from it.

She well knew and respected my motives for joining the Communist Party. She knew it was basically for herself and the kids. When I'd first joined the Labour Party she'd scarcely raised an eyebrow but when I joined the Communist Party she did – but that was all it was, just an eyebrow. She thought that left to myself it would eventually go the same way as the Labour Party had gone, that I would eventually tire of it and then drop it altogether. As she saw it I was but going through a phase – the political phase or the angry young man phase – belatedly maybe – but that it would pass. That's what she had thought.

But as the months had gone by and began to turn into years and my enthusiasm for the cause showed no signs of abating, she herself began to show signs of impatience. She was becoming heartily sick of sharing her husband and home with Marx, Engels, Lenin, Kruschev, Kennedy, Churchill, Castro, Keynes, Uncle Joe Stalin and all. She was also mightily sick of the fact that in the evenings I was either out at meetings or had my nose stuck into a book trying to get the hang of Historical Materialism or discover how its philosophical opposite The Immanent Will worked, or some other high-flown, unimportant, intellectual rubbish as that. She wanted her husband back! So one day she decided to have it out with me.

She gave me no ultimatums or anything like that. For one thing she knew me better than that and for another that wasn't her way. She argued her side of the picture with a quiet concern and a logic which shattered my defences completely. It went something like this.

There might be a nuclear war or there might not. If there was one, then we, the family, would quite likely all go together in the same blast and quite likely scarcely even know a thing about it and that would be the end of that. On the other hand, if there wasn't a nuclear war – and it was her opinion that there would not be one for the very good reason that those at the top who started such things would this time stand every bit as good a chance of going the same way as the rest of us – I was wasting my time and my life, and hers too, worrying about it. Far better that I spent them and my money on being happy like everybody else we knew.

In the meantime and for the forseeable future, the establishment hatred for and intolerance of communists, as unfair and wrong as it might seem to me, would continue, and as my name wasn't a common Smith, Robinson or Brown but was a very uncommon and easily memorable Framp and as Scunthorpe was but a small provincial town, the communist and anti-establishment connection with the name would linger in people's minds and might well rebound to the disadvantage of anyone else bearing the same name – my own children, for example. True, they were as yet but children but soon, in only a few short years, they would be looking forward to careers or jobs of their own – and there were always some establishment minded nutters about who would be biased and vindictive enough to visit the sins of the father upon the children and there were many subtle ways in which the establishment could discriminate against people without making it obvious – and finally, is that what I wanted for my children?

No, it bloody well was *not* what I wanted for the children! She'd hit me for six and she knew it. For of course she was right on every count. She knew she could safely leave the final decision to me and in the end the Communist Party did go the same way as the Labour Party. I've never joined another political party since then.

I didn't resign my membership of the branch immediately, I simply stopped attending its meetings. I felt very guilty about finishing with it, as if I was ratting on mates in their hour of need. My resignation I knew would be a big blow to the branch, so small in numbers was it – it had no more than eight or nine members all told, including several women.

After a period of time had elapsed, maybe two or three weeks, they began to inquire about my absence from the meetings I could only mumble shamefacedly about family ties and commitments having priority and that my political and trade union activities were putting too great a strain on my marriage and family life – at least more than I was prepared to tolerate. They nodded understandingly – my situation was no uncommon one in the Communist Party of that time, many members fell by the wayside for pretty much the same reasons as I had done. Even so, many of those, though they resigned their membership and took no active part in Party affairs, continued to support it financially – you could always raise enough cash from these faithfuls to pay the rent of a meeting hall and the cost of advertising the meetings. Some of them also contributed regularly to the Daily Worker, perhaps only a few shillings each time, but it was all grist to the mill and it helped to keep that paper going.

'Fellow Travellers' such friends and supporters of the Communist Party and the Peace Movement were cuttingly and derisively called by their enemies and the press in the cold war jargon of the time, but, as one of them said to me, he didn't in the least object to being called a 'fellow traveller' as long as it was made clear by the caller that he wasn't calling him a *Tory* fellow traveller!

I didn't go around announcing my resignation from the Communist Party to all and sundry, any more than I'd gone around announcing that I'd joined it in the first place, mostly because nobody cared a damn about it one way or the other. I didn't loom very large in anybody's eyes and it was damn all to do with them anyway. As far as I was concerned thay could put whatever tag on me they'd a mind to and I'd go on voicing my thoughts and beliefs in the same way as I always had done when I thought the occasion called for it.

16.

THE ROTOR FURNACE

ALTHOUGH THE BULK OF THE WORK of the Bricklayers Department was confined to the Melting Shop, building and repairing the Company's seven open-hearth furnaces, its work generally ranged over the whole of the works from the blast furnaces to the coke-ovens.

Our men were to be seen everywhere – in the mills, in the power houses, in the boiler-houses, in the sinter plant, under the ground, on the ground and quite often up to a hundred feet above it. The jobs themselves ranged in size from a half dozen bricks in a works-loco smoke box to the complete rebuild of a blast furnace, involving the use of several hundred thousand bricks or their equivalent in blocks and the temperatures the men worked in ranged from freezing to frying.

I have seen more than a few men suddenly leap from their work with their clothes smouldering ready to burst into flames at any moment. I have also seen wooden sections of the scaffolds they worked upon suddenly burst into flames.

It was the Bricklayers' Department which was charged with the task of caging and containing that unholy terror of the steel industry – the raging, roaring, hissing, spitting inferno which reduced cold scrap by the score of tons to a mass of boiling liquid steel in scarcely any time at all. It was a task which called for character as well as know-how – it certainly was no job for faint hearts.

The open-hearth furnace above the level of the raised stage from which it is charged and tended by its crew is comprised of the 'bath' which holds the charge and the huge domed roof above it. The whole may be likened to the empty shell of a tortoise – if the reader can imagine one as large as a small bungalow!

It is the furnace roof and the squat outer lining which fills the space between it and the bath which takes the brunt of the wrath of the caged beast within – the same fierce heat which reduces the charge of cold steel scrap to liquid in a matter of a few hours also reduces the thickness of the 'outer shell' of the furnace from feet to inches in a matter of a few weeks.

It is the job of the bricklayers to keep that heat caged for as long as possible by keeping the roofs and linings of the furnaces in good and reasonable repair. A hot repair to a furnace roof or outer lining can be as nasty and as tough a job of work as I imagine is to be found in any industry anywhere.

Hot repairs are commenced as soon as it is humanly possible to get at them, before the furnace as a whole loses too much of its precious heat. This is usually the moment the furnace has discharged the last of its 120 ton charge of molten metal and slag into the huge 120 ton steel ladle placed ready to receive it.

The repair team will vary in size and number from perhaps only four men to forty – a full shift – depending on the size of the job to be done.

The average hot repair involves eight men, four brickies and four mates, and may take a couple of hours to complete. As tightly as Eskimos wrap up to keep out the cold, as tightly do the members of a hot repair team wrap up to keep out the furnace heat. Faces are completely swaddled in sweat towelling, leaving only the eyes visible below the peaks of caps. Hands and arms are protected by full length, thick leather fettling gloves. Corrugated tin sheets – of which there are always plenty about the place – may also be used as shields against the fierce heat.

The team is divided into two equal parts. One half works while the other half 'cools off'. Each half of the team works at top speed on the repair for perhaps fifteen minutes – by which time it has had enough. Then, drowned in sweat and with hearts pounding fit to burst their rib cages, the men retire and the other half of the team immediately takes over the work – and so on and repeat until the repair is completed. By which time all the members of the team will each have lost several pounds in weight and be absolutely 'arse 'oled'!

The late 1950s and early 1960s had been years of change in the steel industry. The new oxygen blowing processes of making steel had advanced by leaps and bounds – chiefly in Germany. The writing was clearly on the wall for the open-hearth process and us steelworkers with it – especially the bricklayers.

When the rest of the steel industry had been de-nationalised in 1953 by the Conservative Government then in office, the Richard Thomas and Baldwin group had been left in public ownership. Nobody wanted us – it appeared that too much of our plant and machinery was too aged and worn to make us an attractive proposition to investors – which ageing and wearing had been scarcely noticed by the workforce at Redbourn, many of whom had themselves become aged and worn with it. It seemed alright to us, but not to somebody else high up in the affairs of the group.

About the same time as I was elected shop steward for the bricklayers, it was announced that we – Redbourn, that is – were going to be 'modernised' at a cost of £22 000 000.

Included in the modernisation programme, we were subsequently informed, was a new mill, a sinter plant and a Rotor furnace – and everybody went about asking what was a Rotor furnace? And nobody at Redbourn knew, and with good reason – there was only one in the world and that was in far away South Africa where nobody had been.

By mid-1962 we knew exactly what a Rotor furnace was. We'd got one of our own and it was like nothing we'd ever seen before. It was without a doubt the weirdo of the furnace world, like something straight out of Disneyland!

The Rotor furnace consisted of an enormous steel drum about sixty feet in length and twelve feet in diameter. This rested horizontally on a steel structure known to us as the 'cradle'. There were two of these drums or barrels – when one was in production on the cradle, the other was undergoing reline and repair by the brickies.

In action, the Rotor furnace immediately reminded you of those particular circus performers who lay on their backs, stuck their legs in the air and juggled with a barrel – albeit no circus performer ever juggled with a barrel of such enormous dimensions as did our Rotor furnace. Even so, it could do anything they could with its barrel, apart from tossing it in the air, that is.

It could turn it over and over for ever and a day; it could twist it round from end to end for as many times as its operators wanted to twist it round from end to end; it could stand the barrel upright on its end to one side and then keel right over and pick up the spare barrel at its other side, also from the perpendicular position, and juggle with it just the same. It was a complete circus act in itself and until we became accustomed to it, men from all parts of the works left their own places of work – to the intense exasperation of their foremen – to come and watch it perform. It would have been a star attraction at any seaside resort or even in the big top itself – given a little imagination it could quite easily have been disguised and advertised as perhaps 'King Kong Juggling with Giant Barrel' – I'm sure it would have made a fortune for its owners in such a role!

But that same Rotor furnace which everybody had found to be so fascinatingly entertaining upon its first arrival at Redbourn was, especially to us bricklayers and mates who had the job of re-lining the barrels after each productive cycle, to become a nightmare. As an entertainer it was top, as a furnace it was a flop, and like poor old King Kong himself it too was to be the last of its kind – after it nobody ever built another, the beast became extinct.

The circus analogy didn't end with the performance of the Rotor furnace itself, it continued afterwards with the wrecking out of the old, burnt linings of the vessels after each one's cycle of production on the cradle. But this time it was we bricklayers and mates who were thrust into the role of performers – we had to become combined acrobats and trapeze artists and perform the most amazing feats of agility even to get into the vessels, where the real performance began.

Basically the trouble was the scaffold. It was fine to work on when we were installing the linings in the vessels but it became a nightmare to work upon it when we wrecked out the linings after their turn on the cradle.

That Rotor and particularly the scaffold, as a problem, became to us what the leaning tower of Pisa was to the Italians – every solution brought in its wake other equally brain-racking problems and we never really did conquer them in the whole of the twelve years reign of the Rotor at the Redbourn Steelworks.

The thickness of the linings was about thirty inches, which effectively reduced the working area in the vessel from a diameter of twelve feet to one of seven feet. Our scaffold, suspended on wire ropes from the top of the vessel fifty feet above us, was electrically operated, it lifted or lowered at the touch of a button. It was circular itself, obviously, and was comprised of sectional steel grids which, when assembled by the 'riggers', gave it an overall diameter of six feet six inches – which was a sufficiently good clearance of the lining to enable it to be lifted or lowered without snagging. For the building work it was just the job, everything went fine, but when it came to the wrecking the scene was changed dramatically and our nightmare began.

When the vessels were retired from their campaign on the cradle to be relined they were allowed to stand for twenty-four hours in order to 'cool off'. Even so, they were still pretty hot when they were pronounced to be cool enough for the wrecking work to commence.

For the wrecking we began at the top of the vessel and worked downwards. The men worked in pairs comprised of a bricklayer and a mate – in the case of the Rotor we worked two pairs at a time. Carrying our four feet long steel wrecking bars and seven pound sledge hammers, we'd climb the succession of steps and ladders to the top of the vessel sixty feet up, which itself could be a fairly taxing business. The ends of the vessels were slightly domed, with a four foot diameter aperture in their centres through which the vessel was charged when in production. We scrambled up the sloping steel plates – still hot – to this aperture and one by one climbed through it and down onto the scaffold within with the aid of a short wooden ladder which rested

194.

on the scaffold and poked a little way through the entry hole.

Because most of the original lining had burnt away, the scaffold which had fitted it so snugly before now had a clearance all round it of between eighteen and twenty four inches. That gap all round the scaffold was as essential to the wrecking out of the old refractory lining as was the scaffold itself, since through it fell all the rubble of the lining as it was wrecked, to the bottom of the vessel and so through the aperture at the other end, to be removed later by a mechanical shovel.

Because our scaffold was suspended on wire ropes like a conker on a string – it could do everything that a conker on a string could – it could twist right round and back again, it could tilt to the most alarming angles and it could swing from side to side, thus doubling the size of the gap at one side of it from twenty-four inches to fourty-eight inches or four feet. And it could do all those things at the same time – and above drops which ranged in depth from more than fifty feet to but a few feet.

Any man who has swung a seven or ten pound sledge hammer at a target no bigger than an old fashioned halfpenny such as the end of a steel bar will know just how difficult it is to hit it – even from a solid footing with the bar held perfectly still. But to hit the same target while swinging the hammer horizontally from a footing which was never stable for more than two or three seconds at a time – that same man would undoubtedly argue that if the task wasn't completely impossible then certainly it would be dangerous. Then if you were to tell him you knew of men who did that just for a living, he'd possibly believe you, but if you were to add any more – such as, while perched on the edge of forty or fifty foot drops, the odds are he'd either call you a bloody liar or them bloody fools!

Nor yet is that the half of it – all magnesite refractory bricks and blocks are much heavier than their building trade equivalents and they do not always come away cleanly a few at a time from the remains of the old lining. Sometimes a whole half ton of lining would suddenly break away from the rest and come crashing down, much of it, often most of it onto the scaffold, so setting it bucking and gyrating madly like some crazy Western bronco, while you, perhaps alerted by the quick, warning shouts of your mates a couple of seconds before the crash, clung for dear life to one of the steel uprights in the centre of the scaffold to which the pulley wheels were attached and waited in the utterly blinding fog of dust which accompanied and followed the fall for the heaving and the whirling around to cease and the fog to disperse.

Of course we wore safety harnesses as we wore safety helmets, safety gloves, safety boots, face masks and all the rest of it – but we still tried every possible method, including retractable arms, to stabilise that scaffold without at the same time rendering it immovable, but no matter what we did we only ever achieved partial success. That Rotor furnace not only broke hearts, it also broke brains. Somebody in 1974 came up with the best idea of all – it was broken up and put into a furnace itself. Nobody I know mourned its passing.

But life at Redbourn's wasn't all hard slog and danger, there were those times when all the furnaces, including the Rotor, were in good repair and in full production and then our foremen were hard put to find enough work for all of us brickies to do. Such an interlude occurred in 1962 at the time of the Cuban missile crisis.

I shall never forget that day when the final act of that world-shaking missile crisis was played out in the Atlantic, not only because of the enormous tension and trauma of the event itself but also because of the totally contrasting, belly-shaking little comedy which came to be enacted at the Redbourn steelworks where I worked, on that same day.

Castro had won his revolution. The American-backed Bay of Pigs fiasco was behind him and the Russians were installing rocket bases on the island with the obvious intention of threatening the USA – which threat, when it was discovered, so alarmed the US Government that it demanded the immediate dismantling of the bases and the complete withdrawal of the rockets and to back up its demands it mobilised its own forces along the Atlantic seaboard facing Cuba. In the meantime, several Russian ships, allegedly carrying more rockets for the island, were sailing se-

196.

renely across the Atlantic towards Cuba. These ships too the American Government demanded to be turned about and their rockets sent back to Russia. The whole world awaited the outcome with baited breath.

That day also happened to be the final day of the Redbourn steelworks 'Good Housekeeping Week'. Every department on the works, maintenance and production, from the blast furnaces to the coke-ovens and from the melting shop to the rolling mill was involved. Each department had that week devoted what time it could to the cleaning and general tidying up of its own work area in readiness for the great inspection on the final day by a panel of judges comprised of equal numbers of works' managers and works' trade union officials. The department which, in the opinion of the panel, had achieved the best result would be adjudged to be the winner.

The great day of the final inspection by the judges arrived – and nobody cared a damn, they'd other things on their minds – like nuclear war!

The bricklayers' department wasn't very busy that day. All the open-hearth furnaces were in production and none under repair. Men stood about in small groups discussing in low voices the latest news of the crisis in the Atlantic and studying the banner headlines which exploded in their faces from the papers they'd bought on their way to work that morning. The Russian ships still held their course and the Americans continued to mobilise their forces on the east coast and in Florida. The world had never before stood in such mortal danger – this could well be the day it died.

The judges were due round the bricklayers' work area at any moment – if the 'bomb' didn't obliterate it first!

It was just about then that the burly figure of one of our foremen – who was no more noted for his understanding of the affairs of his own department than he was for his grasp of world affairs generally – hove into sight.

Hands clasped behind his back, eyes everywhere, slowly he ambled towards us. He was himself making a last minute check of the area ahead of the judges. No more than three or four yards away from us his gaze alighted upon a single brick which had fallen from the corner of one of the several neatly arranged stacks of bricks in the area. Instantly a look of utter horror appeared upon his face and he pounced on the brick and hastily replaced it upon the stack. He then swung savagely upon us lot watching. 'Why couldn't one of you have done that?' he demanded angrily, 'that could have cost us five points!'

Did you laugh or did you cry? You could of course go and find a quiet corner somewhere and go mad in it!

Well, as everybody knows today, the Cuban crisis was resolved when the Russians agreed to be good boys and to turn their ships around and also to take their rockets out of Cuba, and for their part the Americans also agreed to be good boys and not to invade Cuba any more – and the whole world heaved a huge sigh of relief, including the Europeans, who had won for themselves a few extra rockets, as it was pretty certain the Russians wouldn't let perfectly good missiles go to waste.

If there was blood, toil, tears and sweat to be found at Redbourn, there was laughter and humour too. Most of the tears I saw shed were the results of eye wedges but many too were simply tears of laughter – there was always a laugh to be had somewhere on the works.

Every department had its own folklore – its own little fund of anecdotes and stories built up over the long years and passed on from men to boys. The best of these broke the departmental boundaries and entered into the larger folklore of the works generally. There was the one about Alf the boilersmith. Alf weighed somewhere in the region of twenty-two or three stone and he was so fat he had difficulty in even getting about. One day his foreman handed to Alf a list of jobs to be done that day in various parts of the melting shop. Alf took the list, studied it for a moment or two and then turned to his mate and remarked angrily, 'He must think I'm a bloody greyhound!'

Or the one about George the fitter's mate. For two weeks running the wages office overpaid him by about ten shillings each time and George never said a word about it to anybody. By the third week the wages office had discovered the mistake and so stopped a pound from George's wages to recover the over-payments. George shot up to the wages office to have it out with the paying officer, who gave him the reason for the pound stoppage and then asked George why he hadn't complained when he'd been overpaid on the previous two weeks – to which George replied that anybody could make a mistake, even the wages office. He hadn't minded when they'd made one mistake in his wages, he'd even been prepared to overlook the second mistake the week after but it was now getting to be every bloody week that came and he was buggered if he was going to put up with that!

'Thumper' was a melting shop foreman. He was a large man of uncertain temper and his nickname was derived from his readiness to thump anybody who too strenuously or too often disagreed with him. Thumper could neither read nor write. One night, when he was in charge of the 10.00 pm to 6.00 am shift, the melting shop manager had left a note for him in the foreman's office, knowing he would find somebody to read it for him. Thumper enlisted the aid of his second foreman on the shift, who was scarcely more literate than he himself was. The two of them pored over the note for some time. 'Well, what does it say?' demanded Thumper impatiently. 'It says,' answered his second, 'we've got to get more work done – the other shifts are starting to complain about us!' Thumper's temper exploded. 'D'yer know,' he said to his mate, 'if I was an educated man I'd write arseholes right across that!'

Many other men besides Thumper had earned themselves nicknames – many of them totally unaware of the fact. The nicknames often themselves paid a striking tribute to the directness and the perspicacity of the ordinary steelworker.

There was 'Squeak', a small man with a small squeaky voice; 'Crackers', a man totally irrational in argument and behaviour; 'T.6', an abbreviation of 'Tanky Thompson the two-ton teararse', a fat man noted not for his work speed but for the speed of his leaving it at meal breaks and at the end of the shift!; 'Blank One', a one-eyed man; 'Warthog', an extra ugly foreman; 'The Ghoul' or 'Ghouly', an unshaven character with blood-shot eyes and a mouthful of broken and blackened teeth; 'Owd Sojer', an ex-Army regular; 'Chicken' of the long beak nose, long neck and large splayed feet – when you heard the name you at once saw the resemblance.

Poor old Chicken died a horrible death after a steel ladle filled to the brim with molten steel slapped some of it over him – as indeed did Owd Sojer, when he fell into the fifteen-inch space and became wedged between two red-hot six ton ingot moulds and was roasted alive before the horrified gaze of his mates.

I was there the night when Chicken, burning like a torch and screaming with the agony of his pain and shock, raced crazily along the narrow, brick-cobbled, teeming stage with his mates in close pursuit. You don't forget nights like that.

17.

THE SHOP STEWARD

TOWARDS THE END OF 1959 I'd been elected to the position of shop steward by the one hundred or so bricklayers employed at Redbourn – our mates, the bricklayers' labourers, who were about half as many again in number, were in a different union. They were organised by the British Iron and Steel and Kindred Trades Association (BISAKTA) and they had their own departmental representative or shop steward – this BISAKTA post was held by my father at the time of my election to the office of bricklayers shop steward.

I think it is worth recounting the circumstances of this election and the events subsequent to it, inconsequential though at first sight they may appear to be in relation to the far greater issues of national democracy and industrial relationships generally. It may be that there will be those amongst my readers who, having no first hand experience of heavy industry, would like to take a closer look at just what does go on on the shop floors of some of our great industries besides the actual manufacturing and productive processes themselves.

Even though I had severed my links with the Communist Party some time previously, I was at the time of the election still regarded by those who knew me, or thought they knew me, as a 'dyed in th wool' communist. I neither did nor said anything to correct that somewhat mistaken belief – why should I have done? I was not either then or later ashamed of my political beliefs. I was but being myself and so far as I was concerned other people, whether for me or against me, could make of me what they wished – that was their business.

Closely watching the events taking place in the Bricklayers' Department was the Redbourn Management. The last thing they wanted in such a crucial area was a 'commie' shop steward – they viewed the possibility with deep alarm. Their alarm was shared by the retiring shop steward, resigning his union office in order to become a foreman. An attempt was made by him to foist his own chosen succcccessor upon the bricklayers by the simple act of nominating him for the office himself and thus obviating the need to hold a formal election.

Perhaps at another time he'd have got away with it – it was no uncommon practice on the works for retiring shop stewards to 'appoint' their successors in this way, and as a general rule nobody cared a damn one way or the other, but this time I at least within the department was determined that there would be an election, even if it meant standing for office myself!

One could understand the management's concern at the prospect of my being elected to union office within the department – at that time the trades unions in the industry were safely tucked into their pockets.

At national level the Executive Union members were kept sweet by an unprecedented flow of union subscriptions into their coffers consequent upon the post-war phenomena of full employment and the industry-wide growth of the closed shop. They too, provided they sung the right tunes, were in line for knighthoods and other honours upon their retirements – in some cases even before. There were also places found for them on the boards of other publicly owned industries, such as water, at, in some cases, grossly inflated salaries.

At shop floor level it seemed to me the managements had put most of the shop stewards into their pockets – by flattering their importance, by allowing them a 'cushy' time on the shop floor and by ever dangling before them the prospects of promotion, providing they too sang the right tunes. Most of them did. When I looked at the terrible conditions in many parts of the industry – at the low pay of most of the unskilled workers, only made tolerable by the very, long hours they were allowed to work in order to make it good – at the paucity, or even total lack, of welfare facilities on the plants – at Redbourn at that time the main labouring gang didn't even possess a mess room, the men ate their meals for the most part behind and below the furnaces, more often than not plagued to death by hordes of rats, mice and crickets, not to mention the stinking fumes and constant danger from flying liquid metal – at the lack of shower facilities – there were none, to the best of my knowledge, anywhere on the works at all – and as for safety, it was a laugh! When I came to look at all this and bearing in mind also that this was a nationalised industry, I was sickened. It seemed to me there was something very rotten, not only in the state of Denmark, but in that of England also, and the blame for this state of affairs I chiefly lay at the door of the unions – one wouldn't expect the managements to be overly concerned about the welfare of their workers or the low pay – even if they managed a publicly owned industry. Labour, when they'd nationalised the industry, had left the same people in charge. But for the unions to look the other way and pretend not to know was more than I could stomach. Exactly as before, when I'd joined the Communist Party to fight for the 'Peace', I well knew there would be little I could do to effect a change but that too seemed to me to be no good reason for not trying – what the hell, I wasn't going any place, I'd nothing better to do with my time.

Once the issue was forced to an election the opposition, aided, not all that surreptitiously, by the management in the background, did their best to discredit me by circulating all kinds of alarmist stories about the consequences which would follow my election to office – it would deal a very severe blow to the good relations which at present existed in the department between men and management – I would be out to ban or, at the very least, curtail their overtime – I could even be the cause of strike action in the department. At the very least I wouldn't have the management's confidence which in turn would seriously affect departmental negotiations – which really was one big guffaw since there had been no meaningful negotiations initiated in the department by the men for decades, not since before the war.

The campaign against me backfired badly. I was elected by a substantial majority.

The very first thing I did on being confirmed in office was to abolish the 'one man band' system of dealing – I won't say negotiating – with the managment. I formed a departmental committee comprised of one man from each shift, chosen by the men of each shift. The purpose of this was to enable the men to be kept in touch at all times with what was being done and said in the departmental office in their name by the shop steward – now myself. It would also allow me to have a finger upon the departmental pulse at all times and thus gauge the strength of its feeling upon any particular issue at any particular time.

Secondly, I let it be known there would be no more 'snap' union meetings called in the messroom under the noses of the bosses and which very often were over and done with before many of the men of the department were even aware they'd been called.

I let it be known that all departmental meetings would in future be held *off* the job, either in the branch offices in the town or in other places of our own choosing and all men would be given equal opportunity to attend – including, if he wished, the Departmental Manager, who still retained his union card and had been known to attend cabin meetings. He never did.

All of which unprecedented activity by a shop steward thoroughly alarmed the management. It confirmed their worst fears – I was setting up a 'communist cell' within the department, which fact, if something wasn't done about it and done quickly, could have very serious repercussions throughout the whole works. This insidious spread of communism must be halted at once, strangled at birth, nipped in the bud or whatever.

Accordingly, within a week of the election, I was summoned to the departmental office to a meeting with the Departmental Manager. I collected the shift representative on route and together we went to the office. I knocked on the door and awaited the manager's call to enter. It came and we went in.

He was working, or pretending to, at his desk. Seated by his side was the departmental second-in-command. He continued with his work, we continued with our waiting for him to finish and the departmental second-in-command continued with his silent, frosty surveillance of the two of us.

Eventually the 'Boss' put his pen down and looked up from

204.

his work. The curt 'good morning' almost froze on his lips as he noticed I hadn't removed my cap. He stared meaningfully at it for a long moment – I ignored the stare. The second-in-command seated by his side then pointedly tapped his own head with one finger, indicating I should remove the cap. That gesture too I ignored.

Eventually, seeing that I wasn't going to remove the cap, the departmental head requested us to be seated – there were several spare chairs in the office. That was the first hint of politeness or consideration shown to us and accordingly, when I'd seated myself, I removed the cap and placed it on the table between us. The Manager glanced at it distastefully – it was a dirty old thing – but he made no comment and for my part I hoped the gesture was clear – I would give respect for respect.

The Manager cleared his throat and then commenced to inform us of the purpose of the meeting. As I'd feared, it was intended to be of no help or comfort to me, indeed, precisely the opposite.

He informed us that from that day forward, henceforth and for evermore, we the bricklayers of the department were to lose all our 'privileges'.

What he meant by 'privileges' were the so-called 'gentlemen's agreements' which had been agreed between himself and the previous shop steward – and those before him. These 'gentlemen's agreements' mainly applied to the hot work on the furnaces, soaking pits, ladles, etc. Upon completion of these jobs, rarely lasting longer than a few hours, our men were allowed to go home without waiting to the end of the shift. If the completion of these hot jobs coincided with or went over the end of the shift the men were paid a couple of hours at a time and a half rate in lieu of 'cooling off' time. There were other 'gentlemen's agreements' but most were confined to the hot working practice of the department.

Discipline was also going to be tightened up throughout the department, we were further informed – no more going home early at the end of each shift, no more late comings at the start of each shift, no more this, no more that! I listened grimly and with

205.

inwardly mounting anger to this catalogue of petty humiliations and ultimatums being heaped upon my head. The implications were quite plain – the bricklayers were going to be punished for electing the wrong shop steward and only by getting rid of him again would they be able to restore the situation.

I tried not to show my feelings but I was hard put not to do so. What he, our manager, was calling our 'privileges' in effect operated entirely to the managment's benefit.

After hot repairs to the furnaces or whatever, the men were almost always without exception completely exhausted and soaked through to the skin and there were no showers nor even nearly adequate toilet facilities for them to clean up afterwards or dry their sweat soaked clothes. The idea of letting them go home upon completion of the hot repairs had been agreed with the departmental manager to avoid their having to sit out their 'cooling off' time in the cold, draughty cabins. That is what he called a 'privilege' – I think the poor chap really believed it was.

I didn't argue with him there or then. I heard him out to the finish and then I picked up my cap from the table and departed the office. But I'd be back – I knew it even if he didn't.

Over the next few days I conferred with my committee in order to get an agreed response to this gauntlet which had so rudely been thrown down to us by the managment.

Their first reaction, both individually and collectively, was one of dismay. They suggested that I return to the office and in effect plead with the manager to restore the 'privileges. I'd have died first!

When they'd calmed down I put it to them that the Departmental Manager had been quite right when he'd described our so-called privileges' or gentlemen's agreements as 'hangovers from the past' – that was exactly how we should regard them too.

What we wanted, I argued, was not a system of privileges or gentlemen's agreements which gave all the benefits to the management and scarcely any to the men and which could be withdrawn or suspended at a moment's notice by the managers but a system of properly written agreements covering all the aspects of our work, especially the hot work. In addition, I went on, we should demand as our right the provision of better welfare facilities, including showers, individual lockers and better and roomier messing accomodation.

What I argued for was so obviously correct that I was given the full backing of the committee in my determination to bring the 'privilege' game to an end and to negotiate in its stead a system of properly written agreements, not forgetting the welfare side of the business.

Accordingly, I informed the manager through his clerk and general dogsbody, who shared the office with him and minded it in his absence, that I would like to have another meeting with him. Incidentally, this character always faithfully mirrored his master's attitude towards myself at all times. When I was in the doghouse with the boss, which was much if not all of the time, I was in it with him too. On those rare occasions when the boss smiled upon me, so did he. He also ran the boss' errands – it was almost always he who was sent to find me or anyone else who might be wanted in the office. He would suddenly appear at my side, blurt out his message – usually a curt 'You're wanted in the office' – and then scurry away as fast as his legs could take him before I'd even had time to acknowledge its receipt, let alone discover the reason behind it.

Perhaps later that same day I was informed by this character that the Departmental Manager would see me in his office. I knocked at the door and awaited the invitation to enter. Our second encounter was almost a carbon copy of our first but this time minus the head tapping by the second-in-command. Only when he – the manager – had invited us to have a seat did I remove the cap and, as before, I placed it on the table between us – which place, I was as well aware as he was, wasn't the proper place for it – there were numerous hat pegs scattered around the office walls. I was but giving grudging courtesy for grudging courtesy.

The meeting got under way and this time it was my turn to do most of the talking. He and his second both, almost fell out of their chairs when I came to the bit about I and the departmental committee being in complete agreement with his view of our 'privileges' and departmental 'gentlemen's agreements' as being 'hangovers from the past'. Their reaction was comical to behold. I then went on to inform them of our intentions to negotiate a proper system of written agreements in their place, the details of which I would be submitting later in written form to the Labour Office.

I also raised the business of welfare. That too I informed them we would be raising at the highest level. Particularly would we be demanding the provision of a proper shower room, individual lockers for each man and greatly improved messing accomodation generally.

Never for a moment had this pair anticipated such a reaction to their ultimatum and petty insults of the previous meeting. They were completely floored by it and not a little alarmed as well.

There were times when I almost felt sorry for the two of them. I say this with no air of superiority – I really did, so little grasp did they have of even the rudiments of industrial relations, even of man management. Such knowledge had never in their experience been called for – both were the products of the early twentieth century north Lincolnshire countryside, brought up in the shadow of the landed gentry of that isolated part of the world. They readily accepted its values and particularly so in relation to its class structure – both knew their places and both of them thought they knew the places of everybody else. The two of them had entered the steelworks as ordinary building workers during the war-scare years of the late 1930s and had worked with men throughout the years of the second world war, many of whom had been so afraid of losing their immunity from the call-up, which they would have done had they been for any reason dismissed from their employment on the steelworks, that they all but licked the boots of their foremen and other supervisors throughout all those years and both men believed that that was how it always had been and how it always would be and should be, especially now that they were the gaffers.

My elevation to the shop steward's job in the department had turned their world topsy-turvy. In their eyes I became the living proof of the evil of communism, and that in their department! It was scarcely credible.

Perhaps a couple of days later the errand boy appeared at my side. 'You're wanted in the office,' he said, and made his usual rapid departure. I'd been expecting the call and I had in my pocket the prepared list of our claims.

The procedure was exactly as before – knock, wait, enter, wait again, sit down, cap, etc.

The manager cleared his throat and I thought I detected a little uncertainty in his manner. There was almost the hint of a smile as he opened the meeting.

He began by saying that perhaps after all he'd been a little hasty in withdrawing our privileges and upon further consideration he'd decided to restore them in their entirety. I knew exactly what that meant – he'd been ordered to by the Labour Officer with whom he'd consulted between the two meetings. But if he and those above him in the management chain liked to maintain the myth that he and he alone ran the department, it was no skin off my nose. I thanked him politely for changing his mind and told him that we for our part would be prepared to accept that as the status quo position pending the signing of the new agreements. I then reached into my pocket and handed him the papers upon which our claims were set down.

He looked both surprised and angry. He glanced at the documents – they weren't all that detailed or very scholarly set out. 'Surely you're not going to press ahead with these now?' he exclaimed angrily. 'You've got your privileges back, what more do you want?'

I told him it was all in the papers and that we'd be obliged if he would pass them on to the Labour Office and arrange the meetings accordingly. I then made my departure before he had apoplexy.

Well, to cut a long story short, we did get to meet the Labour Officer and bring those particular claims to a successful conclusion over the next two or three months. We were helped considerably by our mates, the bricklayers' labourers, who, under the leadership of my father, associated themselves with all our claims. For our Departmental Manager and his staff the dam had well and truly burst. Of course, we didn't get everything we'd wanted, but we did achieve most of our objectives, incuding an increase in wages, in written agreement form, and the promise of better welfare facilities including showers, lockers and better messing accomodation.

So delighted were the men of the department with the final settlement of these particular claims that they clubbed together and bought me a beautiful leather briefcase embossed in gold with my initials and containing a proper minute book and a pen and pencil set. It's one of the nicest things that's ever happened to me in my life.

Even so, I wasn't going to be allowed to rest on my laurels – there was a great deal still waiting to be done in the department. The neglect of decades wasn't to be repaired by one comparatively small success – it was but the first step on a long, long road.

Overtime working in the department was totally out of control and I would say almost as much from the management stand-point as from the unions – though perhaps the higher echelons of the management weren't then fully aware of that. From time to time we even had the ludicrous situation in which at the end of the working week men were claiming pay for more hours than there actually were in the whole week.

Much of the overtime was phony – some men spent entire shifts of it at home in bed, only appearing back on the job to show their faces before clocking off and then returning once more to resume their rest or go fishing or something.

These were the boom years of steel – they were also the years of the lotus eaters.

18.

AN UNHOLY ALLIANCE

WHENEVER A FURNACE, an open hearth furnace that is, was taken out of commission for repairs – and at any given time there was almost always one of the seven, occasionally even two, undergoing repairs – the sole objective was to get it back into production as quickly as possible, seemingly at any cost. Overtime limits didn't exist. At such times men accused each other of living on the job – some, even many, all but did. Health and safety standards, never at any time the first consideration, went almost completely by the board.

Overtime working in our department, and in many other departments also, was the root cause of much friction and jealousy, not only between men and men, shift and shift, foremen and foremen, but between the departments themselves and also on a wider scale between the production workers, who scarcely worked any and the maintenance and labouring gangs who worked much.

These jealousies between men gave rise to the greatest friction on those rare occasions when all the furnaces were in production. Then their overtime was curtailed, sometimes even cut back to zero. Rarely did such periods last longer than a week or a fortnight before the whole sad business began again.

But so addicted were many of the men to their overtime – in some cases it formed the larger part of their pay packets each week – that they'd get up to all sorts of dodges in order to manufacture phony overtime. The most common was to slow time or by some means delay the completion of a job which they knew had to be completed before they could leave it, so to run the work over into the next shift and thus into time and a half pay.

Often they were aided and abetted in this practice by the foremen who, albeit that only three or four of their men were involved, stayed on the extra time with them to 'supervise' the work.

This practice led to much cronyism on the shifts and, as may be imagined, much friction between the men who were selected for this work and the men who were not – it paid to keep well in with the foremen.

In the old days before the war the steelworks management had been able to increase the size of their labour force in the 'busy' periods by the simple expedient of raiding the dole queues for men, and conversely in the 'slack' periods they'd been able to reduce its size by standing the men off again.

Every steelworks in the area had its own 'shadow gang' outside the gates, which could be whistled back at a moment's notice and returned to the dole queues when the work was done.

Under the conditions of full employment which obtained in the post–war era this practice became impossible. The only way to increase the output of the gangs was to expand the number of hours each man worked – not nearly as efficient! For, by doubling the number of hours worked, you didn't necessarily double output or effort, not nearly. Even so, the management did obtain some extra effort and, obviously, as the method continued for a long number of years, they must have been reasonably satisfied with the returns.

Then who was I to fault and condemn a system so valued by both men and management? I was the prize fool shop steward of Scunthorpe, quite prepared to rush in where men and angels feared to tread, that's who I was!

In my eyes overtime working in the department was totally out of control, both from the union point of view and – had they been more astute – from the management's, not that I was shedding any tears for them.

Apart from the degrading spectacle of having to witness men constantly at one another's thoats over the issue, I had several other reasons for wanting to impose some control, some orderliness, on an otherwise totally chaotic situation. To begin with, the fact that overtime was so readily available and in such great quantity blinded men to the realities of the bare working week of forty-four hours, to the need to maintain its worth in the pay packet, ready for the day when overtime disappeared or could no longer be relied upon to the same degree to top up an otherwise low wage system. Already by the early 1960s the open hearth method of producing steel was under very serious threat from the new oxygen blowing process then sweeping Europe. For the open hearth furnaces – and us with them – the writing was already on the wall.

Another thing – I wanted to negotiate a day rota agreement with the management. Our day workers, as opposed to our shift workers, had no continuous working week agreement. Their hours of work were from Monday to Saturday – half day Saturday, that is.

Their work too, the management wanted to cover the whole of the seven days of the week – but from Saturday 12 o'clock noon until 7.30 am Monday morning by overtime working.

Most of these day workers – about 20% of our total workforce – were the older, longer serving members of the department – not so keen on the overtime as their shiftworking brothers in the melting shop. But if they wouldn't cover their jobs by overtime working at the weekend there were plenty of men in the same department who would only too willingly stand in for them. Thus in this way did the management use men against men, so undermining their bargaining power. I wanted that stopped also, and the control of overtime was the key to this.

The obstacles to getting control of that overtime working were not nearly as formidable as at first sight they'd appeared to be – though I was always conscious of the howls of fury which would go up from a substantial number of the men – and the management too – once they realised what I was about – but I also had a great faith in the sturdy commonsense of the bulk of my members, who could always be brought to see the truth of any works situation once the facts of it were clearly and honestly elucidated for them.

You can't run a steelworks without some overtime – leastwise such a steelworks as Redbourn was at that time. I knew that – my aim wasn't to bring overtime working to an end – although that was what I was accused of – I was neither so bloody-minded nor as big a fool as that. Rather I wanted to be able to control it – albeit to begin with ever so gently. The benefits to be derived from such a control would be enormous and not least at the negotiating table. A short-sighted management had made itself almost as dependent upon the overtime as had the men – and though time was running out for the open-hearth furnaces, we still had a few years left, which was time enough, or so I thought.

To begin with, the labourers of the department, half as many again as ourselves, the brickies, were unable to bring any pressure to bear upon me as they were in a different union. That was three fifths of the opposition bundled out of the way at a stroke – although in truth it must be said, I had many strong supporters in their ranks also, not least amongst them their own trades union representative, my father.

I was then left with the comparatively simple task of convincing my own members, the bricklayers, of the soundness of the move.

Once it was explained to them they readily saw that by working unlimited overtime when the furnaces were off and so getting them back into production that much quicker they also at the same time brought to an end the case for working the overtime – in effect, cutting their own throats. The remedy, I argued, was to limit the number of overtime hours worked by each man in these 'crisis' periods, thereby ironing out the peaks and levelling up the troughs in overtime working at one and the same time, which in turn would compel the management and the departmental foremen to share the overtime more fairly amongst the men. In essence, we would be replacing the managerial hand on the overtime 'tap' with our own. I got my overtime limit – it was up to me and the departmental committee to use it wisely.

I think we did. As a result we were able to negotiate a day rota agreement with the management. We were also able to negotiate a system of extra bonus payments related to the time it took to get the furnaces back into production. But above all we were eventually able to bring to an end the pernicious system of seven day week working – we banned the working of overtime in both the shift rota and day rota rest periods.

Only that minority of men who had previously 'lived on the job' were able to argue that they'd lost money through the control of the overtime changing hands. No really great amounts of money were involved in the negotiation with the managements – I knew my limits – but I think it's pretty safe to say that in general terms the men gained both in their pay packets and in their social life and the company lost nothing – the furnaces continued to be turned round as quickly as ever.

Of course, events never went as smoothly as all that and our successes were often hardly earned. I had many fierce arguments and fights, not only with the management but also with the shop stewards of other trades unions on the plant – not least – and perhaps that which caused me most distress – with a sizeable section of my own membership – sizeable but never at any time anywhere near a majority. None of these were ever able to topple me from my perch, though it certainly wasn't for the want of trying, especially in the early days of my stewardship.

A new spirit was abroad in the Bricklayers Department. Our mates, the labourers, broke away from the general BISAKTA branch of the Redbourn Works to form one exclusively their own. As a consequence they too now had their own departmental committee and always, or almost always, acted in concert with the bricklayers. Between us we became a pretty formidable force for change on the works.

And what was happening in our department wasn't going unnoticed in other departments. The men there began to prod their shop stewards for similar action. In consequence they too won day rotas for themselves – which business of course was considered very bad business by sections of the management at Redbourn.

Twice they launched major counter attacks – if I may use the term – upon the men of the Bricklayers Department, the major cause of their discomfort as they saw it – and twice they were decisively repelled.

The first time occurred in 1961 – just when in 1961 I'm not quite sure, nor does it really matter. If my memory serves me right the scenario was this. One of the blast furnaces on which the open hearth furnaces depended for their supply of iron had to be taken out of commission for extensive repairs due to an explosion or something. With the supply of iron so reduced, the pressure for the quick turn round of the open hearth furnaces was greatly reduced also. Redbourn now had open hearth furnace capacity to spare. Blast furnaces are not as easily or as quickly restored as are steel furnaces – it was estimated that this particular blast furnace would be out of commission for at least three months.

It seemed to someone somewhere in the Redbourn management hierarchy that the opportunity was too good to be missed – the explosion at the blast furnace had not only shattered the furnace itself, it had also shattered the bricklayers' bargaining strength at the same time and that too of the other maintenance unions who were beginning to climb onto their band waggon. Now, if ever, was the time to strike back, to recover at least some of the gains made by the men over the last couple of years.

With the sole exception of the Bricklayers' Union all other maintenance unions – Engineers, Electricians, Woodworkers, Boilersmiths, Blacksmiths etc. – were united in one negotiating body. This was the Allied Trades Committee and it was comprised of representatives from each of its constituent unions. At works level these were the shop stewards of each union, from amongst whom one was chosen to be their convener and chief spokesman.

In accordance with the negotiating procedures of the Steel Industry – which, as we were the smallest union in the industry, always left the bricklayers to the last – the Labour Officer summoned the works' Allied Trades shop stewards to a meeting in his office.

At that meeting the Allied Trades shop stewards were informed by the Labour Officer of the very serious consequences of the blast furnace failure for the rest of the Redbourn steelworks.

216.

It was suggested by him that it could quite possibly mean the taking out of commission of two, perhaps even three, of the open hearth steelmaking furnaces, which in turn would have a knock-on effect in the rolling mill and so on and so on.

The Allied Trades stewards listened to this catalogue of gloom and doom with growing alarm, wondering all the time what was coming next and what in the end was it going to mean for them and their members?

What it did mean for them came almost as an anti-climax. After he, the Labour Officer, had dwelt as long as he'd dared to on the bad news without overdoing it, he came to the 'good'. He informed the stewards that as grave and serious as the position was the company still had no intention of cutting its workforce, either by standing men off or of short-timing them.

I wasn't there but knowing personally all those who were I can well imagine the huge sigh of relief which went up from the stewards when this was announced – they took the bait, hook, line and sinker.

However, the Labout Officer continued, there would still have to be some sacrifices made by the men. Accordingly, the company had reluctantly decided to withdraw all the men's 'privileges', including their day rota agreements, especially the day rotas which in any case were in breach of the forty-four hour national working week agreement.

When they'd 'negotiated' the day rota agreements with the company, the Allied Trades shop stewards had sought to outshine the Bricklayers. They'd agreed rotas which embraced 49 hours – thus guaranteeing themselves – or so they'd thought – an extra five hours overtime each week. Now they were hoist with their own petard – there was no way in the present circumstances they were going to be able to defend those rotas, even if they'd possessed the will or the wit, which they didn't.

At a stroke the management recovered all the gains made by the Allied Trades members at works level over the previous eighteen months. The loss of their day rotas was a very big loss indeed to the ordinary shop floor workers – all their double time and time and a half working, which they'd thought to be assured for ever and a day, had gone up in smoke and at a single meeting.

However, before the meeting in the Labour Office broke up, the Allied Trades shop stewards were able to extract from the Labour Officer a promise. The promise was this. He would deal every bit as severely with the Bricklayers when their turn came to meet with him. That promise the Labour Officer gave to them.

Craven bunch that they were, thay feared the backlash which would follow their own abject surrender to the demands of the Labour Office from their members, if it became known amongst them – as it surely would if it happened – that the Bricklayers had conducted a successful defence of their agreements.

But as Rabbie Burns had it, even 'the best laid schemes o' mice and men gang aft a–gley' – to which one might add, even when the schemers come in the guise of Allied Trades shop stewards and steelworks Labour Officers – indeed an unholy alliance.

The turn of the members of the Bricklayers' Department to meet with the Labour Officer came a couple of days later. Of course we'd heard by then of the sell out by the Allied Trades Works Committee, so we faced the meeting with some foreboding. Like Britain in 1940, we now stood alone – melodramatic perhaps, but not a whit less true.

Representing the department for the men were, for the bricklayers myself and one committee member and for the labourers, my father and one committee member – four in all.

It was management practice always to match the number of trades union negotiators on their side of the table with equal numbers of their own on theirs – two against two, four against four, as in our case, or six against six and so on.

They, the management, were very 'psychology' conscious – they got up to all sorts of little tricks so to emphasise their own superiority and the inferiority of the union side, like always arranging the meetings on their own ground – in their own offices – always being ready seated, with hats removed, so they didn't have to remove them in the presence of the trades union representatives before these representatives, were admitted into the room,

218.

and always sitting with their backs to the window, so the light from it fell fully on the faces of the trades union negotiators and not on their own. They appeared to think such nicely calculated little 'ruderies' gave them the psychological edge in the subsequent negotiations – maybe they did in most cases but I think not in the case of the Bricklayers Department of the Redbourn Steelworks.

My father was an old trades union campaigner. Both he and I regarded the new breed of college-boy, whizz-kid type of Labour Officer with a deep distrust – 5% whizz, 95% kid was his verdict upon them. He was the originator of the old Scunthorpe joke, way back in the 1920s, in which the shop steward is requested by the manager to remove his cap before stating his business. 'I'm here after a rise, not an effing haircut,' growled back the shop steward. I've heard the joke recounted on numerous occasions without the tellers having the slightest notion of who its originator was.

I remember once, we entered the Labour Office in which, of course, the Labour Officer, flanked on either side by other managerial representatives, was already comfortably seated. He invited us too to be seated and as he made to sit down, the 'old man' let go an almighty sneeze – he liked his snuff, as did many other steelworkers – and the sneeze almost blasted the Labour Officer's neatly arranged papers off the table. They were saved in the nick of time by the Officer himself who then remarked, slightly unnerved and not a little alarmed, 'Oh dear, Mr Framp, have you got a cold?' The 'old man' gave another great blast into his handkerchief and then replied, as he wiped his nose, 'No, I think maybe I'm allergic to some bugger in here.' Following the direction of his eyes nobody could be mistaken just who that 'some bugger' was – so much for his psychological touches.

However, to get on with the story. We were subjected to the same heart–rending account of the company's difficulties as had been the Allied Trades shop stewards and in addition – and this might have brought tears to the eyes of more sensitive and trusting types than ourselves – he informed us of how all the other maintenance unions on the plant had rallied round the company in its hour of need, how they had agreed, so nobly and unselfishly – he didn't use those words but that's how he meant it to be understood – to give up their day rotas and other privileges to save the day for the company. That bunch noble and unselfish! He then continued that he could ask no less of us, therefore it was with very great reluctance that he had to inform us that our day rota too, even though it was properly founded on the 44 hour National Working Week Agreement, must be forfeit. Of course, he made no mention of the promise he'd given to the Allied Trades shop stewards – that emerged later!

We weren't one little bit convinced of the need to forfeit our day rota – it was the pride of our day workers and the departmental committee who had negotiated its introduction. Nor did the Labour Officer's sob story about the company's difficulties ring wholly true to us.

To begin with, at that very time the Company, which was still in public ownership, was engaged in the biggest spend of its entire history – a £22 000 000 splash of public money on, amongst other things, a new rolling mill, and new sinter plant and – what was of the greatest interest and concern to us in the Bricklayers Department – a rotor furnace which was to embrace all the latest oxygen–blowing techniques and which even then we were in the process of claiming for ourselves all the refractory work which would subsequently have to be done upon it. Other unions were also claiming the same work for their members.

It seemed to us, surveying the problem on behalf of the Bricklayers Department, that all this blast furnace malarky fitted in just a little too well – just a little too glibly with the company's other interests, both immediate and long term.

Production was bound to be adversely affected in any case while the contractors were installing the new mill, which would take several weeks, and even when that task was completed it would have to be run in – and with such a complicated mass of machinery there were bound to be teething troubles. It seemed to us, blast furnaces notwithstanding, maximum production wasn't just then the company's highest priority anyway.

In the longer term, when all the work improvements were completed – rolling mill, sinter plant, Rotor furnace etc. – it would be in the company's interest to have a workforce much more amenable to discipline and control. As it was it was getting far too cocky for its own good. The time afforded the company by the combination of blast furnace failure and works extensions was as opportune as any in which to make that particular deficiency good. That's how we of the Bricklayers Department saw the picture – we were in fact being 'set up' by the company.

We didn't argue the toss with the Labour Officer when he announced the company's intention of foreclosing upon our day rota. We played dumb, we just asked him if only day workers were to be affected by the company's cuts. He replied scenting victory, 'Yes, only day workers.' 'All day workers?', we then asked. 'Of course all day workers,' he replied, a little impatiently. 'Alright,' we agreed, 'then all day workers it shall be – including all our contractors' members on the plant!' He almost fell out of his chair – he saw the trap he'd walked into immediately.

The main contractor carrying out the work on the Redbourn extensions employed about forty bricklayers – which forty bricklayers I had recruited into the union. They all worked day work too – seven days a week. I never bothered or interfered with the business of these contract bricklayers, a fair number of whom were known to me personally. They had elected their own card steward and they ran their own business in their own way and as far as I was concerned that was good enough – that is until the moment when the Labour Officer announced his shattering new deal for the day working bricklayers at Redbourn. They, the contract bricklayers, worked on the Redbourn steelworks too – but because they weren't directly employed by the company he'd completely left them out of his calculations.

And not for a moment did he doubt our intention or our ability to involve them also in his decision to end the seven day coverage of day worker's jobs on the plant. After all, it would be on his authority, on his say so – which at that time of full employment could have caused them to pack in their jobs by the dozen in order to seek more lucrative work elsewhere, which in turn would set back by weeks, possibly months, the company's own ambitious plans to greatly expand production and *his* bosses wouldn't thank him for that, His own job now lay on the line.

At that point we, the union side, were asked to vacate the office while they, the management side, had a private discussion amongst themselves concerning this latest turn of events. This was quite normal practice during negotiations – either side could ask at any time for an adjournment in order to discuss amongst themselves in private some point or other which had arisen out of the main discussions between the two sides.

Fifteen minutes later we were invited back into the office – the management team had regained their composure and we were greeted with friendly smiles and as always the Labour Officer did the talking, or most of it. In the matter of negotiations he was the professional.

He informed us that they had reconsidered their position and, as a result, they had decided the Bricklayers Department could after all keep its day rota – we would continue to work as we had done before the meeting was called. For which change of heart we thanked them very much and left the office.

Over the next fortnight the ordinary shop floor members of the Allied Trades Unions were constantly stopping our men to ask them if they still retained their day rota. 'Of course,' our men replied.

Then the penny dropped amongst them – they realised they'd been sold by their own shop stewards. They turned upon them wrathfully – particularly the convenor, whose incredible response to this was to lead a deputation of his shop stewards to plead with the Labour Officer to implement the promise he'd given to them to end the Bricklayers day rota agreement as he had done their own. To which the Labour Officer calmly replied they'd made their deal and the bricklayers had made theirs and that was that, the matter was ended – but it wasn't!

The Allied Trades ordinary members took the business out of

the hands of their shop stewards and into their own – they staged go slows and flatly refused to work any extra time whatsoever, no matter what the emergency.

About three weeks after the meeting with the Bricklayers, the company restored the day rotas right across the works and I and my father, when we learned of the part the Allied Trades shop stewards had played in the negotiations, roasted them as never before had they been roasted, either by bosses or by their own rank and file members.

So ended the first major counter attack by the company upon our new found strength and confidence – but they weren't finished with us yet, as we were to discover.

19.

MANAGEMENT MUST MANAGE

CAME 1962 and with it the completion of the Redbourn Steel-works expansion programme. Early in that year, February – March time, the first steel was tapped from the new Rotor furnace.

We, the bricklayers, had won 'the battle of the Rotor' – though many times afterwards we were to wish we hadn't. But that was afterwards, right then we were cock-a-hoop, we seemed to be going from success to success.

The work of relining the vessels as they were retired from production each time had been given to us – much to the chagrin of the other unions who had also claimed the work. We had negotiated a reasonably satisfactory bonus agreement with the company to cover the relines but, more importantly, we also won an extra tonnage bonus for ourselves, paid on every ton of steel tapped out of the Rotor. This was in addition to our melting shop tonnage bonus paid on the production of the open hearth furnaces and which we'd feared would be drastically reduced with the coming of the Rotor – between them the two extra rotor bonuses made a fairly handsome addition to our pay packets, but we were to discover as time went by they were to be hardly earned.

It had been our fear that the Rotor furnace, embracing as it did all the latest techniques in steel making, would prove to be such a huge success that it would lead to the speedy demise of the open hearth furnaces, particularly if the company was to commission another one, and so to the decimation of our numbers in the Bricklayers' Department. Hence our earlier determination to grab the work of their relines and repairs for ourselves.

But we needn't have feared for the open hearth furnaces just then – the Rotor furnace turned out to be not all it had been cracked up to be and the new mill seemed to be able to cope with all the steel which was fed into it from both the Rotor furnace and the open hearths. One effect however of the Rotor furnace was to take some of the pressure off the open hearths – the need for *their* quick turn round wasn't quite so urgent as it had been and as the Rotor furnace's weaknesses had not been fully exposed at the time, this led the management into believing they could once again safely take a crack at the Bricklayers' Department. With the Rotor on their side they believed this time they'd win – and once again they bungled it badly.

We were surprised one day, my father and I, to receive a summons to attend a meeting at the Labour Office in order to discuss 'manning levels' in the Bricklayers' Department!   'Manning levels,' we thought, what about manning levels was there to talk about?   Unless it was the company's intention to set more men on so to abolish the need for overtime working completely. Although the amount of overtime worked had been much reduced since the old days, there was still plenty of it about. Many, if not most, men – especially amongst the labourers – still managed to average an extra shift per week – perhaps more.

Wonderingly we made our way up to the Labour Office. Our team was comprised of the same number of men it usually was and pretty much the same faces too – myself, my father and a deputy each. These deputies sometimes changed but all of them nowadays were pretty experienced in Labour Office negotiations.

The management team was also unchanged. It consisted of the Labour Officer and his assistant, who took the notes and kept the records of each meeting for their side, but who appeared to us to take so few notes and yet to have such a marvellous recollection of who had said what at each meeting that we strongly suspected him of having a tape-recorder concealed under the desk. Indeed, we sometimes invited him to 'unconceal' it and place it squarely on the desk so we could all see it. At such times he would force a sickly grin and try to pass the matter off as a joke. Not that we were bothered about it – or whatever else he may have had concealed under the desk. Also included in the management team were the Melting Shop Manager and of course, as always, our own Departmental Manager.

Our Departmental Manager had greatly mollified his attitude of open hostility to me of the early days of my shop stewardship. In the three years since I'd taken that trades union office in his department he'd witnessed many changes come to it – mostly as a consequence of my activities. Basically he believed in the old adage 'happy cows give more milk' and certainly since the overtime had been controlled – albeit not by himself – and a day rota introduced into the department and its bonus agreements had been increased and updated too, he nowadays presided over a department which was a much happier place to work in. Furthermore, our winning of the Rotor furnace work had greatly increased his responsibilities and thus the importance of his own position – and no doubt this was reflected in *his* pay packet also.

He'd also discovered in the passage of time I wasn't after all quite the communist ogre he'd imagined me to be – that I too could be generous and forgiving and show a willingness to compromise on occasions – and in any case our battles nowadays weren't so much with him as with the Labour Office.

I think maybe he secretly enjoyed seeing it get egg over its face – as it did from time to time. There was still a little of the old working class bricklayer blood in his veins. Whatever the reasons he was much more friendly towards me than he had been once.

Although ostensibly the meeting had been convened in order to discuss manning levels in the Bricklayers' Department, we quickly discovered that wasn't the case at all. The business had already been well and truly discussed by the management and we had been called there to hear their decision.

Accordingly we were informed that the gang was to be reduced in numbers – of course they gave us all the usual preliminary blah-blah as to why this had to be so – none of it very convincing – and to say that we were surprised by their decision would be an understatement. We were deeply shocked by it.

In vain did we argue that far from decreasing the workload of the Bricklayers' Department, the addition of the Rotor furnace to the steel making capacity of the Redbourn steelworks had increased it, even though the company wasn't as heavily dependent

226.

upon the speedy completion of the open hearth furnace repairs as it had formerly been, there were now less men to complete the repairs as a sizeable proportion of their numbers on each shift had to be diverted onto the Rotor furnace.

Additionally, we argued, the amount of ancilliary work associated with the increased steel production – such as the lining of steel ladles and the repair of the soaking pits etc. had also greatly increased – all of it true but equally all in vain – the company had made up its mind, there was no going back on its decision. We were talking to stone sphinxes.

We had stated our case for the defence and we let it go at that. At least when the full consequences of its action was brought home to the company it wouldn't be able to claim it had not been warned of them in advance.

About eight bricklayers and a dozen mates were to be made 'redundant' – or rather their jobs were. This was the first time I'd heard that word used to denote sackings.

Some of our members wanted immediate strike action to prevent the sackings, but they were only a small minority and in any case I was convinced, if our own case for the defence was to be believed, it wouldn't be necessary. A simple embargo on overtime working should be enough to convince the management of the error of its ways. It might take longer but I was convinced it would be no less effective and without causing nearly as much loss to ourselves and to other workers on the plant.

Before it was decided just who amongst the men would have to go – and we on the union side were determined that if it was to be, then it was going to be decided on a 'last in, first out' basis – the Departmental Second-in-command let it be known he was already working on the list of those who were to be sacked. Everybody knew just what that meant – it meant the list would be composed of those he personally disliked the most – and there was the rub, nobody could be sure of just who they might be, he appeared to 'most dislike' almost everybody – which business caused a great deal of unease in the department and added considerably to the number of those determined on some action – either by striking or by placing an embargo on overtime working to prevent the sackings or, if they did occur, then to get them reversed.

Despite the threat of the overtime ban, the management went ahead with the sackings, on a 'last in, first out' basis, as insisted upon by us, the union side – which was very much to the disappointment of the second-in-command who had been told quite plainly where to stick his own list of names and who, according to several of our men in whom he'd confided, was rapidly coming to believe he counted for nothing in the department. None of the men contradicted him and all wisely kept their own opinion to themselves.

The men were sacked, we imposed the ban and the battle commenced. To begin with it was pretty much like the 'phoney war' of 1939 – nothing happened, nothing at all. The weeks went by and still nothing happened – but all that time the open hearth furnaces were slowly burning away. Every day, every week the linings and the roofs were getting thinner and thinner and the repair schedules were falling further and further behind. I saw this – the management saw it too.

But during the same time a certain section of our men were getting restless and their numbers were growing as the weeks came and went and still nothing happened. Murmurs of discontent began to arise amongst them, they wanted their overtime back. The management saw this – I saw it too.

After about seven weeks had gone by with seemingly nothing happening, one of the four shifts broke completely – it presented me with a petition signed by almost all the men on that particular shift. The petition requested me to convene a special meeting of all the Redbourn bricklayers in order to discuss the lifting of the overtime embargo.

I wasn't all that surprised by the petition. I knew my members well – and the members on this particular shift very well. They were the heart of all the opposition to myself within the department. Even so, it was their right, so accordingly I convened the meeting.

On any controversial issue within the department, and there were many, I could always rely on the 100% support of two of the four shifts, a two to one majority on a third, but on the shift which had presented the petition it was almost always a solid 100% against me. I also had a fairly large majority support amongst the day workers of the department. That was the usual pattern and the basis of my influence in the department.

Another factor which emerged from a study of my support in the gang was this – it was also comprised very greatly of all the war-time ex-servicemen in the gang. Fifteen years after the war had finished, echoes of old war-time comradeships were still sounding in the Bricklayers' Department of the Redbourn steelworks of Scunthorpe. It was a factor perhaps never appreciated by the management who, because of their profession, had mostly never served in the war-time forces.

It was a week later when the meeting took place. I'd been in no hurry to convene it for now the overtime ban was beginning to bite, to really have its effect upon the furnaces – every day counted in our favour.

Several of the open hearths were in a very precarious state of repair and the undermanning in the department was now exposed for all to see – even the most arrogant of 'the management must manage' types and the remotest of Labour Officers would surely be able to see that.

At the meeting the shift which had handed me the petition was easily defeated. The men overwhelmingly reaffirmed their support for the continuation of the embargo. However, they, the defeated shift and what one or two allies they'd managed to recruit from the others, were somewhat mollified when it was pointed out to them that we weren't so much banning the overtime as banking it – when the fight was won and the embargo lifted, there would be overtime for all and for a long time to come. That much was guaranteed by the dreadful and rapidly worsening state of repair into which the open hearth furnaces had been allowed to fall by a bloody-minded management.

The management had fired its last shot. Though its signature had not appeared amongst the others on the petition sheet, its grubby fingerprints were all over the document.

The day after the meeting at which we'd reaffirmed our support of the embargo – another furnace roof had collapsed during the night – I was requested – in the usual way, by the departmental office-cum-errand boy – to attend a meeting, *not* in the departmental office, *not* in the Labour Office, but in the office of the great man himself – the Works General Manager. This was a truly startling turn of events. I wondered just what it meant. I feared I was going to be roasted alive by him – certainly it wouldn't be for the purpose of pinning any medals on my chest for my services to industry that year, that was for sure.

I picked up a deputy, himself an ex-sailor and submariner of the war years and as tough and outspoken a character as you would meet anywhere. I was glad it was he, I felt the need of strong support. Then the two of us made our way to the General Manager's office.

Apart from the fact that it was somewhere in the main office block neither he nor I knew exactly where to find it, despite the fact we'd both worked at Redbourn for some fourteen years. Such lowly and uncultivated forms of steelworks life as we were kept well away from such holy places.

We found the office and were met by the Manager's secretary who showed us almost immediately into his office – office? It was more like a hall. The walls were wood panelled and hung with huge framed paintings and pictures – including one of the Rotor furnace. The carpet was of the very best – Persian or something – walking on it was like walking on soft springs. The furniture – most of it appeared to be of mahogany – was the very best and included an enormous desk or table in the centre of the room, before which were placed two or three enormous easy chairs.

Behind the desk or table or whatever it was supposed to be sat – not the General Manager but the Assistant General Manager. His manner in contrast to our own was relaxed and easy, his greeting warm and friendly. The secretary departed and closed the door behind her, leaving just the three of us in the room. Our mates, the labourers, had not been invited to attend the meeting – or rather 'talk' which is different.

We were invited to sit down and I sank into one of the enormous easy chairs. My deputy disappeared into the other. I don't know how he felt but I never felt more out of place in my life, as if I was trespassing in the Dalai Lama's temple in Tibet or something.

The Assistant General Manager then asked us if we would take tea and biscuits – we said yes. His politeness was killing me, I was on tenterhooks waiting for the bomb to go off. While we waited for the tea to appear he chatted and we sat dumb – he explained that the General Manager was away that day – on business somewhere – and that he was standing in for him.

The tea appeared – served by a proper maid in a little maid's hat and apron – and still he chatted away about nothing in particular. The maid went, closing the door behind her and I was just reaching for a biscuit when he dropped the bomb. I was glad afterwards that I hadn't got the biscuit into my mouth.

He never changed the tone of his voice. He just simply announced, 'we're throwing in the sponge, Charlie. If we give you your men back will you give us the overtime we need?'

I thought I hadn't heard right. I just gaped at him stupidly. I'd been so keyed up expecting another fight it took several moments for his message to sink in – he was still smiling at me.

Then I recovered my senses. 'Of course we will,' I replied, 'if our men are returned to us then the reason for the overtime ban no longer exists.'

He reached out his hand and I took it and shook it. There was no necessity to sign any papers – I knew he'd keep his word and he knew I would. I liked that man.

There was no big bell of Moscow to ring in the department to celebrate the retreat of our Napoleon but the mood in the gang was none the less joyous for all that. I got the overtime restored immediately and to prove our goodwill we allowed one of the shift-workers two days off per week to be included in the o v e r t i m e rotas, so as to get the furnaces back into good repair as quickly as possible.

The end of that fight marked the beginning of a new era at Redbourn. Somebody high up – and it could only have been the General or Works Manager – decided enough was enough and then proceeded office by office, department by department, to give the whole of the industrial relations machinery at Redbourn a thorough shake out.

Joint Production Committees and Safety Committees were introduced into every department on the works. Each of these committees was chaired by the Departmental Managers or, in their absence, by the Assistant Managers. The men's side was represented by the shop stewards and their deputies. The committees met once each month and the records of each meeting were kept by a clerk who also attended the meetings. These, plus spare copies for the notice boards were afterwards circulated amongst the members of the committees in printed form.

Any matter which could not be agreed or for any reason decided upon at departmental level was referred to the Works General Council or, in the matter of safety, to the Works Safety Council. Both these bodies were chaired by the Works General Manager.

The committees provided a much needed safety valve in the departments – or at least in those departments which had steam to let off, not all had. As a result industrial relations on the works improved enormously.

20.

A MIGHTY WORKING CLASS WARRIOR

I DON'T REMEMBER NOW just when or where it was that I first heard used the term 'Workers' Participation in Management' – it may very well have been at one of the monthly meetings of The Redbourn Delegates Committee itself. However, I do remember it was a term which came to be bandied around with ever increasing frequency, especially by the younger members of that body, at our monthly meetings during the run-up to the second nationalization of the steel industry in 1967.

The Redbourn Works' Delegates Committee was a works based body comprised of all the trades union representatives at the Redbourn Steelworks. It met regularly on the first Friday of each month. The trades unions were not represented equally on it but the numerous departments on the works were – the unions whose membership spanned the most departments had the most members on the committee, one from each department however large or small the departments. My own union, for instance, whose members were all confined to a single department – The Bricklayers – had only one representative on the committee, myself. Not that it mattered – the Redbourn Works' Delegates Committee itself had no negotiating rights as such, it functioned purely as a works welfare body.

Its business was almost always of the most trivial nature and its meetings almost always utterly boring, valued more for the two or three hours you were released from work to attend them than for anything which might be accomplished at them. It's pretty fair to say that its deliberations counted for nothing with nobody – indeed, a fair proportion of the Redbourn workforce itself was unaware that it even existed.

To have been an observer at one of our meetings – which occasionally there was – and to have cast your eyes over our stolid, pasty, peasant faces and listened to our broad, mainly north Lincolnshire accents as we ploughed our way laboriously through the business of the meeting – which even all the 'By Godding' and 'By Crikeying' of Jimmy our chairman, wearing his fiercest expression and thumping the table fit to break it could do nothing to de-trivialise – would have been to depart it again with the firm conviction that here was as uninspiring and moribund a body of trades union representatives as might be found in any industry in any part of the country.

A fierce and mighty working class warrior was Jimmy our chairman – all five feet one inch of him. Possessed of an extremely large head, a barrel chest and a deep booming voice, he would have been perhaps inches taller had the bow been taken out of his legs. To see Jimmy draw himself up to his full height, stick his jaw out aggressively and attempt to stand eyeball to eyeball with an opponent, be he manager or trade unionist, was a sight to behold and never to be forgotten. It was claimed by the members of his own department that Jimmy beat the bosses by his 'sheer, bloody ignorance' and I could imagine it was so – Jimmy was afraid of no man.

When this odd business of 'Workers' Participation in Management' began to intrude itself into the business of his committee a little too often for Jimmy's liking – he made his own views on the subject plain – he wanted no part of it. He was firmly convinced that it was but a cunning management ploy to get the workers to pull their chestnuts out of the fire for them. 'Let 'em stew in their own effin' juice!' was his response to it – but a number of us weren't so sure. With the full nationalization of our industry coming up we wanted to take a closer look at the subject – there might be something in it for us, the ordinary steelworker.

In the end, to get the subject off the agenda list, even for one meeting, and to get back to the more relevant business of 'Them Pakis who had been shitting on the lavatory seats agen,' Jimmy agreed to the setting up of a sub-committee to study the subject and report back to the full committee at an unspecified later date – and thereby hangs a tale for it opened up a new chapter in the history of The Redbourn Works' Delegates Committee which was

234.

to introduce its name into half the homes in the land, make it famous throughout the Midlands and send shivers of apprehension up and down the spines of steel bosses everywhere – even in faraway London – whenever its name was mentioned. It may all be forgotten now but The Redbourn Works' Delegates Committee too had its moment of glory.

Within a couple of months of being given our brief, we – for I too had been elected on to the sub-committee – had produced a plan and drawn up a paper entitled 'Industrial Democracy in the Nationalised Steel Industry', in which we visualised the take-over of the industry, not by the politicians, not by Whiehall bureaucrats, not by trades unions, but by the democratic process itself, which for the first time would guarantee the right of the ordinary steelworker, both as an employee within the industry and as a citizen of a great country which prided itself on its democratic traditions, the right to have his say also in the affairs of his industry.

Our sub-committee of four had looked at other plans and ideas, both ancient and modern, all concerned with that seemingly never to be realised dream of generations of working men for a greater say in and control over the economic forces which govern their lives. We looked at Robert Owen's experiments in his Lanarkshire mills, at the ambitions of the Victorian Syndicalists and, more recently, at the German method of including worker representatives on the governing boards of companies – and also at a plan for steel which originated in Sheffield – all of which, though each had something to offer, we rejected as being too dated, too limited or too bureaucratic.

We were looking for a democratic system of industrial control which was simple to understand and simple to operate – primarily because we ourselves were simple types and also because we knew our steelworker, who, like us, was apt to regard complicated matters as being deliberately designed that way so as to confuse him – as many a bonus scheme and piecework agreement was.

In the end we produced a plan of our own. It was simplicity itself – we based it upon bodies which already existed in the industry and whose workings were already well known to and understood by the ordinary steelworkers: the Works Councils and Departmental Committees themselves. We but made them more representative of the works labour force as a whole. On to those bodies for the higher levels of control and direction we tacked Regional Boards – all under the overall direction of a National Board. In order to ensure the professionalism of the bodies at all levels, as well as their accountability, we suggested that each be comprised of appointed members from the top downwards – beginning with Parliament itself and elected members from the bottom upwards – beginning with the shop-floor.

I wouldn't say that our plan was perfect or that it wouldn't have needed some modification or indeed that it would have been practical to have introduced it into the industry in one fell swoop – but I do say it deserved a much better consideration than it got – in a true democracy it would have been given a much fairer hearing.

The plan was employee orientated and not trades union – it left them exactly where they were before and that they didn't like. Consequently we made enemies of the trades union establishments inside and outside the industry. In one breath they argued that the plan's implementation would only enmesh the workers deeper in the capitalist clutch and in the next, drawing upon capitalist propaganda themselves, they argued that it was 'communist' inspired, simply a 'Red Plot' to sabotage relations in the industry.

The bosses, for different reasons, were also against it – they would be, wouldn't they.

But if we made enemies, we also made friends and one such friend was The Institute of Workers' Control which had its centre in Nottingham.

We at Redbourn didn't particularly like the concept of 'workers' control' any more than we had that of 'workers' participation'. Neither summed up our aim as accurately as did the expression 'Industrial Democracy'. We were no more looking for dominance than we were for only a slightly eased subservience in the industry – we aimed at equality, in the political sense of the word, not the social, which counts for nothing. Our aim was a one side of industry, one vote, sort of understanding.

The Insitute of Workers' Control was a much more experienced body than was our own little works committee, it had branches and connections in other parts of the country besides Nottingham and it was also much more skilled in the arts of communication. We were very glad to have its help in making our own views known to the industrial world outside Redbourn – it was to be greatly more successful in this than we'd imagined it would be.

One day in 1969 the Granada Television Company sent its 'World in Action' team to Redbourn in order to find out and film just what was going on there besides the production of steel. However, the management wouldn't allow the television team onto the works in order to film people like myself, who were involved in the Industrial Democracy campaign, at work in their everyday surroundings.

The Granada bosses then threatened to raise the matter of their access onto the works with Parliament itself as the industry was itself publicly owned, and in the event the management gave way, they let the television crew onto the works on the understanding that it would film the opponents of Industrial Democracy on the works equally with the proponents – and we, the proponents, being the true democrats which we were, raised no objections to the deal. And so the interviewing and the filming at last got under way.

It was impossible, because of the conditions inside the Rotor vessels, to film the wrecking process and the only open-hearth furnace out of production was already wrecked, so no wrecking shots of any kind were obtained for the film – the subsequent film gave only a very cursory view of the works. We and our opponents had a rousing debate before the cameras in the Labour Officer's Office – which seemed to me, watching it afterwards on the telly, to generate more heat than light.

After three days and having used up what appeared to me to be several miles of film and also of sound recording tape, the TV camera crew departed – to condense into a half an hour's recording the work of three days.

In the end the only result achieved by our campaign for Industrial Democracy was the appointment of four Worker Directors to the National Board of the BSC – which should and could have been a tremendous step in the right direction had the four been of the right calibre. They were but management and trades union establishment 'Yes' men, recommended for the appointments by their trades union bosses and comfirmed in office at grossly inflated salaries by the BSC – safe men all and, to the best of my knowledge, not one of whom had ever lifted as much as a finger for the cause of industrial democracy.

It was amazing too, how many of our opponents in the town underwent a sudden conversion to the ideals of industrial democracy when they beheld the appointments, made against all their expectations, and the salaries and the perks which accompanied them. Suddenly everybody who was anybody in the town's trade union hierarchy was an industrial democrat – but their enthusiasm didn't last long. When it became obvious to them that they'd missed the bus and that the BSC had no intention of appointing any more 'workers' to its governing board, their enthusiasm for the cause very quickly waned.

Following 'nationalization', there appeared on the industrial horizon yet another long, six-syllabled monstrosity of a word, which by the early seventies had climbed into such great prominence that its enormous shadow hung blackly over the works like the evil portent of a greater evil to come – that word was 'rationalization'.

Rationalization was the 'in' word of the late 1960s and early 1970s in Scunthorpe. It slid easily, smoothly and knowledgeably off the tongues of bosses, bureaucrats and trendy trades union officials anxious to prove their moderation – one of them so anxious indeed that he went so far as to suggest to the BSC that it site its new steelworks, which it was rumoured was to be built at Scunthorpe, at Immingham thirty miles away instead, where he didn't have a single member.

238.

When the BSC did eventually make public its plans for the rationalisation of iron and steel production in the Scunthorpe area it appeared that the fears which had been expressed in the town concerning its future as a steel making centre had largely been laid to rest.

The Anchor Project which, when completed, would give Scunthorpe one of the largest integrated steel making plants in Europe, had been given the go ahead at an estimated cost to the Steel Corporation of £150 000 000. There would, of course, as everybody had known there would be corresponding shut-downs of older plant in the town. Included in the closures were the melting shops and mills of the Appleby-Frodingham and the Redbourn steelworks, as well as much other plant. The town's third largest producer of steel, the Normanby Park steelworks, was unaffected – it was to go on producing and working exactly as before. Its workers therefore could quite safely go back to sleep – which they did!

The job losses due to the closure of the older plant would be largely offset by the job gains at the new Anchor steelworks. Many people took this to mean there would be scarcely any redundancies at all in the town and in the euphoria which accompanied the Steel Corporation's announcement of its intention to site the new steelworks at Scunthorpe after all, the real extent of the gap between the job losses and the job gains was at first largely overlooked – but not by SLAG – the Scunthorpe Left Action Group.

The Scunthorpe Left Action Group – which wasn't really a too clever title to give it – was a loosely organised body of rank and file steelworks trades unionists in the town, many of whom had been involved in our campaign for industrial democracy. They came from every trade union in steel and shared a common dissatisfaction with the trades union set up in their industry generally, and its ability to represent the higher aspirations of us shop floor workers generally, and especially now that the industry was publicly owned. We – for of course I too had become prominent in its debates – wanted a much more representative trades union set up in the industry, one which would not only be able to speak for the steelworkers as a whole but one also which would be much more responsive to their wishes.

There were eleven recognised trades unions in steel split into five separate negotiating bodies – and each union and each negotiating body was fiercely independent and jealous of the others and determined not only to protect its own area of power and influence but where possible to extend it, at whoever's expense.

The trades union organisation in steel was firstly and foremostly an organisation of full-time officials and their works based mouthpieces in the localities, more anxious to preserve their own little gold fish bowl areas of power and influence than they were to sink their differences and forego their little perks in the interest of the ordinary steelworkers they claimed to represent. The BSC was always able to play them off one against the other with ease.

When the BSC revealed its plans for the rationalization of production in the Scunthorpe area, SLAG subjected them to a pretty close scrutiny.

It seemed to us that the job losses to the town due to the closure of the older plant at the Appleby-Frodingham and the Redbourn steelworks would exceed the job gains at the new Anchor works by some 3 000, and though we were in no position to contradict the declared intention of the BSC to keep the Normanby Park Steelworks in full production, it also occurred to us that this could possibly be but a management ploy to keep a large section of the total Scunthorpe labour force quiet until the first phase of its plans for the area had been completed. How, we asked ourselves, could such an old type steelworks with its obsolete open hearth furnaces and its single one hundred ton converter hope for very long to stay alive in the shadow of such a modern colossus as the new Anchor steelworks with its three giant three-hundred ton converters?

Our findings concerning the job losses and our suspicions concerning the Normanby Park Works filled us with a deep disquiet which, when we looked at our trades union organisation in the industry, all but became dismay. We were only too well aware of our own 'unofficial' standing locally and of the intense hostility shown to us by the local trades union establishment – some of whose more prominent members would gladly have given a week of their own phoney worktime for the opportunity to inflict some lasting damage upon us and perhaps also win for themselves an extra approving pat on the head from a top works or trades union boss.

But if our numbers were weak, our hearts were strong! We set to to devise a response to the challenge facing us. The only possible course of action for the trades unions, it seemed to us, was to fight fire with fire, to meet rationalization with rationalization – the rationalization of the steel industry with the rationalization of the trade union organisation in the steel industry also. In place of the five separate negotiating bodies we suggested one. We also suggested that in the event of the BSC refusing to recognise such a body – which of course they would, and who could blame them? – then there would be nothing to prevent the trades unions setting up their own co-ordinating committee in the localities, in the regions and at national level.

Knowing also just how reactionary and bureaucratic the trades union set up in steel had become and the kind of reception it would almost certainly give to our proposals, we addressed our campaign to the ordinary rank and file trades unionist – as we saw him, the 'fall guy' of an equally bureaucratic BSC and trades union organisation within the industry. We also proposed, in the all too probable event of the outright rejection of our suggestions by our trades union bosses, that the Scunthorpe members should be prepared to set an example to the rest of the industry by going it alone. It could have been done – it should have been done!

Our plan, which we christened 'Plan for the Rationalisation of the Trades Union Structure in Steel', we published in the name of The Redbourn Works' Delegates Committee – which body did enjoy at least a semi-official position in the local trade union movement. Several of its members were also very active members of SLAG.

Having tackled the problem of trade union reform, we next

tackled the problem of devising a correct response to the loss of jobs posed by the shut-downs at Appleby-Frodingham and at Redbourn. To this end we produced what came to be called by the local press when it was published, 'A Charter for Steelworkers'. In our 'Charter' we called for a reduction of hours in the working week from the present forty to thirty-two hours, retirement at sixty years of age on adequate pensions for all steelworkers, and redundancies on a voluntary basis only.

Predictably, the reaction of our trades union 'leaders' to our proposals was one of immediate hostility. Even so, even we SLAG members were scarcely prepared for the new low level of absurdity and virulence they evoked in certain quarters of the local trade union establishment. Amongst their more pathetic utterances were these gems: 'They (our proposals) would give to the workers too much leisure time which they wouldn't know how to use.'; 'They would lead to an increase in the crime rate.'; 'They would lead to an increase in the divorce rate.'; 'We couldn't economically afford them.' – just who the 'we' meant in this last wasn't made clear.

With trades union representatives like that on your side of the negotiating table you didn't need bosses on the other!

For such clown-like leadership the Scunthorpe steelworkers were eventually to pay the price.

Let the reader understand this. SLAG was never against the rationalisation of the steel industry, no more than it was against its nationalisation. But it was against both seen as mere exercises in state capitalist management to the total exclusion of any say in them by the ordinary steelworkers. Democracy, like negotiation, is about debate and compromise – all SLAG ever asked on behalf of the steelworkers was the fair hearing and the respect due to them which their trades unions in the industry were of themselves unable to command. If that's so wrong, then what did we fight two world wars for?

242.

21.

IN 1973 THE COMMISSIONING of the new Anchor steelworks and the phasing out of production at the old plant at Appleby-Frodingham and at Redbourn commenced. The switch-over, which involved the transfer and redistribution of several thousands of men, was, with but a few minor hiccups, accomplished skilfully and smoothly by the BSC management. One of these minor hiccups occurred at Redbourn – and where else but in the Bricklayers Department? It was to be our last dying kick before we ourselves became completely submerged in the morass of BSC bureaucracy and trades union acquiescence which accompanied the first rationalisation of steel production in Scunthorpe.

The pay structures at the Appleby-Frodingham works and at the Redbourn works were different – in many instances not greatly so but in a few very much so. These differences needed to be resolved before a common pay structure could be agreed upon which then would apply to the Anchor works.

The difference between the pay structure of the Redbourn bricklayers and the Appleby-Frodingham bricklayers was very great. At Redbourn we operated a collective system of bonus earnings and payments. All our incentive bonus payments, wherever earned on the works, were pooled and shared equally amongst all the men.

At the Appleby-Frodingham Works they operated a piecework system based more upon the individual – every one there more or less worked for himself. In addition, the fastest pieceworkers were selected by the foremen to form an inner piecework gang which was known as the 'Big Eight'. This inner gang was then favoured with the best paying piecework jobs. The idea was to tear your arse out so to become selected for a place in the 'Big Eight' – or if you were already one of the 'Big Eight', then to tear your arse out to avoid being ousted! It was always a source of amazement to us Redbourn bricklayers that any gang of trades unionists anywhere could have fallen for such an old, old trick.

With the fusing of the two works gangs of bricklayers in the offing at the Anchor Works it became imperative to reconcile the differences in work practices and in payments between the two.

It seemed to the new, Appleby-Frodingham dominated management of Anchor there was no real problem, the Redbourn bricklayers would just have to accept the Appleby-Frodingham methods of work and payment – though of course they didn't say this outright. The Labour Officer played his part in the plan admirably, but the Redbourn bricklayers did no such thing. They flatly refused to even consider such a change, no way would they have the Appleby-Frodingham systems of work and payments.

After several meetings like this, wheedling, tearing his hair and thumping the table, the Labour Officer finally informed us we'd no choice – whether we agreed to it or not, whether we liked it or not – the Appleby-Frodingham system of bonus earnings would apply to the Redbourn bricklayers also, commencing at once, long before we even got to Anchor.

The management had calculated that at a time of such uncertainty about the future, when people were afraid for their jobs as never before, they'd get away with the issuing of such an ultimatum. They miscalculated – we withdrew our labour.

I hadn't much confidence we could win our dispute, not in the long run anyway – we'd too many enemies and our brother bricklayers at Appleby-Frodingham could hardly be expected to support us, it was after all their system of work and payment we were striking against – they'd never liked the ridicule we'd heaped upon it – and BISAKTA, the largest union in the steel industry, with ambitions to be its only one, would, we knew, use the opportunity to do us mischief and, as they organised our mates in the Department, they were in a position to do just that. Which they promptly did – they instructed the brickies' mates to stay at work and carry on as normally as possible.

It's to the credit of most of our mates that they refused to service the blackleg labour recruited by the management to replace the bricklayers – but there were still those who did, which sickened me. As I saw it they stood to lose equally with us if the management gained the day.

After little more than a week on strike we agreed jointly with the management to the setting up of a 'Neutral Committee' comprised of two 'neutral' management representatives from other areas and two 'neutral' trades union representatives also from other areas. Both we, the bricklayers, and the Redbourn management agreed in advance to be bound by its findings and its recommendations to resolve the dispute. It seemed to me to be the best deal we could hope to get – time and BISAKTA were both against us and nothing and nobody was for us.

The Neutral Committee's recommendations for the settling of the dispute were: (1) the management should drop its ultimatum to the bricklayers; (2) in return the bricklayers should be prepared to give the Appleby-Frodingham system on bonus earnings a month's trial; (3) 'Big Eights' were out; (4) minimum earnings for the period of the month's trial would be guaranteed not to fall below those of the previous month under the old system of bonus payments; and (5) at the end of the month's trial the two sides should meet again to iron out their remaining differences.

On the basis of those recommendations – accepted both by the Redbourn management and ourselves – we returned to work.

For the month's trial all our members were instructed to work normally – neither to slow-time nor to fast-time, so to affect the results of the experiment. What we found at the end of the month confirmed our suspicions – our own Redbourn system of bonus payment was worth more to us by some £6 per man per forty hour week than was the Appleby-Frodingham system for the same amount of work – which gave us plenty of ammunition with which to return to the Labour Office.

As the day drew nearer and ever nearer when we would see the end of the Redbourn Steelworks as I'd known them over the last twenty eight years and the break up and transfer of our men to the new Anchor works, I decided I wanted no part of it. I volunteered to take the redundancy.

I was fifty two years of age – still thirteen years away from official retirement – and unless I chose to do something about it I was faced with another thirteen years of the muck and the dust, the noise and the heat of the steelworks. This seemed to be my chance to make the break – my girls had grown up and married, my boy was at university, the only dependent I had was Jean, my leg, though not so strong as the other, had not let me down for years past and out there away from the steelworks were green fields with wide blue skies above and lots and lots of clean fresh air to breathe between the two. That's what I wanted, that's what I would have – twenty eight years in the steel industry was long enough. It was a decision which Jean not only supported but actively encouraged.

22.

A COUNTRY COTTAGE

AFTER TWENTY EIGHT LONG YEARS of the clang and the crash, the smoke and the dust and the heat and the stench of the steelworks, it was sheer joy each day upon my first awakening just to be able to stay right where I was and listen to the early morning traffic bearing the much less joyful clangers, crashers, smokers, dusters, heaters and stenchers themselves to work for the first shift of the day and to savour the delight of knowing that my own long stint on the works was over and that never again would I have to turn out on the cold winter mornings – or, even worse, on the bright summer mornings – to dance attendance upon the burnt out furnaces, soaking pits, ladles or whatever at Redbourn – I was free!

It seemed to me, as I turned over and drifted off to sleep again, that there was much to be said in favour of the drop-out way of life, the carefree existence of looking solely after number one. Even if I wasn't cut out to be one of life's yes-men, I didn't have to be so damned much of a no-man. I could, I would, from now on take a back seat – some other silly bugger ccould worry about the steelworks, the state of the nation, the cold war and all that crap!

Materially I'd never been better off. I'd collected close on £2500 severance pay, my children had grown up and flown the nest, we'd changed houses and because of the price difference between the two I'd been able to buy my present one outright. I still had my war pension and Jean also had a part-time job.

What with no rent to pay, no kids to provide for and money in the bank – more than we'd ever had before – I had truly never had it so good. The only problem now was 'what next?' and the answer came back, sublime in its simplicity, nothing next! I'd take a break, a long, long break – to hell with work, manual work anyway.

I decided to become a writer – I'd write a novel. There didn't seem to be so much to it – who knew? There might just be a Steinbeck or a Tolstoy in me trying to get out, though I doubted it. In any case, I'd no intention of aiming that high – not to begin with at least. I'd read a lot of slush in my time and it seemed that all you wanted was a beautiful heroine and a passably good-looking hero and you were in business.

I needed to brush up on my sex and violence – I bought a few books to get the feel of things, *The Confessions of a Window Cleaner; Who Was Jack The Ripper?; The Brides in the Bath Murders; The Perfumed Garden; The Kamasutra* and several other such steelworker classics – which reading matter caused Jean some alarm, especially when it got me going.

For about three months I slogged away hard at it, everything else was pushed to one side. During which time friends and acquaintances of ours were constantly stopping Jean in the street to inquire, with worried looks on their faces, after my health, rumour had it I'd gone queer – not 'gay' queer, just ordinary queer. They'd heard I scarcely ever left the house but spent all my time writing and was it true? Yes, it bloody well was true! And I didn't care who knew it – the pitying looks would soon disappear from their faces when my book was published.

At the end of the three months I got a university-educated acquaintance of mine to read the completed work and criticise it for me. When, a month after that, I finally managed to force out of him his full and truthful opinion of my work, I knew he told me the truth – I'd written a load of shit! So ended my career as a novelist – which really all along I'd known wasn't for me.

I decided next to return to work, proper work, in the building trade and the prospect pleased me. The summer was coming and I'd had no problems either with my back or my leg for donkeys years. True, I still wore a caliper and had a pronounced limp but other people were always more aware of that than I was. There would, of course, be the slight problem of re-adjusting myself to the trade – after all, a whole generation and a toddler into the next had gone by since I'd last worked in it, during which time there had been changes in materials and practices which I should have to acquaint myself with and to master – but all in all I anticipated no great problems.

I needn't have worried. Nobody wanted me. They said I was too old or I wasn't fit or this or that – anything to avoid giving me a start. I knew they weren't being completely honest. Scunthorpe was a small provincial town and its building trade community were all well known to each other, by name if not always by sight – my notoriety had gone before me. In the best of times there had been little love lost between the completely trades union organised bricklayers on the steelworks and the almost completely non-unionised bricklayers in the building trade proper outside the works. I'd come up against a pretty solid wall of prejudice and dislike – and in the eyes of the local building trade bosses I was especially tainted – I could tell that from the expressions on their faces and the tone of voice in which they asked, 'Haven't I seen you somewhere before?' or 'Haven't I heard your name mentioned somewhere before?' Of course they had! Goodness knows, both had received enough publicity on the telly and in the local press and in other ways – they were just checking to make sure they'd got the right man before putting the boot in, and they couldn't even do that honestly.

In my boyhood apprentice days in the building industry before the war I'd often watched 'tramp bricklayers' come on to the sites in search of work. These characters travelled the country, mostly on bicycles, and mostly alone, with no more tools than a trowel and a brick hammer stuck in their belts, a pair of line-pins and a two-foot wooden rule in their jacket pockets and a wooden plumb rule strapped to the crossbar of the bike. If they obtained work, be it only for a couple of days or a couple of weeks, they slept 'rough' on the site, usually in the site cabin.

They were all – almost without exception – excellent tradesmen and good workers – and completely trustworthy – it was part of their 'code of the road' to leave every job 'clean', so as not to prejudice the job prospects of the next tramp brickie who came along to the site – or indeed their own at some future time. Most building bosses were well aware of their worth and, providing their work load justified it, they didn't hesitate to hire them. In this way too, they got a nightwatchman on the site for free.

As a boy I'd always been fascinated by these characters and I'd loved to listen to their tales of the road and, of course, for their part they'd especially cultivated the friendship of the boys on the sites – they could borrow the tools from them they lacked themselves and they could also be used to run their errands – to fetch their fish and chips, baccy, bread and other groceries and in return they taught us many a new trick of the trade. I was nearly always sorry when the time came for them to leave the site and move on to the next town or wherever.

It occurred to me that if I was really serious about returning to the building trade I would either have to become self-employed and take up jobbing on my own or become a tramp-bricklayer myself. Like Mahomet, if the mountain wouldn't come to me, I would have to go to it. I resolved to go to it – I could also, if I wanted to, change my name to Mahomet – but I didn't think my plight, if plight it was, called for that, yet awhile anyway.

The first thing I did was to buy a small second-hand touring caravan to hitch behind the car – there was going to be no sleeping or travelling rough for me – draughty cabins and bumpy bikes were out. I had also talked Jean into accompanying me. She'd been doubtful about it but in the end she'd agreed on the condition that if she didn't like the life I'd bring her straight back – I'd agreed!

Late in May 1974 we locked up the house and left the keys with the neighbours who promised to keep an eye on it. I slung my tools in the back of the car and with Jean beside me, the caravan behind and the open road before us, we set off for 'anywhere'.

Other than the decision to head south, the job prospects apparently being better down there, we'd made no definite plans – I'd go where the work was or the fancy took me. The fancy took me first to Skegness, a mere sixty miles away. The weather was fine and for Jean's sake – she was still doubtful about the venture – I wanted to give it a holiday atmosphere. I myself was in no hurry to find work – our financial circumstances were still fairly comfortable.

After a few days at Skegness we decided to move on further south. On the way we passed by the aerodrome at Sutton Bridge where I'd been stationed during the war. The old concrete pill boxes were still there by the roadside gathering moss, their fields of fire now somewhat obscured by the growth of vegetation about them which had been allowed to spring up since those hectic days and nights of long ago when we'd manned them at the double, ready to repel the German invader. The memories came flooding back to me.

At King's Lynn, for no reason, we turned east and headed for Norwich. At Norwich we decided we wouldn't stay there after all but instead push on to the coast. We pulled into a campsite not very far from Yarmouth for the night and, pretty tired after our drive, we turned in early, so we didn't hear the news until the next morning. The Nypro factory at Flixborough, which was on the outskirts of Scunthorpe, had been blasted clean off the map by an almighty explosion which had also caused a great loss of life and done tremendous damage to property for miles around.

I couldn't get through to Scunthorpe on the telephone that day as all the lines to it were reserved for the emergency services, but I did the next day. I telephoned my brother and he told me that my house, which was about five miles away from the centre of the blast, was undamaged but that shop windows only a hundred yards from it had been broken by the force of the explosion. He himself had been working on a roof when the explosion occurred and the fright it gave him had very nearly caused him to fall off it. His first reaction to it had been that a nuclear war had started, so colossal had been the bang, and then, seeing the direction of the explosion, he'd thought the huge gasometer at the Normanby Park Steelworks, which was only a mile from Flixborough, had gone up. Twenty eight people died in that blast – all of them Nypro factory employees and one or two of whom I knew personally.

After staying a few days in the area we decided to move on.

Jean wanted to see Kent – The Garden of England. I didn't mind, we could also perhaps look in on our boy who was studying at the University of Kent at Canterbury.

On the way down we met a bloke in a cafe who recommended to us a little campsite he'd left that morning. As it seemed to be nicely situated about halfway between Margate and Ramsgate and to be no more than eighteen or twenty miles from Canterbury we decided to give it a try.

It was a nice little camp site too – clean and friendly and with its own little social club. As an added bonus there was another little clubhouse in the lane which ran behind the site – this one belonged to the villagers. We were welcomed as members in both clubs – personally I've always preferred clubs to pubs, if it's only for the concessions on the prices of the beers. I have never quite been able to understand how it is that the county which is so noted for the excellent quality of its hops also manages to brew the worst beer in the country! But no matter – as the man said, there is no bad beer, it's just that some beers are better than others.

After a couple of days spent looking around the area and liking what we saw, I decided it was high time I found myself a job. The obvious starting point for this was the Employment Office in Margate. Jean went along too, she said if there was anything going for her she might just take it.

There were no vacancies for bricklayers advertised that day in the Employment Office but there was a job going for a labourer/handyman at a large toy-making factory in the town and the same factory also wanted a kitchen assistant, which interested Jean. We decided to get ourselves along to the factory and scout the prospects on site. I was shown around the factory by the Labour Officer and his assistant showed Jean the canteen and the kitchen, which acts in themselved impressed us – no Labour Officer in my experience would have taken such trouble to interest a mere labourer and a possible kitchen assistant in the layout and work of their factory.

The factory employed about eight hundred women but only

forty or so men. The wages were low but the work conditions looked to be good and as we'd be together working exactly the same hours, we took the jobs.

My job was to fetch and carry for the women and girls on the assembly line and generally keep the work area clean and tidy – in between times I painted the storage racks. After steelworks conditions it scarcely seemed like work at all and the meals served in the canteen were of really good quality and cheap too.

Women in the mass have always made me nervous – you could never be sure just what it was they found to be so amusing as you passed by them. You knew their eyes were upon you! Their own work confined them to the one seat on the assembly line and was probably utterly boring so they welcomed any little diversion from its routine or any change in the immediate environment – even one of as little consequence as myself. I glanced down hastily – were my flies open? I had suffered that embarrassment before!

I discovered all the women were friendly but one or two I quickly realised were quite willing to be more than just friendly! One shapely young woman, less than half my age, particularly surprised me by her attention. She was always telling me how much she preferred 'older men' – I'm sure she did! As we stood in the queue at the meal breaks she would press herself up against me so tight that it brought me out in a nervous sweat and as often as she could she would seat herself beside me at the meal table. Nor do I think she was just flirting or trying to make a fool out of me – not that I would have needed any help in that respect – few middle-aged men would in similar circumstances – but Jean's eagle eye was forever upon me and also there were others in the queue. Working with women, I was discovering, was vastly different to working with men – not nearly so boring!

By the little clubhouse in the little lane behind the caravan site stood a little cottage beneath several tall trees. The cottage was empty and wanted a lot of repair work doing to it, but the more I looked at it the more I bcame convinced of its possibilities, I could restore it, I was sure. It was a lovely little spot, all day long the lane was filled with birdsong and cuckoos called constantly from the tall trees. Perhaps they – the cuckoos – were trying to tell me something. I am sure they were.

When I began to show too much of an interest in the cottage, Jean became thoroughly alarmed. She was nowhere near as much in love with her job in the factory kitchen as I was with mine on the factory floor, her work was undoubtedly much harder than mine was. She also greatly missed her friends and family back home, Particularly our grandchildren. In short, she was ready for going home – things hadn't for her turned out to be quite what she'd expected them to be. Certainly she'd never envisaged a permanent home here in Kent – Garden of England or not. That had never been a part of our understanding when we'd left Scunthorpe. But I hadn't known then that I was going to find a fairyland cottage in a fairyland world at the end of our journeying. I could have lived there quite happily – maybe not for ever after, but for very much longer than I did – it would be as near as I would ever get to owning a country cottage and a harem of my own. Such was the stuff one working man's dreams and sexual fantasies were made of – once upon a time!

Little more than three months after leaving it we arrived back in Scunthorpe and once more I was out of work.

Money in the bank doesn't last forever – as I was discovering. Once the rest of the world had discovered your secret, it has a million and one ways of clawing it out again and putting it back into its own pocket.

I'd no intention of repeating the humiliating experience of a few months earlier by canvassing the local building firms for a job. Instead, I inserted a little advert in the Situations Wanted column of the local paper. I advertised myself as a freelance bricklayer and general handyman – it brought me in a few small jobs – but come the winter I knew such work would dry up. What I needed was a full time regular job – but such jobs were rapidly disappearing from the market, those within my capabilities anyway. Our financial circumstances were still pretty comfortable, it was just that I wanted to keep them that way. By a mixture of alternate jobbing bricklaying work and signing on at the dole queue I got myself through reasonably comfortably to late February 1975 – when I had a stroke of luck. I found a job with the local Council in its Direct Labour Department. I was delighted with the opportunity to return to the building trade proper – but my delight was shortlived. I became teamed up with one of the most morose and curmudgeonly type characters I've ever met in my life. Working with him, it was said, was as uncomfortable as working with a nail up in your boot – and so it was! It wouldn't have mattered had I been in a larger gang, but every day I was faced with the prospect of sharing a line with him. After little more than a couple of months I'd had enough of him, I asked for my cards. I preferred to take my chances with the uncertainties of the jobbing world rather than put up with his surly manner any longer. No doubt he was as glad to see the back of me as I was of him.

I returned to jobbing building and two things I quickly learned from it. Firstly, the work was there to be had if you ferreted it out and your prices weren't prohibitive – and mine certainly weren't. The second thing I learnt was that I wasn't nearly as dependent on the larger building trade as I'd thought – there was no way I was going to make a fortune at going it alone but I was confident that neither would I starve.

I'm a man who has always handed over to his wife the weekly wage packet. Jean had always been the financial manager and controller in our house and it's an arrangement I've never thought to question in the whole of the forty odd years of our marriage – why should I have done? I've never gone without or been unable to buy myself a pint or a smoke whenever I've wanted one. When I got married the man of the house was expected to be the provider for his family – it didn't occur to him that his wife should also be expected to make a contribution to the household finances. True after the kids had all started school, Jean started work too, but she's only ever gone part-time and each time it's been her own decision – and never when she thought she was needed more at home.

I'm well aware that in these changing times and circumstances of heavy unemployment and 'womens's lib' and all that, roles can become changed by sheer force of circumstances – even so I know a number of men who prefer to stay at home 'Mary-Anning' while their wives go out to work. Me, I'd die of shame!

I'd no intention of dying of shame. I bought an old Land Rover – complete with trailer – extending ladders, a little scaffolding and various other basic requirements of the small jobbing builder and I was back in business. Jobbing building is a pretty carefree way of life – you work pretty much your own hours and set your own earnings target. Mine was always pretty low – as my old mother used to say: 'Enough is as good as a feast!' I'd no ambition to become rich - there are other things in life besides 'money-grubbing' all the time, especially in later life. There was however still that age-old scourge of the building worker to be reckoned with – grim winter – and particularly did it punish the small jobbing builder. Between December and the end of March nobody wants to know him and then suddenly in the spring he's wanted by everybody at once. But that's the game, you play it that way or not at all.

Whenever it was possible I found alternative work in the winter – my experience in Kent had shown me that other jobs could sometimes be fun too, for a while anyway. I have taken such work on a number of occasions. I was able to find the jobs usually because nobody else wanted them because of the low wages which went with them – I was nearly always the sole applicant. One or two jobs I took on in this way turned out reasonably well, but one or two also turned out just the opposite – even disastrous.

One such job I obtained in the central warehouse of a large organisation which owned and controlled a chain of grocery shops and supermarkets. I was one of a number of men charged with the task of unloading the lorries which delivered straight from the factories to the warehouse. From the lorries and vans we stacked the goods onto the seemingly endless and countless shelves within the warehouse – later we unstacked the goods and loaded them onto the company's own transport for distribution around its retail outlets.

I've lifted up plenty of foodstuffs in my time, almost all of it from a plate with a knife and fork, but it's quite another thing to lift those same foodstuffs in bulk from lorries and stack them onto shelves which ranged in height from the excruciatingly high to the excruciatingly low. The goods came in packages of every conceivable shape and size and their weights varied between the ridiculously light to the all but unliftable! The only requirements for the job were – above the neck, nothing; below it, a cast iron back on hinges and a strong pair each of arms and legs. Above the neck I qualified, below it I certainly did not.

I knew the first day I started the job, which was a Monday, that I'd dropped a clanger. By the Friday of the same week my back ached so much I feared I was in for a repetition of my experiences of 1947. Before I'd left work that day I'd given in my notice – a week after that I was back where I'd started, at home nursing my aches and pains, a sadder and a wiser man!

Another job I once obtained for the winter was as a school caretaker. I sometimes felt a little guilty about applying for such jobs, knowing I was going to ditch them again within a few months, but I was able to live with myself – no employer I'd ever known had ever hesitated to ditch his workers when he'd felt he no longer needed them. For this job, however, I did have competition.

When I rolled up for the interview, which was held at the school itself, there were another couple of blokes there waiting to be interviewed for the job. While the first chap was in the room where the interview was being conducted, the second bloke and I talked. He was a bit younger than I was. He asked me what kind of work I'd been doing before and when I told him bricklaying I thought I detected a little smirk appear on his face so then I asked him what *he'd* done before and he told me he'd been a janitor on the steelworks. I well knew that caretakers are only glorified janitors, I thought, there go my chances of the job – my own experience of the work was nil.

I was the last to be interviewed and when I walked into the room where the interviews were being conducted I was greatly surprised to find it almost filled with interviewers. There were six of them, one or two of whom I recognised, including the headmaster of the school and a prominent local councillor. The others apparently represented the governors of the school, the parents association or something and one aggressive looking character who, I discovered later, was their expert on the technical aspects of school caretaking. There were four men and two women. I didn't see the local MP – possible he'd been called away on other business!

I was politely invited to take the only vacant seat in the room, which had been so positioned that everybody could see it and, of course, it's occupant.

They were all very nice people who asked their questions in the friendliest possible manner – with the sole exception, that is, of the aggressive looking technical expert. He asked me the most awkward technical questions without a glimmer of humour on his face, questions such as: What experience did I have of industrial cleaning equipment? What would I do if the central heating system developed a leak? What would I do if the electricity supply failed? I got right sick of him and his smart aleck questions! I learned later that the correct answers to almost all his questions should have been: 'Telephone the appropriate Borough Emergency Service Department' – it was as simple as that! He never once asked what I would do if the telephone service broke down.

I much preferred the questions of the others, such as, if I'd just cleaned a large area of the floor and then in came the children and paddled all over it, what would be my reaction? If I'd answered that one truthfully I'd have replied, 'Give 'em one round the earhole with a wet mop!' but of course I'd more sense than to answer in that way and cock up the interview for sure. I parried it well enough I think, but perhaps some slight hesitation on my part before I did answer the question prompted the next one from one of the women. She asked, with a slightly alarmed look on her face, wasn't I fond of children? 'Oh yes,' I replied, 'very fond of

258.

them.' And of course I was fond of the little brats as long as they behaved themselves.

I was very pleasantly surprised, a few days after the interview, to learn through the post that I'd been given the job – it really seemed to be the case after all that I was smarter than the average man when it came to interviews!

Within a couple of days of starting on my new job I learned the real reason behind my appointment from the head cleaning lady who knew everything about everybody in the school. The headmaster of the school – who himself had been the only one who had asked no questions of me at the interview – had plumped solidly for me. Indeed, if I was to believe the cleaning lady, he'd all but laid his own job on the line for me.

It appeared he'd been deeply impressed by my total ignorance of the requirements of the job, which had been in stark contrast to the expert knowledge of it displayed by the other two applicants. What they hadn't known about industrial cleaning equipment or about faulty boiler valves and leaky central heating systems just wasn't worth the knowing. But the real clincher in my case, so far as the headmaster had been concerned, was the fact that I was lame. He was, too. He'd only one leg, the other was false, and he was just plain sick to death of expert cleaners and floor polishers who sent him skating all over the place whenever he ventured from his study! And when, because I limped and because I wore a caliper, I'd gone swaying and clanking with all the grace of a mechanical digger into the interviewing room, his interest had been aroused immediatly.

Here, it appeared, was a fellow sufferer, almost as unsteady on his feet as he was himself, one who almost certainly would share his own hatred of highly polished floors! And as the interview had progressed to reveal in even greater detail my total lack of experience and general ignorance of all things caretaking, he'd hugged hmself more and more with delight. Here was the very man to be his next caretaker – one he would be able to train from scratch to his own ways, one who would need little prompting to grit the school's exits and entrances on the icy days of winter, or

259.

salt the kids' playground slides. How he'd sold me to the others of the panel I'm not sure and the cleaning lady, if she knew, wasn't letting on, but it stands to reason he must have said something good about me. No matter, it was I who had the job.

I'd attended the same school as a boy and it was strange at first to be wandering in and out of the same old classrooms as the ageing caretaker, where once, almost half a century earlier, I'd sat at my desk as a small boy learning my lessons. Everything was pretty much the same as it had been then, including the desks and the carving on them but the old open fireplaces had gone from the fronts of the classrooms, which had warmed only the teachers – theirs being the only desks near enough the fires to fully benefit from their warmth.

The old school bell which, as one of the privileged older boys, I'd been so proud to ring in my turn to proclaim to the other schoolkids still dawdling on their way to school that they'd only ten minutes left to make it on time, was still there, but now, removed from its belfry, it stood, a relic of days long gone, on a table in the school hall, silent as a ghost itself. I remembered the teacher's joke – 'Send not to know for whom the bell tolls, it tolls for thee.' When the bell ceased to ring dead on nine o'clock, if you weren't in the playground then you were late – and then, as you raced fearfully into the school yard, you like as not received a quick thwack across your trouser seat from the fat old headmaster's cane which awaited all latecomers by the school gates. Happy days!

And happy were those I spent there as caretaker. When the spring came I handed in my notice – I had lingered in the job a little longer than I'd intended. The old headmaster tried hard to get me to change my mind – he almost succeeded, in the time I'd been there he and I had become good friends – but, unable to persuade me otherwise, when the day came for me to go he shook me by the hand and wished me luck and I did the same for him. You can't wish lameness on anybody but I hoped at least he'd find somebody to be his next caretaker who would be as inexperienced and therefore as amenable to his own training as I had been. I

260.

know he didn't.

In August 1976 dad died and a little over a year later mum followed him. They'd been a tough old pair. Both born 'in the 1890s, they'd seen many ups and downs in their lifetimes and many changes – and much war too – but neither of them had ever whined about their lot in life, they'd both fought their own battles and stood on their own two feet from the cradle to the grave. They both retained all their faculties right to the end and their children, grandchildren, and great grandchildren may fairly be proud to come of such sturdy stock.

In the late 1970s unemployment was beginning to get out of hand – so much so that I feared in the spring of 1980 to leave the secure job I'd obtained with the Post Office for the uncertain world of jobbing building outside. The job was the most utterly boring one I've ever had but I was resolved to stay on until I was certain either of a better one or that the jobbing prospects were sufficiently good to justify my taking a chance on them – which right then looked to be very doubtful.

I was employed by the Post Office as a cleaner. This time at the interview I was the expert, drawing on my previous experience as a caretaker I'd managed to convince the couple of chaps who interviewed me that what I didn't know about industrial cleaning equipment, about boiler valves, faulty or otherwise, and leaky central heating systems just wasn't worth the knowing, which did the trick, I got the job. I was then requested to sign the Official Secrets Act – just in case I had a notion to pass on to the Russians our latest, top secret floor swamping techniques – which I hadn't. I was then admitted to full membership of that great elastic band of brothers – the Union of Post Office Workers.

It was no alarm clock job, I didn't have to be at work until 9.30 am each day and not at all on Saturdays and Sundays. Of course the wages for such work were as usual rock bottom but they did at least have the merit of being wages – you could look any barman straight in the eye when you spent your share of them, or for that matter, any Tax Inspector when he spent his.

In the late spring of 1980, providing the weather was fine

during my midday meal breaks, I regularly took to walking down to the Job Centre, which wasn't too far from the Post Office where I worked, in order to scan the job vacancies advertised on the boards.

The place was always packed with people on the same errand, men and women, old and young. The changing economic climate itself was reflected in the wording of many of the job adverts – a new arrogance had appeared in them and a few seemed to me to border on the insolent. 'Wanted bricklayer. Must also be able to plaster and do some joinering. Must have own transport. Must be prepared to work long hours. Nobody over forty years of age need apply.' was one example. The job offered no better pay than anyone under forty could have obtained elsewhere and without having to be three tradesmen rolled into one, or being compelled to work long hours and having to provide his own transport to, and no doubt between, jobs!

There were also numerous 'vacancies' for self-employed salesmen paid on a commission only basis – which was nice work if you could get it indeed – for the main agent or organiser.

Every get-rich-quick spiv in the area it seemed, having scented the changed conditions brought about by a shrinking job market, had hastened to the 'water-hole' provided by the Job Centre in order to make a 'killing'. Of course, such vacancies so advertised were by no means the norm but where once they would have been laughed off the boards they were now on the increase.

One particular vacancy attracted my eye. It was for a Bricklayer Supervisor on the Youth Opportunities Scheme set up by the local authority. The job was to supervise a half dozen school leavers on the building and repairing of council-owned property, such as garden walls, garden paths and other such simple building work.

In answer to my query about the job, the clerk informed me that it was reserved for the unemployed, which I wasn't – and that, I thought, was that.

A couple of months went by, during which time the same

advert appeared on the board every single day. I again enquired after it of the same clerk – surely, I thought, if it was still unfilled after all that time the employers would be willing to consider me for the job even if I wasn't unemployed, especially as in the event of my filling the vacancy there would be another immediately created at the Post Office which almost certainly would be filled much more easily – but no! I couldn't persuade him to pick up the phone and make the enquiry for me. I was a fool, I should have done it myself.

A month later the vacancly was still being advertised. I approached the same clerk. This time I told him that I would be unemployed within the week as I intended to give in my notice to the Post Office. I asked him to check with the advertiser that the same conditions as before still applied to the vacancy. He told me to come back when I was actually unemployed.

I decided to take the chance – after all, the vacancy hadn't been filled in three months of advertising, it seemed unlikely that it would be during the one week it would take me to work out my notice.

I gave in my notice at the Post Office and worked the week it took to expire. Then the following Monday morning bright and early I was back at the Job Centre. I told the clerk – the same one – that I was now unemployed. Now would he phone the job advertisers and let them know he'd found them a man for the job? He gave me a pitying look. Had I, he asked, registered my claim for unemployment benefit at the Employment Office? I told him I hadn't as I didn't intend to be unemployed for very long. He gave me another pitying look – I must first register my claim for benefit before he could consider me as a suitably qualified applicant for the job.

I knew it would be a waste of time arguing with him. To such little bureaucrats their rules are commandments – common sense comes a poor second, and common humanity last of all.

So off to the Unemployment Office I went and stood in a queue fifty yards long which wound its way from the counter inside, out through the door, and along the side of the building.

In the late summer and early autumn of 1979–80 the steel-works and the steelworks contractors were laying men off by the hundreds each week – so many that the Unemployment Office, it-self a large modern building, had had to hire a large church hall and bring in extra staff to man it in order to cope with the extra work.

After standing in the queue for goodness knows how long, in a fever of impatience wondering all the time if somebody would pinch 'my' job at the Job Centre while I stood there, I at last reached the counter and my claim was registered – but still they weren't done with me. I was directed to the annexe at the Church Hall where again I had to stand in a queue and go through pretty much the same procedure while my claim was further processed.

Several hours later I was back at the Job Centre, the paper proof of my unemployment in my hand, and at long last, after first studying the papers, the little Job Centre bureaucrat con-sented to get on the phone to the advertisers of the vacancy.

I was sitting on a chair at one side of his desk and he on a chair at the other. The phone was on the desk between us. Lan-guidly he picked it up and dialled the number. I saw the look of boredom suddenly disappear from his face as he spoke to who-ever it was on the other end of the line – to be replaced by one of consternation.

The vacancy had been withdrawn a month earlier but some-one had 'forgotten' to inform the Job Centre!

For several long moments, as I digested this piece of informa-tion, I just sat and stared stupidly at him while the full enormity of my folly sank deeper and ever deeper into me. After a while he gave me an uncomfortable little smirk – like he'd prefer me to see the matter as a joke. I didn't strike him when my temper finally exploded – mainly because there was his wide desk between us and also because he'd fallen off his chair when I jumped to my feet – but the real reason was because I blamed myself more than him for what had occurred. I should have known better than to have trusted an issue which was of such great importance to my-self to the words of such an obvious little bureaucrat as he. All the warning bells in my head had been ringing all the time but I'd ignored them. Even though I'd been unable to persuade him it would have been so easy for me to have checked on the vacancy myself before handing in my notice at the Post Office.

Having picked himself up from the floor and also having reassured himself I'd no intention of striking him, the clerk was now anxious to make amends for his previous lack of interest. He fished out another vacancy for a bricklayer – also with the local council in the Maintenance Section of their Building Department, which wasn't a bad job if you could get it. He wrote me out an introduction to the Building Works Manager and off I went to see that worthy.

I didn't get to see him – only his receptionist. She handed me one of their official application forms for the job which I filled in there and then in a little side room. They would, said the receptionist, let me know in due course of time whether my application for the job had been successful or not. Then I went home – it had been a long, long day.

Maybe a week later I received a letter which informed me that my application had been unsuccessful – no explanation of why, it just said they regretted the fact that they were unable to offer me a job *at the present time.* It was signed by the Borough Surveyor.

I couldn't understand it. I'd been the first one to apply for the job, that I knew. Moreover, the letter seemed to suggest that they would be able to offer me a job at some future time. I decided to go back to the office and check it out.

At the office I asked the receptionist if I could see the manager – she said she would look into his office to see if he was in, which she did – it was right next to her own little cubby hole. She came back to say he was out. I said I'd wait and seated myself on a chair by her open window. She looked decidedly uncomfortable. After I had sat there for perhaps five minutes she looked up from her work and said 'If it's about that job you applied for, it's no good your waiting. 'Oh!' I said, surprised, 'and why not?' 'Well,' she said, and I quote her exact words, 'It was thought because of your war wounds you wouldn't be able to do any bending'! And that was it – condemned without either a trial period of work or a proper medical examination and by a man apparently too afraid to leave his office and tell me himself. He was there alright, I'm pretty certain of that.

I'd had to declare my disability on the application form and give the cause of it, otherwise I'd have made no mention of it at all. I'd applied for the job on my ability to do it and not on the grounds of my disability – I could have eaten it.

I had some fierce correspondence with the Borough Surveyor over the matter – several letters each way – but it seemed it was to be my year for bureaucrats. They win their battles by the sheer weight of paper, they love the stuff – you only play their game by exchanging it with them and particularly do you find them in government and local authority service – or that's been my experience. There they live insulated in their cosy little centrally heated office worlds, many of them as remote from the world of real people as the Dalai Lama himself. That's been my experience too.

23.

THE WISHING WALL

HEIGH-HO! It was back to jolly old jobbing for me and, as I'd feared, the trade was not only declining rapidly but there was also much more competition for what work was available. The smaller building firms and the self employed two-and-one gangs were now willing to take on work they'd hitherto considered to be not worth their while. Even so, I found jobs. I could always get under their prices, some of which, even with the times as bad as they were, were outrageously high – and neither was I VAT registered.

Literally no job was too small for me – a slate on a roof, a half dozen wall tiles wanted in a bathroom or a yard of brickwork which wanted re-pointing would bring me out.

The worst time for business was when I was just getting started again – during the steel strike of 1980. Fortunately for me it coincided with the traditionally slack time of the building trade, January to April, so perhaps the harm it did to me was minimised – even so, it still cost me jobs.

Even though the steelworkers of Scunthorpe loyally supported their unions' call, the strike was far from popular with them. It was about the wrong issues at the wrong time. At a time when the threat of closure quite clearly hung over many steelworks and the unions, as late in the day as it was, should have been seeking reduced hours of work, retirements at sixty on adequate pensions and redundancies on a voluntary basis only, they chose instead to call a national stoppage over the issue of pay.

They got their increase, but it cost them. Only a couple of years later the number of hours worked in the industry had been slashed by half because the workforce itself had been slashed by that amount and scarcely a man over fifty-five, let alone sixty, still had a job in the industry – certainly not in the Scunthorpe area. Men had been bundled out of their livelihoods by the thousands, voluntarily or otherwise.

Everything which happened to the steel industry in the 1980s was predictable in the 1970s – certainly following the referendum of 1975 which confirmed Britain's status as a full member of the EEC. Had the steel unions on behalf of their members taken the appropriate action then, much of the sting could have been taken out of the closures which came later.

The jobbing game isn't a particularly exciting one, most of the time I worked by myself building garden walls, an occasional garage or a small extension to a house or bungalow. Sometimes I worked inside the houses knocking two rooms into one or perhaps building a stone fireplace. Most of the people I worked for were professional or business people themselves and, as often as not, both the man and his wife went out to work. If my work took me inside their houses they nearly always trusted me with the key.

When the wives were at home I was usually kept well supplied with tea – and just occasionally, very occasionally, one of them would indicate that she would be willing to supply more – which should have put some excitement back into the game. But it rarely did – not that I'm a particularly moral man, I ain't. Nor would I kiss and tell if I had lapsed – it was rather the case that these one or two particular housewives were way past their best and pretty desperate. They had to be to fancy me! Apart from the fact that I was no oil painting, I was also doddering on in years a bit myself. I was also happy with my own marriage and I much preferred the cash for my services – no offence intended, missus, or taken! It's all in the game!

I was still jobbing around the town – and behaving myself – when MacGregor announced the closure of the Normanby Park Steelworks in 1981, so throwing almost five thousand steelworkers out of work at a stroke.

It came as no surprise to me – it had long been on the cards. Nor did the lack of real resistance to the closure by the steelworkers come as any great surprise to me – they were by now a pretty demoralised workforce.

Many of the displaced middle-aged men were found alternative jobs at the Anchor steelworks and to make room for them as many – and more – of the older workers there were made redundant, almost all voluntarily. The severance pay for them was pretty reasonable – for the longer serving ones that is – up to £20 000. In addition, their dole pay would be made up to 90% of their former earnings for the first year of unemployment and up to 80% for the second year. There was little hope for the vast majority of ever finding other jobs but most saw two years of paid holiday stretching away before them and more money in the bank than they'd ever had before. Most too had small works pensions and that was sufficient – they volunteered for the redundancies by the hundreds, and who knowing the industry could really blame them? They wanted nothing more than to be out of it. Not all, of course – there were those who resisted, even amongst the older men, but most of the opposition to the closures, as you would expect, came from the younger, shorter-serving steelworkers, many accused the older men and their unions of betrayal – but it was all too late, much, much too late.

It did surprise me when those 'favoured' by the closure of the Normanby Park Steelworks organised a counter demonstration march to that organised by the protesters – it was led by none other than the former Worker Director for the area – indeed were the unions in the eyes of their younger members well and truly discredited.

As the curtain mercifully descended upon this final act of ignominy in the long running saga of the rationalization of the steel industry in Scunthorpe I couldn't help but reflect upon the whole sorry chain of events leading up to it which in Scunthorpe alone had cost more than 10 000 jobs and left the town dazed and shattered, scarcely knowing where to start to pick up the pieces.

It's fate had been the brutal rationalization of the eyrie – the destruction and cannibalization of the smaller chicks by the larger – of the weaker competition by the stronger – in Scunthorpe the destruction and the cannibalization of the Redbourn and the Normanby Park steelworks by the larger, seemingly all powerful

Appleby-Frodingham works.

Nobody should condemn the smaller chicks for putting up the fight they did for their own survival before going under – but of course there were those who did – including some so-called trades unionists.

Rationalization there had to be – everybody knew that – once Britain had opted to become a full member of the EEC in the referendum of 1975 it was inevitable. But did it really have to be so brutally carried out? Surely there are more ways than one of rationalizing just as there are more ways than two of responding to that rationalization, other than the one of outright opposition on the one hand and the one of meek acceptance on the other.

In one way I suppose it could be said we steelworkers had asked for all we got. As everybody knows it pays to keep your wits about you when visiting the market place, otherwise you may very quickly get ripped off by unscrupulous traders, or even more quickly get your pockets picked by other unsavoury forms of market life – there was no reason to believe simply because it commanded capital letters the Common Market was any different from the general run of the mill market places.

Its aims and intentions had years earlier been quite clearly spelled out for all to see – in the Treaty of Rome of 1966 – they included neither a commitment to full employment or to the continuance of the policy of successive British Governments of feather bedding the monolithic, nationalized British Steel Industry – in effect we were warned in advance of the possible – in the case of our own industry – even the likely consequences of leaving our wits behind when Britain entered the Common Market – it was a warning we chose to ignore and so we got ripped off and our pockets picked of the change into the bargain.

The sudden influx into the town of money brought about by the redundancies coupled to the currrent sale of council houses at knock-down prices was at least good for the jobbing building trade. Housewives who had long wanted this or that improvement or alteration to the house now found the house had suddenly become theirs to do with as they liked and furthermore the money was also there to do it with.

Trade in 1981 and 1982 was reasonably good, I found all I wanted – indeed right into 1983. There was never a spring as long or as wet as the springtime of 1983 – the wettest since records had begun, so it was said. Indeed, I would have gone further and said ever since Noah built the Ark! It rained almost every day – the moment you took a shovel full of earth from the ground the hole filled with water, the moment you had mixed a barrow of mortar the heavens opened up. Most days it was all but impossible to work outdoors and by the June of that year I'd only earned a fraction of what I would have done in a normal year.

Rained off one day I decided to look in on the Job Centre – more to kill time than with any expectation of finding another way of making a living. My luck was in – a vacancy for a bricklayer had been notified to the Job Centre that same day. There were no conditions attached to the job, age limits or anything like that. The Manpower Services Commission, who were just setting up a project at Brigg, a small town about seven miles from Scunthorpe, wanted a bricklayer urgently and because my name was still on the Job Centre list of bricklayers seeking employment, the clerk thought I might well qualify for the job despite my age. I shot off to Brigg at once, it was an opportunity not to be missed – I didn't mind being rained off on pay, my earnings each week would be assured if I landed the job – which I did.

It was a Church sponsored programme and the work was mainly on churches, church properties and chapels. The Church provided all the materials and the Manpower Services Commission provided the labour.

To begin with I was the oldest employee on the programme by forty years, all the others were youths and young men between the ages of eighteen and twenty-two or twenty-three, but as the programme got under way and more and more work came in from the churches, chapels and other bodies, more men were recruited to the programme each week until by the end of the first six months it was providing work for seventy or eighty men.

We were divided into teams, each about a dozen strong and

usually comprised of a couple of qualified tradesmen – perhaps a bricklayer or joiner and a painter – and the rest was made up of the youths and young men. Each team worked under the direction of its own supervisor.

Many of the youths and young men had scarcely worked at all since leaving school at sixteen – and it was pretty evident they hadn't by their general behaviour on the jobs, their lack of knowledge of even the most rudimentary work practices and on the job codes of conduct which often got them into trouble with the supervisors. Their jobs were not only temporary – a year was all they got – but they were also part-time – a couple or three days each week. Consequently they didn't regard them as 'proper jobs' and tended to treat the whole business as a lark, as if they were still at school and this attitude exasperated some of the older tradesmen as well.

My sympathies were generally with the youngsters. I believed they'd been badly let down by the older generation. At their age and long before it I'd been doing a man's job in a man's world and I'd been respected accordingly – these youngsters had never had the chance of that – society's rejects they were and they were also aware of it. If their development was stunted, it was the society they grew up in which had stunted it. Basically there was little wrong with the lads.

A week after I started work on the Project the weather faired up and it scarcely ever rained again that summer.

I enjoyed the year I spent with the MSC – the work on the churches, wet and dry stonewalling mostly, was a change from the usual run of building work and the surroundings of the village churches were pleasant to work in.

Right by one of the churches was the village school and I often worked to the accompaniment of the children singing in the classrooms. After the steelworks it was a sheer delight to hear them and to be out in the sunshine and the good clean air.

At another church, amongst all the other work I did inside, outside and about it, I built a wet stone wall backed by ordinary brickwork – which is a pretty unusual kind of wall. As it was almost my last job for the MSC I built it good and strong – if it's not removed it should last for a thousand years.

The wall marks the boundary between the churchyard and the roadway which runs by it – which circumstances prompted me to compose a little verse and bury it deep and well-protected in the interior of the wall, maybe to be found hundreds of years hence. For what it's worth I quote:

> This wall was built
> To separate the dead from the living.
> If it may have a soul
> Then let it be as forgiving
> As I trust will be those
> On both of its sides,
> Come the day one from the other
> It no longer divides.

One other thing about the wall – I made it a 'wishing wall' – or that's what I told the smaller village children it was going to be when I'd finished it as the stones I was using to build it had themselves all come from an old wishing well. I left a small hole in the wall, about the size of a sheep's eye, and then in the wet cement about the hole I traced a shallow indent full circle. When the wall was completed and its cement was set I showed the kids how to wish – a number of them had become very interested in the whole business. They were, I told them, firstly to trace the circle three times round with a finger and then whisper their wish into the hole - and then, provided they kept the wish a secret to themselves, it would one day come true.

Shortly after I'd done with the wall I had the satisfaction one day of witnessing from a distance several children trying it out. Who knows, I may have just begun something in the village which could carry on for generations? Perhaps five hundred years hence, when maybe the world has matured and capitalists and communists – 'caps and comms' – has become but a kids game like Cowboys and Indians is to the kids of today, the village children will still be wishing at my wall. I'd like to think so – long may they at least continue to believe in the magic of the world.

In the summer of 1984 my year with the MSC came to an end – I would have stayed on but a year was your ration.

I went to the Unemployment Office to sign on. I couldn't draw any dole as during the years previous to my employment with the MSC I'd only paid self employment stamps but I signed on just the same for the full employed person's stamp each week – I'd no intention at my age of going back to self-employment. They did tell me at the dole office that I could apply for Social Security Benefit but I didn't bother – apart from the fact that I'd never drawn that in the whole of my working life, I still had my war pension and Jean worked a few hours part-time each week. Whatever they might have allowed me would have been but a pittance – certainly not worth the humiliation of having to reveal my most private affairs to some slip of a girl scarcely a couple of years out of school or college. I wasn't that hard up.

I resolved to return to jobbing building – as I would be drawing no state benefit I saw no reason why I shouldn't continue to sign on each week for the stamp – and for the record. After twelve months of signing on I should qualify for another year with the MSC – always supposing they were still in business

But it was to be another mice and men job. They changed the rules – that year MSC made it a condition that you had to be in receipt of a state benefit before you could be employed by it, war pensions didn't count, no matter how long you'd been unemployed.

But I needn't have worried. Scarcely had I resumed jobbing building than I began to suffer severe back pain. It had been carrying on for the past couple of years but by resting at the weekends I'd managed to keep it at bay. In the end I was compelled to see the doctor who, after examining me, referred me to the hospital for an X-ray examination. The result of that surprised me, I'd assumed my trouble was caused by the old injuries I had suffered when I was young – that and advancing years I'd thought was the problem. But no, said the doctor at the hospital, I was suffering from arthritis.   I didn't think so but you don't argue with doctors on their own pitch.   He had a corset made for me which resembled a strait-jacket – had I a desk job I might have been able to work in it but I hadn't and I couldn't.   It finished my career as a builder and I haven't worked since – not manually that is. But it doesn't matter now. This year 1987, I've retired officially.

EPILOGUE

TODAY I live no more than eighty yards from the house where I was born in the next street. It, like me, has seen many changes come to the town – especially since the end of the Second World War.

There are no bright crimson night skies above it now like ones both it and I once knew – the techniques of steelmaking and of slag disposal changed years ago and the old open hearth furnaces are all gone. True, you may occasionally notice a faint red flush in the skies above the Anchor works but so brightly lit is the town nowadays – even into the ten-foots behind the streets – that you scarcely notice it. Sometimes too, when I awake in the night and all is quiet, I fancy I can hear the low rumble of the Anchor mills – but it is, I think, but a fancy – age has 'dimmed' my hearing as well as my eyes.

The times have changed greatly and with them too the town, the steelworks – and also the steelworkers. They no longer now wear the sweat towelling about their necks as they once did nor the heavy hob-nailed boots on their feet which were once the hallmark of the steelworker. Nor do you see them cycling to and from work in their thousands at the change of shifts – the majority now travel to work in cars and if it wasn't for the direction in which they travelled, you wouldn't be able to tell which lot were going to work and which leaving it.

The modern steelworker is much better paid and catered for in the way of welfare facilities than was his father, but he still hasn't won a real reduction in the hours of his working week since my time in the industry, nor yet retirement at sixty on a decent pension – which, considering the massive unemployment in the country generally and the nature of the industry particularly, is in my view a sad reflection upon his trades unions particularly and upon society generally.

Nowadays you never hear any mention of industrial democracy in the town – unless maybe you happen to bump into one of your old workmates in the street or the club or somewhere. Then perhaps, as the two of you reminisce about old times, some incident connected with it will be recalled by one or the other of you to remind you that it was once a very real and very live issue amongst the town's steelworkers. But as something worth having and worth fighting for, it seems to be something of a 'dead duck' amongst todays steelworkers. Perhaps they are right, perhaps it was but the vain dream of a few – in the way we visualised it anyway. Perhaps some kind of profit-sharing scheme or works shareholding idea will be as close to an industrial democracy as I shall ever see come to the steelworks in my time - at the moment of writing it looks that way. But who can tell? It's possible the steelworkers will get the bug again.

For myself, I've always been aware that you can't have a practical working democracy either in industry or in the country which involves so many people in the decision taking process that control and initiative become stifled and responsibility fragmented – of course you can't!

Democracy – industrial or political – is about accountability firstly, and numbers secondly.

An economy in which production and distribution for private profit has become enshrined as the central article of faith, will automatically have an in-built resistance to any greater accountability than that which each company has to its shareholders on the one side of industry, and each trades union has to its own members on the other.

During my lifetime British democracy, that great ideal and institution for which the dead of two world wars allegedly gave their lives, has very largely been a democracy of society's 'big guns' – mainly of the two sides of industry, of organised capital on the one side and of organised labour on the other – and not a democracy of the 'little man', of the ordinary citizen, especially when that ordinary citizen also happens to be a very ordinary working man as well.

Even at this stage of our democratic development he may still be regarded by industry as being one of its more expendable items when difficulties occur – pretty much as the balloonist regards the ballast he carries on board his craft as something which quite morally may be heaved overboard whenever he wishes to shed weight in order to gain height or buoyancy or for whatever reason.

It could, of course, in the case of industry, be argued with equal logic that the same results might be achieved if the 'balloonists' were to exchange places with the 'ballast' – it's a system which appears to work pretty well amongst those most ardent of devotees to the competitive spirit – the clubs of the Football League.

It seems to me that the time is well overdue for the democratic ideal to be extended to industry itself, so to give the ordinary working man – both as a citizen and as an individual in his own right – a say in the decision taking processes where it matters most to him – at his place of work.

I can hear the cries of the objectors to this already – say they, 'Managements have to be ruthless in order to ensure the survival of their companies and thus the jobs of at least a proportion of their employees. Given a say in the running of their companies could the workers fairly be expected to be party to a management recommendation to axe jobs – very possibly including their own?'

My answer to that is – yes, they could. When the choice is stark, your ordinary man is every bit as capable of reaching common sense decisions as is his boss – it is but a matter of sound leadership at the top and of a sound 'safety net' at the bottom, a couple of items one might fairly expect to find in any democracy – although at the time of writing both appear to be in need of some repair in this one of our own.

With regard to the question of leadership, Churchill once had nothing to offer the entire British people but 'blood, toil, tears and sweat' and to a man and to a woman they responded in exactly the way he knew they would and wanted them to. If leadership is honest and positive then the ordinary people will respond to it as honestly and positively.

Perhaps those amongst our present day political and trades union leaders and captains of industry, who are doubtful about the benefits to be derived from the introduction of democracy into industry, are really doubtful about their own capacity to lead in such circumstances.

It cannot be that they doubt the enthusiasm of the ordinary British people for democracy or their ability to live up to the responsibilities it thrusts upon them – if that be the case then already the history of the twentieth century proves them to be wrong and – should we have to wait that long – so will that of the twenty-first century when it comes to be written!

I have been in and out of many furnaces in my life – almost all of them on the steelworks and all of them with almost all the heat taken out of them. But two furnaces I have passed through with the heat full on.

The first of these was the white-hot furnace of war. The second was the red-hot furnace of Marxist-Socialist thought and literature.

I passed through the first when I was little more than a callow youth and through the second when my mind was still largely virgin territory, as an empty land waiting to be peopled. I emerged from both experiences I think a better man for each one.

From books you may learn much about men – but from war you may learn about the man himself – especially about **the** man – yourself.

It is said that every man has three characters – the one he shows to others, the one he thinks he is and the one he really is. Or, put another way, every man has three faces – the one you see, the one he sees and the one God sees.

War – prolonged war, that is, may not do much to alter the face you see, or indeed, the one God sees, but by God it will wipe the smirk off the face he himself sees – nor will the character he really is ever again be able to hide behind the one he thinks he is.

When I talk of war I really mean combat – the two are

different. And then again prolonged exposure to combat conditions is different from a short spell of it. A man may be one man for a month of it and quite a different man after a year of it – a hero for a month and a stuttering wreck in a year. I have watched the process at work on men, I've seen them crack up. I have known men inflict the most dreadful wounds upon themselves in order to get away from the miseries of the front line and I have known men briefly desert their comrades in their moments of greatest need – and eventually desert them for ever. Indeed, I have read on good authority that there were 15 000 British deserters alone, hiding out in Italy by the end of the war – almost all of whom were infantrymen. But none of that amazed me nearly as much as did the steadiness and strength of character shown by the vast majority of ordinary blokes when faced with the most appalling conditions of trial and tribulation punctuated by sudden death over long periods of time – often for months.

In war you see your mates through new eyes. You learn to have a new respect for the bloke you scarcely noticed before when you witness examples of selflessness and compassion by him which shame you. Above all, you learn the proper meaning of the word humility because in the fullness of your experience you learn that each and every man, including yourself, has only so much to give and when he's given it – however little or however much it may be – he has nothing left, only the shell remains. So, when your mate cracks up, or shoots himself, or simply deserts, you know that there, but for the grace of God, go you – character lost, face lost – to all except those who themselves have been through the same furnace. War teaches men how to take other men to pieces and put them back together again in more ways than one.

What war can do to a man in one way, books can do to him in another. They too can deeply disturb his peace of mind, can sear his soul.

After I left school in 1936 at the age of fourteen, books played no more part in my life for the next twenty years. It was the

Communist Party of the mid-1950s which then opened my eyes to the world of books and learning.

At first my reading was almost exclusively Marxist in content but after that I read anything and everything by anybody – reading became an obsession. I'd go to great lengths in order to get hold of a book I particularly wanted to read which wasn't available to me through the customary channels of libraries or the booksellers. But it is to the British Communist Party that I owe the greatest debt of gratitude for that first awakening of my interest in reading and learning and for the heightening of my awareness of the larger world outside my own little workaday world of the steelworks, pubs, clubs and the back garden.

But as wide and prolonged as my reading has been over the years, I can make no pretensions to scholarship for there has been no plan or system to it – I have but read whatever books became available to me, regardless of subject or continuity. Economics, History, Physics, Philosophy or whatever, I gulped them all down and then reached for more of the same. I am therefore well aware that my contact with the world of learning is but sketchy – as a view imperfectly obtained through the keyhole and the cracks in an otherwise barred and bolted door might be. Even so, I have been privileged to hear much great and learned debate and perhaps also to have learned something from it – but for the main, like Omar Khayyám, I must confess;

'Myself when young did eagerly frequent
    Doctor and Saint and heard great Argument
About it and about; but evermore
    Came out by the same door as in I went.'

So, at the end of it all, I remain pretty much what I have always been – just another working bloke: or rather, ex-working bloke – my working days are over. I still live in the same community into which I was born sixty-five years ago. It was here I went to school as a boy and grew to manhood – it was from here I went to the war – it was to here I returned when the war was done – and it is here I have remained and worked ever since. It is my home, it is part of me as I am part of it – I fit perfectly into the background of its everyday life, seeing and seen, knowing and known – and I am happy in it.

It is, therefore, out of no spirit of vainglory or of discontent with my lot that I would like to leave the reader with a view of my own belief about life – of its meaning and the meaning of this world in which it exists, for meaning it surely has. Nor do I offer it as some great, brain-shattering new truth or anything like that. The reader may take it or leave it as he chooses and I shall be neither surprised nor offended if it is the latter, for my own view of life's truths has too often been at odds with that as seen by my fellows – albeit I have enjoyed the debates, I am accustomed to rebuff.

I have never been a religious man and I have never voluntarily attended church worship. The only time I ever see the inside of a church is when I have my arm twisted – when it's a matter of 'hatch, match or dispatch', a christening, a wedding or a funeral, that is.

For me, God, as portrayed by the Church, is altogether too absolute. He leaves impossibly unanswered the sixty-four thousand dollar question, 'If He made everything, then where did He come from?'

But if I don't particularly believe in the God of the Church, I do believe in a God, though I know of no religious body or organisation which would endorse my view of what God is, or is about.

Does the universe have to be all God as the church insists or no God as the materialists insist? I believe not!

Whatever theories may be advanced to explain how the universe came into being, however it actually began, however much it has changed and developed since then to become what it is now, whatever it may be in the process of becoming, one thing is for certain – we human beings are part of it and right now, here on Earth, I believe there is much more going on than mere hot and cold wars and the gratifying of human egos. Here, at least, if not anywhere else in the universe, intelligent life in the form of

282.

Man has made its appearance – in man creation has become fully conscious of itself.

It is my belief this little planet Earth of ours, this sun-warmed home of man – this hatch-patch of life and intelligence may well be destined to play a much larger part in the ever unfolding story of the universe than has yet been imagined.

Already to the brain of man is added the brainchild of man – the computer – and who is to doubt the enormous possibilities opened up for him by that achievement in his own never ending quest for ever greater knowledge and understanding of the universe.

If any materialist were to say to me, 'There is no God.' I wouldn't contradict him – not because he was necessarily right but because at the present level of human knowledge and understanding it would be impossible to prove him wrong, at least to his satisfaction.

If then he were to say to me, 'There never has been a God.' I still wouldn't argue the matter with him for the same reason.

But if then, perhaps emboldened by my timidity, he were to say to me, 'There can never be a God.' Then, most assuredly I would take up cudgels with him.

Man the Thinker has already begun to throw off the restraining bonds of his earthly cot, his future in space seems to be already assured – beyond that beckons his future as a creature of the entire galaxy – who can doubt it! – and beyond that again beckons his future as – what?

No matter – even such an enlargement of his grasp as we can reasonably visualise must inevitably be accompanied by a corresponding reduction of his Earthliness, even to his earthly body, and once the process has begun, what may it not lead to - perhaps in the fullness of time even to his complete release from it, that he may become – what?

In the sense that the child is the father of the man, may not Man be the father of the God? It pleases me to believe that he may and that somewhere, sometime in the yet far distant future, Man, virgin born of David the Sun and Mary the Earth, has a rendezvous to keep with his maker.

I can see our little planet – Earth the Wanderer – bearing its precious cargo of life and hope – journeying on through the limitless expanses of time and space for many hundreds of thousands, perhaps even millions of years yet, before it finally arrives at its meeting point with destiny - but that it will one day safely deliver its charge into the arms of the waiting God I firmly believe!

This is the God of my belief – it is one I can see all around me on every day of the week, in every man, in every woman and in every child. It follows then as night the day that anyone who sins against them – whoever – wherever – they be, commits a greater sin against the God I believe in for, unlike the God of the Church who may be sinned against on every day of the week and twice on Sundays without His coming to any great harm, He may not be because He is *not* absolute – yet!